BUSINESS REPLY M.

INTEL
PO BOX 5937
DENVER CO 80217-9808

The latest updates to the specifications contained in the *Pentium® II Processor Developer's Manual* are now available. These updates are valuable to PC manufacturers and software developers needing up-to-date technical information. Use this reply card to order your complimentary copy of the current updates. Please allow 3-4 weeks for your copy to reach you.

☐ Please send me the current *Pentium® Processor Specification Update* (242480)

Name _____

Company _____

Address _____
_____

City _____

State _____   Postal Code _____

Country _____

Expires 12/31/98

LITERATURE

For additional information on Intel products in the U.S. or Canada, call Intel's Literature Center at (800) 548-4725 or write to:

INTEL LITERATURE SALES
P.O. Box 7641
Mt. Prospect, IL 60056-7641

To order literature outside of the U.S. and Canada contact your local sales office.

Additional information about Intel products is available on Intel's web site: http://www.intel.com.

CURRENT DATABOOKS

Product line databooks contain datasheets, application notes, article reprints, and other design information. All databooks can be ordered individually, and most are available in a pre-packaged set in the U.S. and Canada. Databooks can be ordered in the U.S. and Canada by calling TAB/McGraw-Hill at 1-800-822-8158; outside of the U.S. and Canada contact your local sales office.

Title	Intel Order Number	ISBN
SET OF NINE DATABOOKS (Available in U.S. and Canada)	**231003**	**N/A**
CONTENTS LISTED BELOW FOR INDIVIDUAL ORDERING:		
EMBEDDED MICROCONTROLLERS	270646	1-55512-248-5
EMBEDDED MICROPROCESSORS	272396	1-55512-249-3
FLASH MEMORY (2 volume set)	210830	1-55512-250-7
i960® PROCESSORS AND RELATED PRODUCTS	272084	1-55512-252-3
NETWORKING	297360	1-55512-256-6
OEM BOARDS, SYSTEMS AND SOFTWARE	280407	1-55512-253-1
PACKAGING	240800	1-55512-254-X
PENTIUM® AND PENTIUM PRO PROCESSORS AND RELATED PRODUCTS	241732	1-55512-251-5
PERIPHERAL COMPONENTS	296467	1-55512-255-8
ADDITIONAL LITERATURE: (Not included in databook set)		
AUTOMOTIVE PRODUCTS	231792	1-55512-257-4
COMPONENTS QUALITY/RELIABILITY	210997	1-55512-258-2
EMBEDDED APPLICATIONS (1995/96)	270648	1-55512-179-9
MILITARY	210461	N/A
SYSTEMS QUALITY/RELIABILITY	231762	1-55512-046-6

A complete set of this information is available on CD-ROM through Intel's Data on Demand program, order number 240897. For information about Intel's Data on Demand ask for item number 240952.

January 1996
Order Number: 000900-001

Intel Application Support Services

World Wide Web [URL: http://www.intel.com/]

Intel's Web site now contains technical and product information that is available 24 hours a day! Also visit Intel's site for financials, history, current news and events, job opportunities, educational news and much, much more!

FaxBack*

Technical and product information are available 24 hours a day! Order documents containing:

- Product Announcements
- Product Literature
- Intel Device Characteristics
- Design/Application Recommendations
- Stepping/Change Notifications
- Quality and Reliability Information

Information on the following subjects are available:

- Microcontroller and Flash
- OEM Branded Systems
- Multibus and iRMX Software/BBS listing
- Multimedia
- Development Tools
- Quality and Reliability/Change Notification
- Microprocessor/PCI/Peripheral
- Intel Architecture Labs

To use FaxBack (for Intel components and systems), dial **(800) 628-2283** or 916-356-3105 (U.S./Canada/APAC/Japan) *or +44{0} 1793-496646 (Europe)* and follow the automated voice-prompt. Document orders will be faxed to the fax number you specify. For information on how the Intel Application Support team can help you, order our Customer Service Agreement, document #1201. Catalogs are updated as needed, so call for the latest information!

Bulletin Board System (BBS)

To use the Intel Application BBS (components and systems), dial **(503) 264-7999** or **(916) 356-3600** (U.S./Canada/APAC/Japan) *or +44{0} 1793-432955 (Europe)*. The BBS will support 1200-19200 baud rate modem. *Typical modem configuration: 14.4K baud rate, No Parity, 8 Data Bits, 1 Stop Bit.*

CompuServe *Just type* 'Go Intel'

Intel maintains several forums where people come together to meet their peers, gather information, share discoveries and debate issues. For more information about service fees and access, call CompuServe at 1-800-848-8199 or 614-529-1340 (outside the U.S.). The INTELC forum is set up to support designers using various Intel components.

General Information Help Desk

Dial 1-800-628-8686 or 916-356-7599 (U.S. and Canada) between 5 a.m. and 5 p.m. PST for help with Intel products. For customers not in the U.S. or Canada, please contact your local distributor.

Intel Literature Centers

U.S.	+1-800-548-4725	France	+44{0} 1793 421777
U.S. (from overseas)	+1-708-296-9333	Germany	+44{0} 1793 421333
England	+44{0} 1793 431 155	Japan (fax only)	+81{0} 120 47 88 32

Intel Distributors

Check the back of an Intel data book or request one of the following distributor listing FaxBack documents: #4083 (U.S. Eastern Time Zone), #4084 (U.S. Central Time Zone), #4085 (Mountain Time Zone), #4086 (U.S. Alaska/Pacific Time Zone), #4209 (Europe) or #4403 (Canada).

*Other brands and names are the property of their respective owners.

January 1996
Order Number: 000901-001

intel®

Pentium® Pro Family Developer's Manual

Volume 1: Specifications

NOTE: The *Pentium® Pro Family Developer's Manual* consists of three books: *Specifications*, Order Number 242690; *Programmer's Reference Manual*, Order Number 242691; and the *Operating System Writer's Guide*, Order Number 242692.
Please refer to all three volumes when evaluating your design needs.

1996

intel.

TABLE OF CONTENTS

CHAPTER 4
BUS PROTOCOL

TABLE OF FIGURES

TABLE OF TABLES

intel®

1

Component
Introduction

CHAPTER 1
COMPONENT INTRODUCTION

The Pentium® Pro microprocessor is the next generation in the Intel386™, Intel486™, and Pentium family of processors. The Pentium Pro processor implements a Dynamic Execution microarchitecture — a unique combination of multiple branch prediction, data flow analysis, and speculative execution while maintaining binary compatibility with the 8086/88, 80286, Intel386, Intel486, and Pentium processors. The Pentium Pro processor integrates the second level cache, the APIC, and the memory bus controller found in previous Intel processor families into a single component, as shown in Figure 1-1.

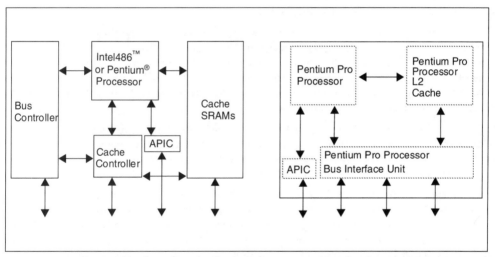

Figure 1-1. The Pentium® Pro Processor Integrating the CPU, L2 Cache, APIC and Bus Controller

A significant new feature of the Pentium Pro processor, from a system perspective, is the built-in direct multi-processing support. In order to achieve multi-processing for up to four processors and maintain the memory and I/O bandwidth to support them, new system designs are needed which consider the additional power requirements and signal integrity issues of supporting up to eight loads on a high speed bus.

The Pentium Pro processor may be upgraded by a future OverDrive® processor and matching voltage regulator module described in Chapter 17, *OverDrive® Processor Socket Specification.*

Since increasing clock frequencies and silicon density can complicate system designs, the Pentium Pro processor integrates several system components which alleviate some of the previous system requirements. The second level cache, cache controller, and Advanced Programmable Interrupt Controller (APIC) are some of the components that existed in previous Intel processor family systems which are integrated into this single component. This integration results in the Pentium Pro processor bus more closely resembling a symmetric multi-processing (SMP) system bus rather than a previous generation processor-to-cache bus. This added level of integration and improved performance results in higher power consumption and a new bus technology. This means it is more important than ever to ensure adherence to the specifications contained in this document.

The Pentium Pro processor may contain design defects or errors known as errata. Current characterized errata are available upon request.

1.1.   BUS FEATURES

The design of the external Pentium Pro processor bus enables it to be "multiprocessor ready." Bus arbitration and control, cache coherency circuitry, an MP interrupt controller and other system-level functions are integrated into the bus interface.

To relax timing constraints, the Pentium Pro processor implements a synchronous, latched bus protocol to enable a full clock cycle for signal transmission and a full clock cycle for signal interpretation and generation. This latched protocol simplifies interconnect timing requirements and supports higher frequency system designs using inexpensive ASIC interconnect technology. The Pentium Pro processor bus uses low-voltage-swing GTL+ I/O buffers, making high-frequency signal communication easier.

All output pins are actually implemented in the Pentium Pro processor as I/O buffers. This buffer design complies with IEEE 1149.1 Boundary Scan Specification, allowing all pins to be sampled and tested. An output only buffer is used only for TDO, which is not sampled in the boundary scan chain. A pin is an output pin when it is not an input for normal operation or FRC.

Most of the Pentium Pro processor cache protocol complexity is handled by the processor. A non-caching I/O bridge on the Pentium Pro processor bus does not need to recognize the cache protocol and does not need snoop logic. The I/O bridge can issue standard memory accesses on the Pentium Pro processor bus, which are transparently snooped by all Pentium Pro processor bus agents. If data is modified in a Pentium Pro processor cache, the processor transparently provides data on the bus, instead of the memory controller. This functionality eliminates the need for a back-off capability that existing I/O bridges require to enable cache writeback cycles. The memory controller must observe snoop response signals driven by the Pentium Pro processor bus agents, absorb writeback data on a modified hit, and merge any write data.

The Pentium Pro processor integrates memory type range registers (MTRRs) to replace the external address decode logic used to decode cacheability attributes.

The Pentium Pro processor bus protocol enables a near linear increase in system performance with an increase in the number of processors. The Pentium Pro processor interfaces to a multiprocessor system without any support logic. This "glueless" interface enables a desktop system to be built with an upgrade socket for another Pentium Pro processor.

The external Pentium Pro processor bus and Pentium Pro processor use a ratio clock design that provides modularity and an upgrade path. The processor internal clock frequency is an n/2 multiple of the bus clock frequency where n is an integer equal to or greater than 4 but only certain bus and processor frequency combinations are supported. Additional combinations are reserved by this specification to provide future upgrade paths. See Section 9.2., "Clock Frequencies and Ratios" for the bus and processor frequencies and combinations.

The ratio clock approach reduces the tight coupling between the processor clock and the external bus clock. For a fixed system bus clock frequency, Pentium Pro processors introduced later with higher processor clock frequencies can use the same support chip-set at the same bus frequency. An investment in a Pentium Pro processor chip-set is protected for a longer time and for a greater range of processor frequencies. The ratio clock approach also preserves system modularity, allowing the system electrical topology to determine the system bus clock frequency while process technology can determine the processor clock frequency.

The Pentium Pro processor bus architecture provides a number of features to support high reliability and high availability designs. Most of these additional features can be disabled, if necessary. For example, the bus architecture allows the data bus to be unprotected or protected with an error correcting code (ECC). Error detection and limited recovery are built into the bus protocol.

A Pentium Pro processor bus can contain up to four Pentium Pro processors, and a combination of four other loads consisting primarily of bus clusters, memory controllers, I/O bridges, and custom attachments.

In a four-processor system, the data bus is the most critical resource. To account for this situation, the Pentium Pro processor bus implements several features to maximize available bus bandwidth including pipelined transactions in which bus transactions in different phases overlap, an increase in transaction pipeline depth over previous generations, and support for deferring a transaction for later completion .

The Pentium Pro processor bus architecture is therefore adaptable to various classes of systems. In desktop multiprocessor systems, a subset of the bus features can be used. In server designs, the Pentium Pro processor bus provides an entry into low-end multiprocessing offering linear increases in performance as CPUs are added to scale performance upward allowing Pentium Pro processor systems to be superior for applications that would otherwise indicate a downsized solution.

1.2. BUS DESCRIPTION

The Pentium Pro processor bus is a demultiplexed bus with a 64-bit data path and a 36-bit address path. This section provides more details on the bus features introduced in the preceding section:

- Ease of system design
- Efficient bus utilization
- Multiprocessor ready
- Data integrity

1.2.1. System Design Aspects

The Pentium Pro processor bus clock and the Pentium Pro processor internal execution clock run at different frequencies, related by a ratio. Section 9.2., "Clock Frequencies and Ratios" provides more information about bus frequency and processor frequency.

The Pentium Pro processor bus uses GTL+. The GTL+ low voltage swing reduces both power consumption and electromagnetic interference (EMI). The low voltage swing GTL+ I/O buffers also enable direct drive by ASICs and make high-frequency signal communication easier and cheaper to implement.

The Pentium Pro processor bus is a synchronous, latched bus. The bus protocol latches all inputs on the bus clock rising edge, which are used internally in the following cycle. The Pentium Pro processor and other bus agents drive outputs on the bus clock rising edge. The bus protocol therefore provides a full cycle for signal transmission and an agent also has a full clock period to determine its output.

1.2.2. Efficient Bus Utilization

The Pentium Pro processor bus supports multiple outstanding bus transactions. The transaction pipeline depth is limited to the smallest depth supported by any agent (processors, memory, or I/O). The Pentium Pro processor bus can be configured at power-on to support a maximum of eight outstanding bus transactions depending on the amount of buffering available in the system. Each Pentium Pro processor is capable of issuing up to four outstanding transactions.

The Pentium Pro processor bus enables transactions with long latencies to be completed at a later time using separate deferred reply transactions. The same Pentium Pro processor bus agent or other Pentium Pro processor bus agents can continue with subsequent reads and writes while a slow agent is processing an outstanding request.

1.2.3. Multiprocessor Ready

The Pentium Pro processor bus enables multiple Pentium Pro processors to operate on one bus, with no external support logic. The Pentium Pro processor requires no separate snoop generation logic. The processor I/O buffers can drive the Pentium Pro processor bus in an MP system.

The Pentium Pro processors and bus support a MESI cache protocol in the internal caches. The cache protocol enables direct cache-to-cache line transfers with memory reflection.

The Pentium Pro processors and bus support fair, symmetric, round-robin bus arbitration that minimizes overhead associated with bus ownership exchange. An I/O agent may generate a high priority bus request.

1.2.4.   Data Integrity

The Pentium Pro processor bus provides parity signals for address, request, and response signals. The bus protocol supports retrying bus requests.

The Pentium Pro processor bus supports error correcting code (ECC) on the data bus and has correction capability at the receiver.

The Pentium Pro processor supports functional redundancy checking (FRC), similar to that of the Pentium processor. FRC support enables the Pentium Pro processor to be used in high data-integrity, fault-tolerant applications. In addition, two Pentium Pro processors can be configured at power-on as an FRC pair or a multiprocessor-ready pair.

1.3.   SYSTEM OVERVIEW

Figure 1-2 illustrates the Pentium Pro processor system environment, containing multiple processors (MP), memory, and I/O. This particular architectural view is not intended to imply any implementation trade-offs.

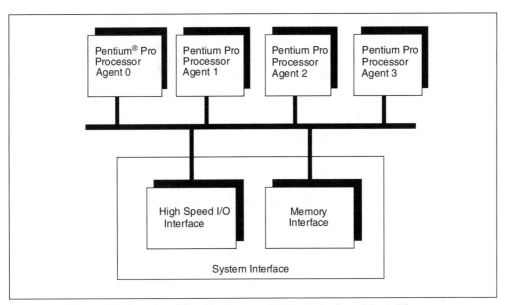

Figure 1-2. Pentium® Pro Processor System Interface Block Diagram

Up to four Pentium Pro processors can be gluelessly interconnected on the Pentium Pro processor bus. These agents are bus masters, capable of supporting all the features described in this document. The interface to the remainder of the system is represented by the high-speed I/O interface and memory interface blocks. The memory interface block represents a path to system memory capable of supporting over 500 Mbytes/second data bandwidth. The high-speed I/O interface block provides a fast path to system I/O. Various implementations of these two blocks can provide different cost vs. performance trade-offs. For example, more than one memory interface or high-speed I/O interface may be included.

An MP system containing more than four Pentium Pro processors can be created based on clusters that each contain four processors. Such a system can use cluster controllers that connect Pentium Pro processor buses to a global memory bus. The Pentium Pro processor bus provides appropriate protocol support for building external caches and memory directory-based systems.

1.4. TERMINOLOGY CLARIFICATION

Some key definitions and concepts are introduced here to aid the understanding of this document.

A '#' symbol after a signal name refers to an active low signal. This means that a signal is in the active state (based on the name of the signal) when driven low. For example, when FLUSH# is low a flush has been requested. When NMI is high, a Non-maskable interrupt has occurred. In the case of lines where the name does not imply an active state but describes part of a binary sequence (such as address or data), the '#' symbol implies that the signal is inverted. For example, D[3:0] = 'HLHL' refers to a hex 'A', and D#[3:0] = 'LHLH' also refers to a hex 'A'. (H= High logic level, L= Low logic level)

Pentium Pro processor bus agents issue ***transactions*** to transfer data and system information. A bus agent is any device that connects to the processor bus including the Pentium Pro processors themselves.

This specification refers to several classifications of bus agents.

- ***Central Agent.*** Handles reset, hardware configuration and initialization, special transactions, and centralized hardware error detection and handling.

- ***I/O Agent.*** Interfaces to I/O devices using I/O port addresses. Can be a bus bridge to another bus used for I/O devices, such as a PCI bridge.

- ***Memory Agent.*** Provides access to main memory.

A particular bus agent can have one or more of several roles in a transaction.

- ***Requesting Agent.*** The agent that issues the transaction.

- ***Addressed Agent.*** The agent that is addressed by the transaction. Also called the Target Agent. A memory or I/O transaction is addressed to the memory or I/O agent that recognizes the specified memory or I/O address. A Deferred Reply transaction is addressed to the agent that issued the original transaction. Special transactions are considered to be issued to the central agent.

- **Snooping Agent.** A caching bus agent that observes ("snoops") bus transactions to maintain cache coherency.

- **Responding Agent.** The agent that provides the response on the RS[2:0]# signals to the transaction. Typically the addressed agent.

Each transaction has several phases that include some or all of the following *phases*.

- **Arbitration Phase.** No transactions can be issued until the bus agent *owns* the bus. A transaction only needs to have this phase if the agent that wants to drive the transaction doesn't already own the bus. Note that there is a distinction between a **symmetric bus owner** and the actual **bus owner.** The actual bus owner is the one and only bus agent that is allowed to drive a transaction at that time. The symmetric bus owner is the bus owner unless the priority agent owns the bus.

- **Request Phase.** This is the phase in which the transaction is actually issued to the bus. The **request agent** drives ADS# and the address in this phase. All transactions must have this phase.

- **Error Phase.** Any errors that occur during the Request Phase are reported in the Error Phase. All transactions have this phase (1 clock).

- **Snoop Phase.** This is the phase in which cache coherency is enforced. All caching agents (snoop agents) drive HIT# and HITM# to appropriate values in this phase. All memory transactions have this phase.

- **Response Phase.** The response agent drives the transaction response during this phase. The **response agent** is the target device addressed during the Request Phase unless a transaction is deferred for later completion. All transactions have this phase.

- **Data Phase.** The response agent drives or accepts the transaction data, if there is any. Not all transactions have this phase.

Other commonly used terms include:

A **request initiated data transfer** means that the request agent has write data to transfer. A request initiated data transfer has a **request initiated TRDY# assertion.**

A **response initiated data transfer** means that the response agent must provide the read data to the request agent.

A **snoop initiated data transfer** means that there was a hit to a modified line during the snoop phase, and the agent that asserted HITM# is going to drive the modified data to the bus. This is also called an **implicit writeback** because every time HITM# is asserted, the addressed memory agent knows that writeback data will follow. A snoop initiated data transfer has a **snoop initiated TRDY# assertion.**

There is a **DEFER#** signal that is sampled during the Snoop Phase to determine if a transaction can be guaranteed in-order completion at that time. If the DEFER# signal is asserted, only two responses are allowed by the bus protocol during the Response Phase, the **Deferred Response** or the **Retry Response**. If the Deferred Response is given, the response agent must later complete the transaction with a **Deferred Reply** transaction.

1.5. COMPATIBILITY NOTE

In this document, some register bits are Intel Reserved. When reserved bits are documented, treat them as fully undefined. This is essential for software compatibility with future processors. Follow the guidelines below:

1. Do not depend on the states of any undefined bits when testing the values of defined register bits. Mask them out when testing.

2. Do not depend on the states of any undefined bits when storing them to memory or another register.

3. Do not depend on the ability to retain information written into any undefined bits.

4. When loading registers, always load the undefined bits as zeros.

intel.

2

Pentium® Pro Processor Architecture Overview

CHAPTER 2
PENTIUM® PRO PROCESSOR
ARCHITECTURE OVERVIEW

The Pentium Pro processor has a decoupled, 12-stage, superpipelined implementation, trading less work per pipestage for more stages. The Pentium Pro processor also has a pipestage time 33 percent less than the Pentium processor, which helps achieve a higer clock rate on any given process.

The approach used by the Pentium Pro processor removes the constraint of linear instruction sequencing between the traditional "fetch" and "execute" phases, and opens up a wide instruction window using an instruction pool. This approach allows the "execute" phase of the Pentium Pro processor to have much more visibility into the program's instruction stream so that better scheduling may take place. It requires the instruction "fetch/decode" phase of the Pentium Pro processor to be much more intelligent in terms of predicting program flow. Optimized scheduling requires the fundamental "execute" phase to be replaced by decoupled "dispatch/execute" and "retire" phases. This allows instructions to be started in any order but always be completed in the original program order. The Pentium Pro processor is implemented as three independent engines coupled with an instruction pool as shown in Figure 2-1.

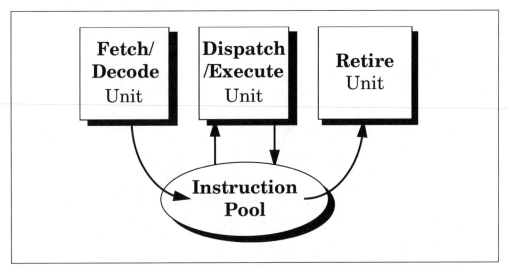

Figure 2-1. Three Engines Communicating Using an Instruction Pool

2.1. FULL CORE UTILIZATION

The three independent-engine approach was taken to more fully utilize the CPU core. Consider the code fragment in Figure 2-2:

```
r1 <= mem [r0] /* Instruction 1 */
r2 <= r1 + r2 /* Instruction 2 */
r5 <= r5 + 1 /* Instruction 3 */
r6 <= r6 - r3 /* Instruction 4 */
```

Figure 2-2. A Typical Code Fragment

The first instruction in this example is a load of r1 that, at run time, causes a cache miss. A traditional CPU core must wait for its bus interface unit to read this data from main memory and return it before moving on to instruction 2. This CPU stalls while waiting for this data and is thus being under-utilized.

To avoid this memory latency problem, the Pentium Pro processor "looks-ahead" into its instruction pool at subsequent instructions and will do useful work rather than be stalled. In the example in Figure 2-2, instruction 2 is not executable since it depends upon the result of instruction 1; however both instructions 3 and 4 are executable. The Pentium Pro processor executes instructions 3 and 4 out-of-order. The results of this out-of-order execution can not be committed to permanent machine state (i.e., the programmer-visible registers) immediately since the original program order must be maintained. The results are instead stored back in the instruction pool awaiting in-order retirement. The core executes instructions depending upon their readiness to execute, and not on their original program order, and is therefore a true dataflow engine. This approach has the side effect that instructions are typically executed out-of-order.

The cache miss on instruction 1 will take many internal clocks, so the Pentium Pro processor core continues to look ahead for other instructions that could be speculatively executed, and is typically looking 20 to 30 instructions in front of the instruction pointer. Within this 20 to 30 instruction window there will be, on average, five branches that the fetch/decode unit must correctly predict if the dispatch/execute unit is to do useful work. The sparse register set of an Intel Architecture (IA) processor will create many false dependencies on registers so the dispatch/execute unit will rename the IA registers into a larger register set to enable additional forward progress. The retire unit owns the programmer's IA register set and results are only committed to permanent machine state in these registers when it removes completed instructions from the pool in original program order.

Dynamic Execution technology can be summarized as optimally adjusting instruction execution by predicting program flow, having the ability to speculatively execute instructions in any order, and then analyzing the program's dataflow graph to choose the best order to execute the instructions.

2.2.   THE PENTIUM® PRO PROCESSOR PIPELINE

In order to get a closer look at how the Pentium Pro processor implements Dynamic Execution, Figure 2-3 shows a block diagram including cache and memory interfaces. The "Units" shown in Figure 2-3 represent stages of the Pentium Pro processor pipeline.

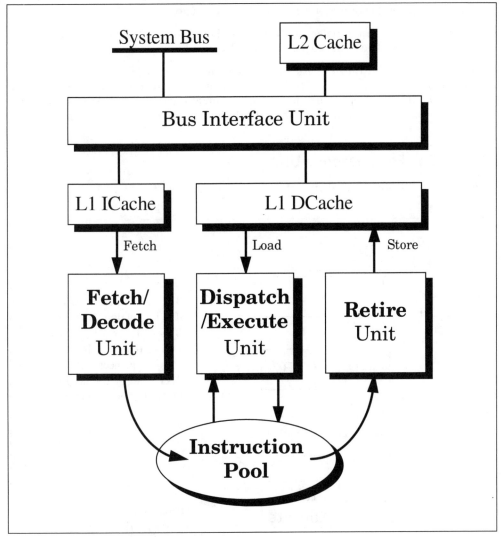

Figure 2-3. The Three Core Engines Interface with Memory via Unified Caches

- The FETCH/DECODE unit: An in-order unit that takes as input the user program instruction stream from the instruction cache, and decodes them into a series of micro-operations (μops) that represent the dataflow of that instruction stream. The pre-fetch is speculative.

- The DISPATCH/EXECUTE unit: An out-of-order unit that accepts the dataflow stream, schedules execution of the μops subject to data dependencies and resource availability and temporarily stores the results of these speculative executions.

- The RETIRE unit: An in-order unit that knows how and when to commit ("retire") the temporary, speculative results to permanent architectural state.

- The BUS INTERFACE unit: A partially ordered unit responsible for connecting the three internal units to the real world. The bus interface unit communicates directly with the L2 (second level) cache supporting up to four concurrent cache accesses. The bus interface unit also controls a transaction bus, with MESI snooping protocol, to system memory.

2.2.1. The Fetch/Decode Unit

Figure 2-4 shows a more detailed view of the Fetch/Decode Unit.

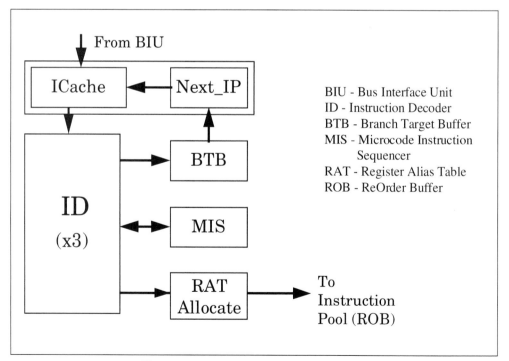

Figure 2-4. Inside the Fetch/Decode Unit

The ICache is a local instruction cache. The Next_IP unit provides the ICache index, based on inputs from the Branch Target Buffer (BTB), trap/interrupt status, and branch-misprediction indications from the integer execution section.

The ICache fetches the cache line corresponding to the index from the Next_IP, and the next line, and presents 16 aligned bytes to the decoder. The prefetched bytes are rotated so that they are justified for the instruction decoders (ID). The beginning and end of the IA instructions are marked.

Three parallel decoders accept this stream of marked bytes, and proceed to find and decode the IA instructions contained therein. The decoder converts the IA instructions into triadic µops (two logical sources, one logical destination per µop). Most IA instructions are converted directly into single µops, some instructions are decoded into one-to-four µops and the complex instructions require microcode (the box labeled MIS in Figure 2-4). This microcode is just a set of preprogrammed sequences of normal µops. The µops are queued, and sent to the Register Alias Table (RAT) unit, where the logical IA-based register references are converted into Pentium Pro processor physical register references, and to the Allocator stage, which adds status information to the µops and enters them into the instruction pool. The instruction pool is implemented as an array of Content Addressable Memory called the ReOrder Buffer (ROB).

This is the end of the in-order pipe.

2.2.2.   The Dispatch/Execute Unit

The dispatch unit selects µops from the instruction pool depending upon their status. If the status indicates that a µop has all of its operands then the dispatch unit checks to see if the execution resource needed by that µop is also available. If both are true, the Reservation Station removes that µop and sends it to the resource where it is executed. The results of the µop are later returned to the pool. There are five ports on the Reservation Station, and the multiple resources are accessed as shown in Figure 2-5.

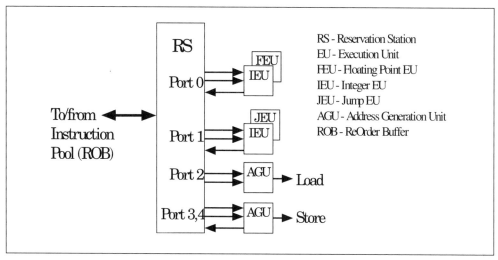

Figure 2-5. Inside the Dispatch/Execute Unit

The Pentium Pro processor can schedule at a peak rate of 5 μops per clock, one to each resource port, but a sustained rate of 3 μops per clock is typical. The activity of this scheduling process is the out-of-order process; μops are dispatched to the execution resources strictly according to dataflow constraints and resource availability, without regard to the original ordering of the program.

Note that the actual algorithm employed by this execution-scheduling process is vitally important to performance. If only one μop per resource becomes data-ready per clock cycle, then there is no choice. But if several are available, it must choose. The Pentium Pro processor uses a pseudo FIFO scheduling algorithm favoring back-to-back μops.

Note that many of the μops are branches. The Branch Target Buffer will correctly predict most of these branches but it can't correctly predict them all. Consider a BTB that is correctly predicting the backward branch at the bottom of a loop; eventually that loop is going to terminate, and when it does, that branch will be mispredicted. Branch μops are tagged (in the in-order pipeline) with their fall-through address and the destination that was predicted for them. When the branch executes, what the branch actually did is compared against what the prediction hardware said it would do. If those coincide, then the branch eventually retires, and most of the speculatively executed work behind it in the instruction pool is good.

But if they do not coincide, then the Jump Execution Unit (JEU) changes the status of all of the μops behind the branch to remove them from the instruction pool. In that case the proper branch destination is provided to the BTB which restarts the whole pipeline from the new target address.

2.2.3. The Retire Unit

Figure 2-6 shows a more detailed view of the Retire Unit.

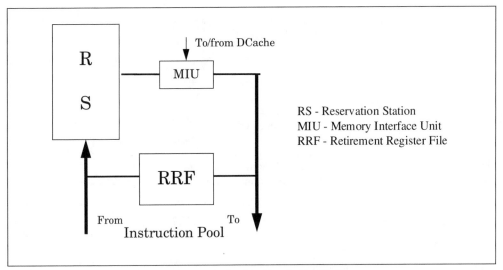

Figure 2-6. Inside the Retire Unit

The retire unit is also checking the status of µops in the instruction pool. It is looking for µops that have executed and can be removed from the pool. Once removed, the original architectural target of the µops is written as per the original IA instruction. The retirement unit must not only notice which µops are complete, it must also re-impose the original program order on them. It must also do this in the face of interrupts, traps, faults, breakpoints and mispredictions.

The retirement unit must first read the instruction pool to find the potential candidates for retirement and determine which of these candidates are next in the original program order. Then it writes the results of this cycle's retirements to both the Instruction Pool and the Retirement Register File (RRF). The retirement unit is capable of retiring 3 µops per clock.

2.2.4. The Bus Interface Unit

Figure 2-7 shows a more detailed view of the Bus Interface Unit.

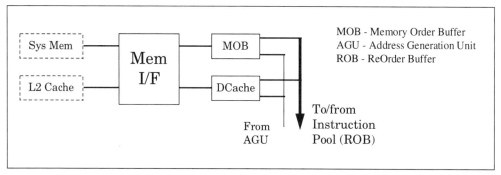

Figure 2-7. Inside the Bus Interface Unit

There are two types of memory access: loads and stores. Loads only need to specify the memory address to be accessed, the width of the data being retrieved, and the destination register. Loads are encoded into a single µop.

Stores need to provide a memory address, a data width, and the data to be written. Stores therefore require two µops, one to generate the address, and one to generate the data. These µops must later re-combine for the store to complete.

Stores are never performed speculatively since there is no transparent way to undo them. Stores are also never re-ordered among themselves. A store is dispatched only when both the address and the data are available and there are no older stores awaiting dispatch.

A study of the importance of memory access reordering concluded:

- Stores must be constrained from passing other stores, for only a small impact on performance.

- Stores can be constrained from passing loads, for an inconsequential performance loss.

- Constraining loads from passing other loads or stores has a significant impact on performance.

The Memory Order Buffer (MOB) allows loads to pass other loads and stores by acting like a reservation station and re-order buffer. It holds suspended loads and stores and re-dispatches them when a blocking condition (dependency or resource) disappears.

2.3.   ARCHITECTURE SUMMARY

Dynamic Execution is this combination of improved branch prediction, speculative execution and data flow analysis that enables the Pentium Pro processor to deliver its superior performance.

intel ®

3

Bus Overview

CHAPTER 3
BUS OVERVIEW

This chapter provides an overview of the Pentium Pro processor bus protocol, transactions, and bus signals. The Pentium Pro processor supports two other synchronous busses, APIC and JTAG. It also has PC compatibility signals and implementation specific signals. This chapter provides a functional description of the Pentium Pro processor bus only. For the Pentium Pro processor bus protocol specifications, see Chapter 4, *Bus Protocol*. For details on the Pentium Pro processor bus transactions, see Chapter 5, *Bus Transactions and Operations*. For the full Pentium Pro processor signal specifications, see Appendix A, *Signals Reference* and Table 11-2.

3.1.   SIGNAL AND DIAGRAM CONVENTIONS

Signal names use uppercase letters, such as ADS#. Signals in a set of related signals are distinguished by numeric suffixes, such as AP1 for address parity bit 1. A set of signals covering a range of numeric suffixes is denoted as AP[1:0], for address parity bits 1 and 0. A # suffix indicates that the signal is active low. A signal name without a # suffix indicates that the signal is active high.

In many cases, signals are mapped one-to-one to physical pins with the same names. In other cases, different signals are mapped onto the same pin. For example, this is the case with the address pins A[35:3]#. During the first clock of the Request Phase, the address signals are driven. The first clock is indicated by the lower case a, or just the pin name itself: Aa[35:3]#, or A[35:3]#. During the second clock of the Request Phase other information is driven on the request pins. These signals are referenced either by their functional signal names DID[7:0]#, or by using a lower case b with the pin name: Ab[23:16]#. Note also that several pins have configuration functions at the active to inactive edge of RESET#.

The term *asserted* implies that a signal is driven to its active level (logic 1, FRCERR high, or ADS# low). The term *deasserted* implies that a signal is driven to its inactive level (logic 0, FRCERR low, or ADS# high). A signal driven to its active level is said to be *active*; a signal driven to its inactive level is said to be *inactive*.

In timing diagrams, square and circle symbols indicate the clock in which particular signals of interest are driven and sampled. The square indicates that a signal is driven in that clock. The circle indicates that a signal is sampled in that clock.

All timing diagrams in this specification show signals as they are driven asserted or deasserted on the Pentium Pro processor bus. There is a one-clock delay in the signal values observed by bus agents. Any signal names that appear in lower case letters in brackets {rcnt} are internal signals only, and are not driven to the bus. Upper case letters that appear in brackets represent a group of signals such as the Request Phase signals {REQUEST}. The timing diagrams sometimes include internal signals to indicate internal states and show how it affects external signals.

When signal values are referenced in tables, a 0 indicates inactive and a 1 indicates active. 0 and 1 *do not* reflect voltage levels. Remember, a # after a signal name indicates active low. An entry of 1 for ADS# means that ADS# is active, with a low voltage level.

3.2. SIGNALING ON THE PENTIUM® PRO PROCESSOR BUS

The Pentium Pro processor bus supports a synchronous latched protocol. On the rising edge of the bus clock, all agents on the Pentium Pro processor bus are required to drive their active outputs and sample required inputs. No additional logic is located in the output and input paths between the buffer and the latch stage, thus keeping setup and hold times constant for all bus signals following the latched protocol. The Pentium Pro processor bus requires that every input be sampled during a valid sampling window on a rising clock edge and its effect be driven out no sooner than the next rising clock edge. This approach allows one full clock for inter-component communication and at least one full clock at the receiver to compute a response.

Figure 3-1 illustrates the latched bus protocol as it appears on the bus. In subsequent descriptions, the protocol is described as "B# is asserted in the clock after A# is observed active", or "B# is asserted two clocks after A# is asserted". Note that A# is asserted in T1, but not observed active until T2. The receiving agent uses T2 to determine its response and asserts B# in T3. Other agents observe B# active in T4.

The square and circle symbols are used in the timing diagrams to indicate the clock in which particular signals of interest are driven and sampled. The square indicates that a signal is driven (asserted, initiated) in that clock. The circle indicates that a signal is sampled (observed, latched) in that clock.

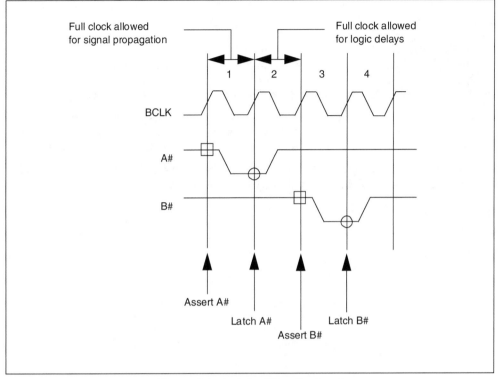

Figure 3-1. Latched Bus Protocol

Any signal names that appear in brackets { } are internal signals only, and are not driven to the bus. The timing diagrams sometimes include internal signals to indicate internal state and show how it affects external signals. All timing diagrams in this specification show bus signals as they are driven asserted or deasserted on the Pentium Pro processor bus. Internal signals are shown to change state in the clock that they would be driven to the bus if they were external signals. Internal signals actually change state internally one clock earlier.

Signals that are driven in the same clock by multiple Pentium Pro processor bus agents exhibit a "wired-OR glitch" on the electrical-low-to-electrical-high transition. To account for this situation, these signal state transitions are specified to have two clocks of settling time when deasserted before they can be safely observed. The bus signals that must meet this criteria are: BINIT#, HIT#, HITM#, BNR#, AERR#, BERR#.

3.3. PENTIUM® PRO PROCESSOR BUS PROTOCOL OVERVIEW

Bus activity is hierarchically organized into operations, transactions, and phases.

An *operation* is a bus procedure that appears atomic to software even though it may not be atomic on the bus. An operation may consist of a single bus transaction, but sometimes may involve multiple bus transactions or a single transaction with multiple data transfers. Examples of complex bus operations include: locked read/modify/write operations and deferred operations.

A *transaction* is the set of bus activities related to a single bus request. A transaction begins with bus arbitration, and the assertion of ADS# and a transaction address. Transactions are driven to transfer data, to inquire about or change cache state, or to provide the system with information.

A transaction contains up to six phases. A *phase* uses a specific set of signals to communicate a particular type of information. The six phases of the Pentium Pro processor bus protocol are:

- Arbitration
- Request
- Error
- Snoop
- Response
- Data

Not all transactions contain all phases, and some phases can be overlapped.

3.3.1. Transaction Phase Description

Figure 3-2 shows all of the Pentium Pro processor bus transaction phases for two transactions with data transfers.

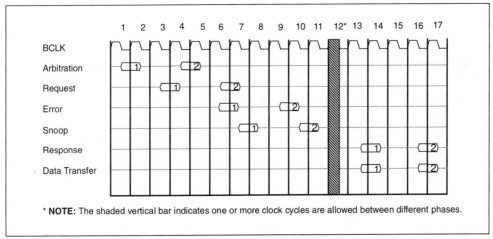

* **NOTE:** The shaded vertical bar indicates one or more clock cycles are allowed between different phases.

Figure 3-2. Pentium® Pro Processor Bus Transaction Phases

When the requesting agent does not own the bus, transactions begin with an Arbitration Phase, in which a requesting agent becomes the bus owner.

After the requesting agent becomes the bus owner, the transaction enters the Request Phase. In the Request Phase, the bus owner drives request and address information on the bus. The Request Phase is two clocks long. In the first clock, ADS# is driven along with the transaction address and sufficient information to begin snooping and memory access. In the second clock, the byte enables, deferred ID, transaction length, and other transaction information are driven.

Every transaction's third phase is an Error Phase which occurs three clocks after the Request Phase begins. The Error Phase indicates any parity errors triggered by the request.

Every transaction that isn't cancelled because an error was indicated in the Error Phase has a Snoop Phase, four or more clocks from the Request Phase. The snoop results indicate if the address driven for a transaction references a valid or modified (dirty) cache line in any bus agent's cache. The snoop results also indicate whether a transaction will be completed in-order or may be deferred for possible out-of-order completion.

Every transaction that isn't cancelled because an error was indicated in the Error Phase has a Response Phase. The Response Phase indicates whether the transaction has failed or succeeded, whether transaction completion is immediate or deferred, whether the transaction will be retried, and whether the transaction contains a Data Phase. The valid transaction responses are:

- Normal Data
- Implicit Writeback
- No Data
- Hard Failure

- Deferred

- Retry

If the transaction does not have a Data Phase, that transaction is complete after the Response Phase. If the request agent has write data to transfer or is requesting read data, the transaction has a Data Phase which may extend beyond the Response Phase.

Not all transactions contain all phases, not all phases occur in order, and some phases can be overlapped.

- All transactions that are not cancelled in the Error Phase have the Request, Error, Snoop, and Response Phases.

- Arbitration can be explicit or implicit. The Arbitration Phase only needs to occur if the agent that is driving the next transaction does not already own the bus.

- The Data Phase only occurs if a transaction requires a data transfer. The Data Phase can be absent, response initiated, request initiated, snoop initiated, or request and snoop initiated.

- The Response Phase overlaps with the beginning of the Data Phase for read transactions.

- The Response Phase (TRDY#) triggers the Data Phase for write transactions.

In addition, since the Pentium Pro processor bus supports bus transaction pipelining, phases from one transaction can overlap phases from another transaction, see Figure 3-2.

3.3.2. Bus Transaction Pipelining and Transaction Tracking

The Pentium Pro processor bus architecture supports pipelined transactions in which bus transactions in different phases overlap. The Pentium Pro processor bus may be configured to support a maximum of 1 or 8 outstanding transactions simultaneously. Each Pentium Pro processor is capable of issuing up to four outstanding transactions.

In order to track transactions, all bus agents must track certain transaction information. The transaction information that must be tracked by each bus agent is:

- Number of transactions outstanding

- What transaction is next to be snooped

- What transaction is next to receive a response

- If the transaction was issued to or from this agent

This information is tracked in a queue called an In-order Queue (IOQ). All bus agents maintain identical In-order Queue status to track every transaction that is issued to the bus. When a transaction is issued to the bus, it is also entered in the IOQ of each agent. The depth of the smallest IOQ is the limit of how many transactions can be outstanding on the bus simultaneously. Because transactions receive their responses and data in the same order as they were issued, the transaction at the top of the IOQ is the next transaction to enter the Response and Data Phases. A transaction is removed from the IOQ after the Response Phase is complete or after an error is detected in the Error Phase. The simplest bus agents can simply count events rather than implement a queue.

Other, agent specific, bus information must be tracked as well. Note that not every agent needs to track all of this additional information. Examples of additional information that might be tracked follow.

Request agents (agents that issue transactions) might track:

- How many more transactions this agent can still issue?

- Is this transaction a read or a write?

- Does this bus agent need to provide or accept data?

Response agents (agents that can provide transaction response and data) might track:

- Does this agent own the response for the transaction at the top of the IOQ?

- Does this transaction contain an implicit writeback data and does this agent have to receive the writeback data?

- If the transaction is a read, does this agent own the data transfer?

- If the transaction is a write, must this agent accept the data?

- Availability of buffer resources so it can stall further transactions if it needs to.

Snooping agents (agents with a cache) might track:

- If the transaction needs to be snooped.

- If the Snoop Phase needs to be extended.

- Does this transaction contain an implicit writeback data to be supplied by this agent?

- How many snoop requests are in the queue.

Agents whose transactions can be deferred might track:

- The deferred transaction and its agent ID.

- Availability of buffer resources.

This transaction information can be tracked by implementing multiple queues or one all encompassing In-order Queue. This document refers to these internal queue(s) as the Transaction Queues (TQ), unless the In-order Queue is specifically being referenced. Note that the IOQ is completely visible from the bus protocol, but the Transaction Queues use internal state information.

3.3.3.   Bus Transactions

The Pentium Pro processor bus supports the following types of bus transactions.

- Read and write a cache line.

- Read and write any combination of bytes in an aligned 8-byte span.

- Read and write multiple 8-byte spans.

- Read a cache line and invalidate it in other caches.

- Invalidate a cache line in other caches.

- I/O read and write.

- Interrupt Acknowledge (requiring a 1 byte interrupt vector).

- Special transactions are used to send various messages on the bus. The special transaction for the Pentium Pro processor are:

  — Shutdown

  — Flush

  — Halt

  — Sync

  — Flush Acknowledge

  — Stop Clock Acknowledge

  — SMI Acknowledge

  — Branch trace message (providing an 8-byte branch trace address)

- Deferred reply to an earlier read or write that received a deferred response.

Specific descriptions of each transaction can be found in Chapter 5, *Bus Transactions and Operations.*

3.3.4.   Data Transfers

The Pentium Pro processor bus distinguishes between *memory and I/O* transactions.

Memory transactions are used to transfer data to and from memory. Memory transactions address memory using the full width of the address bus. The Pentium Pro processor can address up to 64 Gbytes of physical memory.

I/O transactions are used to transfer data to and from the I/O address space. The Pentium Pro processor limits I/O accesses to a 64K + 3 byte I/O address space. I/O transactions use A[16:3]# to address I/O ports and always deassert A[35:17]#. A16# is zero except when the first three bytes above the 64KByte address space are accessed (I/O wraparound). This is required for compatibility with previous Intel processors.

The Pentium Pro processor bus distinguishes between different transfer lengths.

3.3.4.1. LINE TRANSFERS

A line transfer reads or writes a cache line, the unit of caching in a Pentium Pro processor system. On the Pentium Pro processor this is 32 bytes aligned on a 32-byte boundary. While a line is always aligned on a 32-byte boundary, a line transfer need not begin on that boundary. For a line transfer on the Pentium Pro processor, A[35:3]# carry the upper 33 bits of a 36-bit physical address. Address bits A[4:3]# determine the transfer order, called *burst order*. A line is transferred in four eight-byte chunks, each of which can be identified by address bits 4:3. The *chunk* size is 64-bits. Table 3-1 specifies the transfer order used for a 32-byte line, based on address bits A[4:3]# specified in the transaction's Request Phase.

Table 3-1. Burst Order Used For Pentium® Pro Processor Bus Line Transfers

A[4:3]# (binary)	Requested Address (hex)	1st Address Transferred (hex)	2nd Address Transferred (hex)	3rd Address Transferred (hex)	4th Address Transferred (hex)
00	0	0	8	10	18
01	8	8	0	18	10
10	10	10	18	0	8
11	18	18	10	8	0

Note that the requested read data is always transferred first. Unlike the Pentium processor, which always transfers writeback data address 0 first, the Pentium Pro processor transfers writeback data requested address first.

3.3.4.2. PART LINE ALIGNED TRANSFERS

A part-line aligned transfer moves a quantity of data smaller than a cache line but an even multiple of the chunk size between a bus agent and memory using the burst order. A part-line transfer affects no more than one line in a cache.

A 16-byte transfer on a 64-bit data bus with a 32-byte cache line size is a part-line transfer, where a chunk is eight bytes aligned on an eight-byte boundary. All chunks in the span of a part-line transfer are moved across the data bus. Address bits A[4:3]# determines the transfer order for the included chunks, using the burst order specified in Table 3-1 for line transfers.

A 16-byte aligned transfer requires two data transfer clocks on a 64-bit bus. Note that the Pentium Pro processor will not issue 16-byte transactions.

3.3.4.3. PARTIAL TRANSFERS

On a 64-bit data bus, a partial transfer moves from 0-8 bytes within an aligned 8-byte span to or from a memory or I/O address. The byte enable signals, BE[7:0]#, select which bytes in the span are transferred.

The Pentium Pro processor converts non-cacheable misaligned memory accesses that cross 8-byte boundaries into two partial transfers. For example, a non-cacheable, misaligned 8-byte read requires two Read Data Partial transactions. Similarly, the Pentium Pro processor converts I/O write accesses that cross 4-byte boundaries into 2 partial transfers. I/O reads are treated the same as memory reads.

On the Pentium Pro processor, I/O Read and I/O Write transactions are 1 to 4 byte partial transactions.

3.4.   SIGNAL OVERVIEW

This section describes the function of the Pentium Pro processor bus signals. In this section, the signals are grouped according to function.

In many cases, signals are mapped one-to-one to physical pins with the same names. In other cases, different signals are mapped onto the same pin. For example, this is the case with the address pins A[35:3]#. During the first clock of the Request Phase, the address signals are driven. The first clock is indicated by the lower case a, or just the pin name itself: Aa[35:3]#, or A[35:3]#. During the second clock of the Request Phase, other information is driven on the request pins. These signals are referenced either by their functional signal names DID[7:0]#, or by using a lower case b with the pin name: Ab[23:16]#. Note that several pins also have configuration functions at the active to inactive transition of RESET#.

3.4.1.   Execution Control Signals

Table 3-2. Execution Control Signals

Pin/Signal Name	Pin/Signal Mnemonic	Number
Bus Clock	BCLK	1
Initialization	INIT#, RESET#	2
Flush	FLUSH#	1
Stop Clock	STPCLK#	1
Interprocessor Communication and Interrupts	PICCLK, PICD[1:0]#, LINT[1:0]	5

The BCLK (Bus Clock) input signal is the Pentium Pro processor bus clock. All agents drive their outputs and latch their inputs on the BCLK rising edge. Each Pentium Pro processor derives its internal clock from BCLK by multiplying the BCLK frequency by a multiplier determined at configuration. See Chapter 9, *Configuration* for configuration specifications.

The RESET# input signal resets all Pentium Pro processor bus agents to known states and invalidates their internal caches. Modified or dirty cache lines are NOT written back. After RESET# is deasserted, each Pentium Pro processor begins execution at the power on reset vector defined during configuration. On observing active RESET#, all bus agents must deassert their outputs within two clocks. Configuration parameters are sampled on the clock following the sampling of RESET# inactive. (Two clocks following the deassertion of RESET#.)

The INIT# input signal resets all Pentium Pro processor bus agents without affecting their internal (L1 or L2) caches or their floating-point registers. Each Pentium Pro processor begins execution at the address vector as defined during power on configuration. INIT# has another meaning on RESET#'s active to inactive transition: if INIT# is sampled active on RESET#'s active to inactive transition, then the Pentium Pro processor executes its built-in self test (BIST).

If the FLUSH# input signal is asserted, the Pentium Pro processor bus agent writes back all internal cache lines in the Modified state (L1 and L2 caches) and invalidates all internal cache lines (L1 and L2 caches). The flush operation puts all internal cache lines in the Invalid state. After all lines are written back and invalidated, the Pentium Pro processor drives a special transaction, the Flush Acknowledge transaction, to indicate completion of the flush operation. The FLUSH# signal has a different meaning when it is sampled asserted on the active to inactive transition of RESET#. If FLUSH# is sampled asserted on the active to inactive transition of RESET#, then the Pentium Pro processor tristates all of its outputs. This function is used during board testing.

The Pentium Pro processor supplies a STPCLK# pin to enable the processor to enter a low power state. When STPCLK# is asserted, the Pentium Pro processor puts itself into the stop grant state, issues a Stop Grant Acknowledge special transaction, and optionally stops providing internal clock signals to all units except the bus unit and the APIC unit. The processor continues to snoop bus transactions while in stop grant state. When STPCLK# is deasserted, the processor restarts its internal clock to all units and resumes execution. The assertion of STPCLK# has no effect on the bus clock.

The PICCLK and PICD[1:0]# signals support the Advanced Programmable Interrupt Controller (APIC) interface. The PICCLK signal is an input clock to the Pentium Pro processor for synchronous operation of the APIC bus. The PICD[1:0]# signals are used for bidirectional serial message passing on the APIC bus.

LINT[1:0] are local interrupt signals, also defined by the APIC interface. In APIC disabled mode, LINT0 defaults to INTR, a maskable interrupt request signal. LINT1 defaults to NMI, a non-maskable interrupt. Both signals are asynchronous inputs. In the APIC enable mode, LINT0 and LINT1 are defined with the local vector table.

LINT[1:0] are also used along with the A20M# and IGNNE# signals to determine the multiplier for the internal clock frequency as described in Chapter 9, *Configuration*.

3.4.2. Arbitration Phase Signals

This signal group is used to arbitrate for the bus.

Table 3-3. Arbitration Phase Signals

Pin/Signal Name	Pin Mnemonic	Signal Mnemonic	Number
Symmetric Agent Bus Request	BR[3:0]#	BREQ[3:0]#	4
Priority Agent Bus Request	BPRI#	BPRI#	1
Block Next Request	BNR#	BNR#	1
Lock	LOCK#	LOCK#	1

Up to five agents can simultaneously arbitrate for the bus, one to four symmetric agents (on BREQ[3:0]#) and one priority agent (on BPRI#). Pentium Pro processors arbitrate as symmetric agents. The priority agent normally arbitrates on behalf of the I/O subsystem (I/O agents) and memory subsystem (memory agents).

Owning the bus is a necessary condition for initiating a bus transaction.

The symmetric agents arbitrate for the bus based on a round-robin rotating priority scheme. The arbitration is fair and symmetric. After reset, agent 0 has the highest priority followed by agents 1, 2, and 3. All bus agents track the current bus owner. A symmetric agent requests the bus by asserting its BREQn# signal. Based on the values sampled on BREQ[3:0]#, and the last symmetric bus owner, all agents simultaneously determine the next symmetric bus owner.

The priority agent asks for the bus by asserting BPRI#. The assertion of BPRI# temporarily overrides, but does not otherwise alter the symmetric arbitration scheme. When BPRI# is sampled active, no symmetric agent issues another unlocked bus transaction until BPRI# is sampled inactive. The priority agent is always the next bus owner.

BNR# can be asserted by any bus agent to block further transactions from being issued to the bus. It is typically asserted when system resources (such as address and/or data buffers) are about to become temporarily busy or filled and cannot accommodate another transaction. After bus initialization, BNR# can be asserted to delay the first bus transaction until all bus agents are initialized.

The assertion of the LOCK# signal indicates that the bus agent is executing an atomic sequence of bus transactions that must not be interrupted. A locked operation cannot be interrupted by another transaction regardless of the assertion of BREQ[3:0]# or BPRI#. LOCK# can be used to implement memory-based semaphores. LOCK# is asserted from the first transaction's Request Phase through the last transaction's Response Phase.

3.4.3. Request Signals

The request signals transfer request information, including the transaction address. A Request Phase is two clocks long beginning with the assertion of ADS#, the Address Strobe signal, as shown in Table 3-4.

Table 3-4. Request Signals

Pin Name	Pin Mnemonic	Signal Name	Signal Mnemonic	Number
Address Strobe	ADS#	Address Strobe	ADS#	1
Request Command	REQ[4:0]#	Request[1]	REQa[4:0]#	5
		Extended Request[2]	REQb[4:0]#	
Address	A[35:3]#	Address[1]	Aa[35:3]#	33
		Debug (optional)[2]	Ab[35:32]#	
		Attributes[2]	ATTR[7:0]# or Ab[31:24]#	
		Deferred ID[2]	DID[7:0]# or Ab[23:16]#	
		Byte Enables[2]	BE[7:0]# or Ab[15:8]#	
		Extended Functions[2]	EXF[4:0]# or Ab[7:3]#	
Address Parity	AP[1:0]#	Address Parity	AP[1:0]#	2
Request Parity	RP#	Request Parity	RP#	1

NOTES:

1. These signals are driven on the indicated pin during the first clock of the Request Phase (the clock in which ADS# is driven asserted).
2. These signals are driven on the indicated pin during the second clock of the Request Phase (the clock after ADS# is driven asserted).

The assertion of ADS# defines the beginning of the Request Phase. The REQa[4:0]# and Aa[35:3]# signals are valid in the clock that ADS# is asserted. The REQb[4:0]#, ATTR[7:0]#, DID[7:0], BE[7:0]#, and the EXF[4:0]# signals are all valid in the clock after ADS# is asserted. RP# and AP[1:0]# are valid in both clocks of the Request Phase. The LOCK# signal from the Arbitration Phase is asserted in the clock that ADS# is asserted for a bus locked operation.

The REQa[4:0]# and the REQb[4:0]# signals identify the transaction type as defined by Table 3-5. Note that partial memory read/write transactions can be locked on the bus by asserting the LOCK# signal. Transactions are described in detail in Chapter 5, *Bus Transactions and Operations*.

Table 3-5. Transaction Types Defined by REQa#/REQb# Signals

Transaction	REQa[4:0]#					REQb[4:0]#				
	4	3	2	1	0	4	3	2	1	0
Deferred Reply	0	0	0	0	0	x	x	x	x	x
Rsvd (Ignore)	0	0	0	0	1	x	x	x	x	x
Interrupt Acknowledge	0	1	0	0	0	DSZ#		x	0	0
Special Transactions	0	1	0	0	0	DSZ#		x	0	1
Rsvd (Central agent response)	0	1	0	0	0	DSZ#		x	1	x
Branch Trace Message	0	1	0	0	1	DSZ#		x	0	0
Rsvd (Central agent response)	0	1	0	0	1	DSZ#		x	0	1
Rsvd (Central agent response)	0	1	0	0	1	DSZ#		x	1	x
I/O Read	1	0	0	0	0	DSZ#		x	LEN#	
I/O Write	1	0	0	0	1	DSZ#		x	LEN#	
Rsvd (Ignore)	1	1	0	0	x	DSZ#		x	x	x
Memory Read & Invalidate	ASZ#		0	1	0	DSZ#		x	LEN#	
Rsvd (Memory Write)	ASZ#		0	1	1	DSZ#		x	LEN#	
Memory Code Read	ASZ#		1	D/C#=0	0	DSZ#		x	LEN#	
Memory Data Read	ASZ#		1	D/C#=1	0	DSZ#		x	LEN#	
Memory Write (may not be retried)	ASZ#		1	W/WB#=0	1	DSZ#		x	LEN#	
Memory Write (may be retried)	ASZ#		1	W/WB#=1	1	DSZ#		x	LEN#	

NOTES:

1. All commands must determine response ownership with REQa.

2. For the Pentium® Pro processor, x implies "don't care."

3. All memory commands must be snooped.

4. Special Transactions are encoded by the byte enables. See Table 3-10.

5. D/C# indicates data or code. 0 = Code, 1 = Data.

6. W/WB# = 0 indicates writeback, W/WB# = 1 indicates write.

7. ASZ# indicates address bus size. See Table 3-6.

8. LEN# indicates the length of the data transfer. See Table 3-7.

9. REQa0# active indicates the bus agent will have to provide write data and must have a TRDY#.

10. REQa1# or REQa2# active indicate that the transaction is to memory.

11. DSZ# is driven by the initiator and ignored by the responder. For the Pentium Pro processor, DSZ# = 00.

Table 3-6. Address Space Size

ASZ[1:0]#		Memory Address Space	Observing Agents
0	0	32-bit	32 & 36 bit agents
0	1	36-bit	36 bit agents only
1	0	Reserved	None
1	1	Reserved	None

If the memory access is within the 0-to-(4GByte -1) address space, ASZ[1:0]# must be 00B. If the memory access is within the 4Gbyte-to-(64GByte -1) address space, ASZ[1:0]# must be 01B. All observing bus agents that support the 4Gbyte (32 bit) address space must respond to the transaction only when ASZ[1:0]# equals 00B. All observing bus agents that support the 64GByte (36- bit) address space must respond to the transaction when ASZ[1:0]# equals 00B or 01B.

Table 3-7. Length of Data Transfer

LEN[1:0]#		Length	BE[7:0]#
0	0	0-8-bytes	Specify granularity
0	1	16-bytes	All active
1	0	32-bytes	All active
1	1	Reserved	

The LEN[1:0]# signals determine the length of the transfer. The Pentium Pro processor will not issue a request for a 16 byte data transfer.

In the clock that ADS# is asserted, the Aa[35:3]# signals provide a 36-bit, active-low address as part of the request. The Pentium Pro processor physical address space is 2^{36} bytes or 64-Gigabytes (64 Gbyte). Address bits 2, 1, and 0 are mapped into byte enable signals for 0 to 8 byte transfers.

The address signals are protected by the AP[1:0]# pins. AP1# covers A[35:24]#, AP0# covers A[23:3]#. AP[1:0]# must be valid for two clocks beginning when ADS# is asserted. A parity error detected on AP[1:0]# is indicated in the Error Phase. A parity signal on the Pentium Pro processor bus is correct if there are an even number of electrically low signals in the set consisting of the covered signals plus the parity signal. Parity is computed using voltage levels, regardless of whether the covered signals are active high or active low.

The Request Parity pin RP# covers the request pins REQ[4:0]# and the address strobe, ADS#. RP# must be valid for two clocks beginning when ADS# is asserted. A parity error detected on RP# is indicated in the Error Phase.

In the clock after ADS# is asserted, the A[35:3]# pins supply cache attribute information, a deferred ID, the byte enables and other information regarding the transaction. Specifically, the following signals are supported: ATTR[7:0]#, DID[7:0]#, BE[7:0]#, and EXF[4:0]#. The description for these signals follows.

The ATTR[7:0]# pins describe the cache attributes. They are driven based on the Memory Type Range Register attributes and the Page Table attributes as described in Table 3-8. See Chapter 6, *Range Registers* for a description of the memory types.

Table 3-8. Memory Range Register Signal Encoding

ATTR[7:0]#	Memory Type	Description
00000000	UC	UnCacheable
00000100	WC	Write-combining
00000101	WT	WriteThrough
00000110	WP	WriiteProtect
00000111	WB	WriteBack
All others	Reserved	

The DID[7:0]# signals contain the request agent ID on bits DID[6:4]#, the transaction ID on DID[3:0]#, and the agent type on DID[7]#. Symmetric agents use an agent type of 0. All priority agents use an agent type of 1. Every deferrable transaction (DEN# asserted) issued on the Pentium Pro processor bus which has not been guaranteed completion will have a unique Deferred ID. After one of these transactions passes its Snoop Result Phase without DEFER# asserted, its Deferred ID may be reused. During a deferred reply transaction, the Deferred ID of the agent that deferred the original transaction is driven instead of an address.

Table 3-9. DID[7:0]# Encoding

DID[7]#	DID[6:4]#	DID[3:0]#
Agent Type	Agent ID	Transaction ID

The Byte Enables BE[7:0]# are used to determine which bytes of data should be transferred if the data transfer is less than 8 bytes wide. BE7# applies to D[63:56], BE0# applies to D[7:0]. The byte enables are also used for special transaction encoding (see Table 3-10).

Table 3-10. Special Transaction Encoding on Byte Enables

Special Transaction	Byte Enables[7:0]#
Shutdown	0000 0001
Flush	0000 0010
Halt	0000 0011
Sync	0000 0100
Flush Acknowledge	0000 0101
Stop Grant Acknowledge	0000 0110
SMI Acknowledge	0000 0111
Reserved	all other encodings

The Extended Functions, EXF[4:0]#, supported are listed in Table 3-11.

Table 3-11. Extended Function Pins

Extended Function Pin	Extended Function Signal	Function
EXF4#	SMMEM#	Accessing SMRAM space
EXF3#	SPLCK#	Split Lock
EXF2#	Reserved	
EXF1#	DEN#	Defer Enable
EXF0#	Reserved	

EXF4# (SMM Memory) is asserted by the Pentium Pro processor if the processor is in System Management Mode and indicates that the processor is accessing a separate "shadow" memory, the SMRAM. Each memory or I/O agent must observe this signal and only accept a transaction involving SMRAM if the agent provides the SMRAM.

EXF3# (Split Lock) is asserted to indicate that a locked operation is split across 32-byte boundaries for writeback memory or 8-byte boundaries for uncacheable memory. Note that SPLCK# is asserted for the first transaction in a locked operation only.

EXF1# is asserted if the transaction can be deferred by the responding agent. EXF1# is always deasserted for the transactions in a locked operation, deferred reply transactions, and bus Writeback Line transactions.

3.4.4. Error Phase Signals

The Error Phase signal group (see Table 3-12) contains signals driven in the Error Phase. This phase is one clock long and always begins three clocks after the Request Phase begins (3 clocks after ADS# is asserted).

Table 3-12. Error Phase Signals

Type	Signal Names	Number
Address Parity Error	AERR#	1

The AERR# driver can be enabled or disabled as part of the power on configuration (see Chapter 9, *Configuration*). If the AERR# driver of all bus agents is disabled, request and address parity errors are ignored and no action is taken by the Pentium Pro processor bus agents. If the AERR# driver of at least one bus agent is enabled, the agents observing a Request Phase check the Address Parity signals (AP[1:0]#) and assert AERR# in the Error Phase if an address parity error is detected. AERR# is also asserted if an RP# parity error is detected in the Request Phase.

AERR# must not be asserted by an agent for an upper address parity error (AP1#) when the transaction address is not in the address range of the agent. Thus 32-bit agents must ignore memory transactions unless ASZ[1:0]# = 00B. 36-bit agents must ignore memory transactions unless ASZ[1:0]# = 00B or 01B.

The Pentium Pro processor supports two modes of response when the AERR# driver is enabled. This is the "AERR# observation" which may be configured at power-up. AERR# observation configuration must be consistent between all bus agents. If AERR# observation is disabled, AERR# is ignored and no action is taken by the bus agents. If AERR# observation is enabled and AERR# is sampled asserted, the request is cancelled. In addition, the request agent may retry the transaction at a later time up to its retry limit. The Pentium Pro processor has a retry limit of 1, after which the error becomes a hard error as determined by the initiating processor.

If a transaction is cancelled by AERR# assertion, then the transaction is aborted, removed from the In-order Queue and there are no further valid phases for that transaction. Snoop results are ignored if they cannot be cancelled in time. All agents reset their rotating ID for bus arbitration to the state at reset (such that bus agent 0 has highest priority).

3.4.5. Snoop Signals

The snoop signal group (see Table 3-13) provides snoop result information to the Pentium Pro processor bus agents in the Snoop Phase. The Snoop Phase is four clocks after a transaction's Request Phase begins (4 clocks after ADS# is asserted), or the 3rd clock after the previous snoop results, whichever is later.

Table 3-13. Snoop Signals

Type	Signal Names	Number
Keeping a Non-Modified Cache Line	HIT#	1
Hit to a Modified Cache Line	HITM#	1
Defer Transaction Completion	DEFER#	1

On observing a Request Phase (ADS# active) for a memory access, all caching agents are required to perform an internal snoop operation and appropriately return HIT# and HITM# in the Snoop Phase. HIT# and HITM# are be used to indicate that the line is valid or invalid in the snooping agent, whether the line is in the modified (dirty) state in the caching agent, or whether the Snoop Phase needs to be extended. The HIT# and HITM# signals are used to maintain cache coherency at the system level. A caching agent must assert HIT# and deassert HITM# in the Snoop Phase if the agent plans to retain the line in its cache after the snoop. Otherwise, unless the caching agent wishes to stall the Snoop Phase, the HIT# signal should be deasserted. The requesting agent determines the highest permissible cache state of the line using the HIT# signal. If HIT# is asserted, the requester may cache the line in the Shared state. If HIT# is deasserted, the requester may cache the line in the Exclusive or Shared state. Multiple caching agents can assert HIT# in the same Snoop Phase.

A snooping agent asserts HITM# if the line is in the Modified state. After asserting HITM#, the agent assumes responsibility for writing back the modified line during the Data Phase (this is called an implicit writeback).

The memory agent must observe HITM# in the Snoop Phase. If the memory agent observes HITM# active, it relinquishes responsibility for the data return and becomes a target for the implicit cache line writeback. The memory agent must merge the cache line being written back with any write data and update memory. The memory agent must also provide the implicit writeback response for the transaction.

The Pentium Pro processor and bus supports *self snooping*. Self snooping means that an agent can snoop its own request and drive the snoop result in the Snoop Phase. The Pentium Pro processor uses self-snooping to resolve certain boundary conditions associated with bus-lock operations that hit Modified cache lines, and conflicts associated with page table aliasing. Because the Pentium Pro processor uses self-snooping, the memory agent **must always** provide support for implicit writebacks, even in uniprocessor systems.

If HIT# and HITM# are sampled asserted together in the Snoop Phase, it means that a caching agent is not ready to indicate snoop status, and it needs to stall the Snoop Phase. The snoop signals (HIT#, HITM#, and DEFER#) are sampled again two clocks later. This process continues as long as the stall state is sampled. The snoop stall is provided to stretch the completion of a snoop as needed by any agent that needs to block further progress of snoops.

The DEFER# signal is also driven in the Snoop Phase. DEFER# is deasserted to indicate that the transaction can be guaranteed in-order completion. An agent asserting DEFER# ensures proper removal of the transaction from the In-order Queue by generating the appropriate response. There are three valid responses when DEFER# is sampled asserted (and HITM# is sampled deasserted): the deferred response, implying that the operation will be completed at a later time; a retry response, implying that the transaction should be retried; or a hard error response.

HITM# overrides DEFER# to determine the response type. DEFER# may still affect a locked operation. See Chapter 5, *Bus Transactions and Operations* for details.

The requesting agent observes HIT#, HITM#, and DEFER# to determine the line's final state in its cache. DEFER# inactive enables the requesting agent to complete the transaction in order and make the transition to the final cache state. A transaction with DEFER# active (and HITM# inactive) can be completed with a deferred reply transaction (and a delayed transition to final cache state) or can be retried.

3.4.6.   Response Signals

The response signal group (see Table 3-14) provides response information to the requesting agent in the Response Phase. The Response Phase of a transaction occurs after the Snoop Phase of the same transaction, and after the Response Phase of a previous transaction. Also, if the transaction includes a data transfer, the data transfer of a previous transaction must be complete before the Response Phase for the new transaction is entered.

Table 3-14. Response Signals

Type	Signal Names	Number
Response Status	RS[2:0]#	3
Response Parity	RSP#	1
Target Ready (for writes)	TRDY#	1

Requests initiated in the Request Phase enter the In-order Queue, which is maintained by every agent. The response agent is the agent responsible for completing the transaction at the top of the In-order Queue. The response agent is the agent addressed by the transaction.

For write transactions, TRDY# is asserted by the response agent to indicate that it is ready to accept write or writeback data. For write transactions with an implicit writeback, TRDY# is asserted twice, first for the write data transfer and then again for the implicit writeback data transfer.

The response agent asserts RS[2:0]# to indicate one of the valid transaction responses indicated in Table 3-15.

Table 3-15. Transaction Response Encodings

RS2#	RS1#	RS0#	Description and Required Snoop Result
0	0	0	Idle state. (The RS[2:0]# pins must be driven inactive after being sampled asserted)
0	0	1	Retry response.
0	1	0	Deferred response. The data bus is used only by a writing agent.
0	1	1	Reserved.
1	0	0	Hard failure response.
1	0	1	No Data response.
1	1	0	Implicit writeback response. A snooping agent will transfer writeback data on the data bus. Memory agent must merge writeback data with any transaction data and provide the response. (HITM#=1)
1	1	1	Normal data response

The RS2#, RS1#, and RS0# signals must be interpreted together and cannot be interpreted individually.

The RSP# signal provides parity for RS[2:0]#. RSP# must be valid on all clocks, not just response clocks. A parity signal on the Pentium Pro processor bus is correct if there are an even number of low signals in the set consisting of the covered signals plus the parity signal. Parity is computed using voltage levels, regardless of whether the covered signals are active high or active low.

3.4.7.   Data Phase Signals

The data transfer signals group (see Table 3-16) contains signals driven in the Data Phase. Some transactions do not transfer data and have no Data Phase. A Data Phase ranges from one to four clocks of actual data being transferred. A cache line transfer takes four data transfers on a 64-bit bus. A transfer can contain waitstates which extends the length of the Data Phase. Read transactions have zero or one Data Phase, write transactions have zero, one or two Data Phases.

Table 3-16. Data Phase Signals

Type	Signal Names	Number
Data Ready	DRDY#	1
Data Bus Busy	DBSY#	1
Data	D[63:0]#	64
Data ECC Protection	DEP[7:0]#	8

DRDY# indicates that valid data is on the bus and must be latched. The data bus owner asserts DRDY# for each clock in which valid data is to be transferred. DRDY# can be deasserted to insert wait states in the Data Phase.

DBSY# is used to hold the bus before the first DRDY# and between DRDY# assertions for a multiple clock data transfer. DBSY# need not be asserted for single clock data transfers if no wait states are needed.

During deferred reply transactions, the agent that initiates the deferred reply provides the response for the transaction. If there is data to transfer, it is transferred with the same protocol as read data (in other words, no TRDY# is needed).

The D[63:0]# signals provide a 64-bit data path between bus agents. For a partial transfer, including I/O Read and I/O Write, the byte enable signals, BE[7:0]# determine which bytes of the data bus will contain the valid data.

The DEP[7:0]# signals provide optional ECC (error correcting code) covering D[63:0]#. As described in Chapter 9, *Configuration*, the Pentium Pro processor data bus can be configured with either no checking or ECC. If ECC is enabled, then DEP[7:0]# provides valid ECC for the entire data bus on each data clock, regardless of which bytes are enabled. The error correcting code can correct single bit errors and detect double bit errors.

3.4.8. Error Signals

The error signals group (see Table 3-17) contains error signals that are not part of the Error Phase.

Table 3-17. Error Signals

Type	Signal Names	Number
Bus Initialization	BINIT#	1
Bus Error	BERR#	1
Internal Error	IERR#	1
FRC Error	FRCERR	1

BINIT# is used to signal any bus condition that prevents reliable future operation of the bus. Like the AERR# pin, the BINIT# driver can be enabled or disabled as part of the power-on configuration (see Chapter 9, *Configuration*). If the BINIT# driver is disabled, BINIT# is never asserted and no action is taken by the Pentium Pro processor on bus errors.

Regardless of whether the BINIT# driver is enabled, the Pentium Pro processor bus agent supports two modes of operation that may be configured at power on. These are the BINIT# observation and driving modes. If BINIT# observation is disabled, BINIT# is ignored and no action is taken by the processor even if BINIT# is sampled asserted. If BINIT# observation is enabled and BINIT# is sampled asserted, all bus state machines are reset. All agents reset their rotating ID for bus arbitration, and internal state information is lost. L1 and L2 cache contents are not affected. BINIT# observation and driving must be enabled for proper Pentium Pro processor operation.

A machine-check exception may or may not be taken for each assertion of BINIT# as configured in software.

The BERR# pin is used to signal any error condition caused by a bus transaction that will not impact the reliable operation of the bus protocol (for example, memory data error, non-modified snoop error). A bus error that causes the assertion of BERR# can be detected by the processor, or by another bus agent. The BERR# driver can be enabled or disabled at power-on reset. If the BERR# driver is disabled, BERR# is never asserted. If the BERR# driver is enabled, the Pentium Pro processor may assert BERR#.

A machine check exception may or may not be taken for each assertion of BERR# as configured at power on. The Pentium Pro processor will always disable the machine check exception by default.

If a Pentium Pro processor detects an internal error unrelated to bus operation, it asserts IERR#. For example, a parity error in an L1 or L2 cache causes a Pentium Pro processor to assert IERR#. A machine check exception may or may not be taken for each assertion of IERR# as configured with software.

Two Pentium Pro processors may be configured as an FRC (functional redundancy checking) pair. In this configuration, one processor acts as the master and the other acts as a checker, and the pair operates as a single, logical Pentium Pro processor. If the checker Pentium Pro processor detects a mismatch between its internally sampled outputs and the master Pentium Pro processor's outputs, the checker asserts FRCERR. FRCERR observation can be enabled at the master processor with software. The master enters machine check on an FRCERR provided that Machine Check Execution is enabled.

The FRCERR signal is also toggled during the Pentium Pro processor's reset action. A Pentium Pro processor asserts FRCERR one clock after RESET# transitions from its active to inactive state. If the Pentium Pro processor executes its built-in self test (BIST), then FRCERR is asserted throughout that test. When BIST completes, the Pentium Pro processor desserts FRCERR if BIST succeeds and continues to assert FRCERR if BIST fails. If the Pentium Pro processor does not execute the BIST action, then it keeps FRCERR asserted for less than 20 clocks and then deasserts it.

3.4.9. Compatibility Signals

The compatibility signals group (see Table 3-18) contains signals defined for compatibility within the Intel architecture processor family.

Table 3-18. PC Compatibility Signals

Type	Signal Names	Number
Floating-Point Error	FERR#	1
Ignore Numeric Error	IGNNE#	1
Address 20 Mask	A20M#	1
System Management Interrupt	SMI#	1

The Pentium Pro processor asserts FERR# when it detects an unmasked floating-point error. FERR# is included for compatibility with systems using DOS-type floating-point error reporting.

If the IGNNE# input signal is asserted, the Pentium Pro processor ignores a numeric error and continues to execute non-control floating-point instructions. If the IGNNE# input signal is deasserted, the Pentium Pro processor freezes on a non-control floating-point instruction if a previous instruction caused an error.

If the A20M# input signal is asserted, the Pentium Pro processor masks physical address bit 20 (A20#) before looking up a line in any internal cache and before driving a memory read/write transaction on the bus. Asserting A20M# emulates the 8086 processor's address wraparound at the one Mbyte boundary. A20M# must only be asserted when the processor is in real mode. A20M# is not used to mask external snoop addresses.

The IGNNE# and A20M# signals are valid at all times. These signals are normally not guaranteed recognition at specific boundaries. However, to guarantee recognition of A20M#, and the trailing edge of IGNNE# following an I/O write instruction, these signals must be valid in the Response Phase of the corresponding I/O Write bus transaction.

The A20M# and IGNNE# signals have different meanings during a reset. A20M# and IGNNE# are sampled on the active to inactive transition of RESET# to determine the multiplier for the internal clock frequency, as described in Chapter 9, *Configuration*.

System Management Interrupt is asserted asynchronously by system logic. On accepting a System Management Interrupt, the Pentium Pro processor saves the current state and enters SMM mode. It issues an SMI Acknowledge Bus transaction and then begins program execution from the SMM handler.

3.4.10. Diagnostic Signals

Table 3-19. Diagnostic Support Signals

Type	Signal Names	Number
Breakpoint Signals	BP[3:2]#	2
Performance Monitor	BPM[1:0]#	2
Boundary Scan/Test Access	TCK, TDI, TDO, TMS, TRST#	5

The BP[3:2]# signals are the System Support group Breakpoint signals. They are outputs from the Pentium Pro processor that indicate the status of breakpoints.

The BPM[1:0]# signals are more System Support group breakpoint and performance monitor signals. They are outputs from the Pentium Pro processor that indicate the status of breakpoints and programmable counters used for monitoring Pentium Pro processor performance.

The diagnostic signals group shown in Table 3-19 provides signals for probing the Pentium Pro processor, monitoring Pentium Pro processor performance, and implementing an IEEE 1149.1 boundary scan.

PM[1:0]# are the Performance Monitor signals. These signals are outputs from the Pentium Pro processor that indicate the status of four programmable counters for monitoring Pentium Pro processor performance.

TCK is the Test Clock, used to clock activity on the five-signal Test Access Port (TAP). TDI is the Test Data In signal, transferring serial test data into the Pentium Pro processor. TDO is the Test Data Out signal, transferring serial test data out of the Pentium Pro processor. TMS is used to control the sequence of TAP controller state changes. TRST# is used to asynchronously initialize the TAP controller.

3.4.11. Power, Ground, and Reserved Pins

The Pentium Pro processor bus and Pentium Pro processor dedicate many pins to power and ground signals. Refer to Chapter 15, *Mechanical Specifications* for the pin assignment.

intel®

4

Bus Protocol

intel

CHAPTER 4
BUS PROTOCOL

This chapter describes the protocol followed by bus agents in a transaction's six phases. The phases are:

- Arbitration Phase

- Request Phase

- Error Phase

- Snoop Phase

- Response Phase

- Data Phase

4.1.   ARBITRATION PHASE

A bus agent must have bus ownership before it can initiate a transaction. If the agent is not the bus owner, it enters the Arbitration Phase to obtain ownership. Once ownership is obtained, the agent can enter the Request Phase and issue a transaction to the bus.

4.1.1.   Protocol Overview

The Pentium Pro processor bus arbitration protocol supports two classes of bus agents: symmetric agents and priority agents.

The symmetric agents support fair, distributed arbitration using a round-robin algorithm. Each symmetric agent has a unique Agent ID between zero and three assigned at reset. The algorithm arranges the four symmetric agents in a circular order of priority: 0, 1, 2, 3, 0, 1, 2, etc. Each symmetric agent also maintains a common Rotating ID that reflects the symmetric Agent ID of the most recent bus owner. On every arbitration event, the symmetric agent with the highest priority becomes the symmetric owner. Note that the symmetric owner is not necessarily the overall bus owner. The symmetric owner is allowed to enter the Request Phase provided no other action of higher priority is preventing the use of the bus.

The priority agent(s) has higher priority than the symmetric owner. Once the priority agent arbitrates for the bus, it prevents the symmetric owner from entering into a new Request Phase unless the new transaction is part of an ongoing bus locked operation. The priority agent is allowed to enter the Request Phase provided no other action of higher priority is preventing the use of the bus.

Pentium Pro processors are symmetric agents. The priority agent normally arbitrates on behalf of the I/O and possibly memory subsystems.

Besides the two classes of arbitration agents, each bus agent has two actions available that act as arbitration modifiers: the bus lock and the request stall.

The bus lock action is available to the current symmetric owner to block other agents, including the priority agent from acquiring the bus. Typically a bus locked operation consists of two or more transactions issued on the bus as an indivisible sequence (this is indicated on the bus by the assertion of the LOCK# pin). Once the symmetric bus owner has successfully initiated the first bus locked transaction it continues to issue remaining requests that are part of the same indivisible operation without releasing the bus.

The request stall action is available to any bus agent that is unable to accept new bus transactions. By asserting a signal (BNR#) any agent can prevent the current bus owner from issuing new transactions.

In summary, the priority for entering the Request Transfer Phase, assuming there is no bus stall or arbitration reset event, is:

1.   The current bus owner retains ownership until it completes an ongoing indivisible bus locked operation.

2.   The priority agent gains bus ownership over a symmetric owner.

3.   Otherwise, the current symmetric owner as determined by the rotating priority is allowed to generate new transactions.

4.1.2.   Bus Signals

The Arbitration Phase signals are BREQ[3:0]#, BPRI#, BNR#, and LOCK#.

BREQ[3:0]# bus signals are connected to the four symmetric agents in a rotating manner as shown in Figure 4-1. This arrangement initializes every symmetric agent with a unique Agent ID during power-on configuration. Every symmetric agent has one input/output pin, BR0#, to arbitrate for the bus during normal operation. The remaining three pins, BR1#, BR2#, and BR3#, are input only and are used to observe the arbitration requests of the remaining three symmetric agents.

At reset, the central agent is responsible for asserting the BREQ0# bus signal. BREQ[3:1]# remain deasserted. All Pentium Pro processors sample BR[3:1]# on the active to inactive transition of RESET# to determine their arbitration IDas follows :

• The BR1#, BR2#, and BR3# pins are all inactive on Agent 0.

• Agent 1 has BR3# active.

• Agent 2 has BR2# active.

• Agent 3 has BR1# active.

The BPRI# signal is an output from the priority agent by which it arbitrates for the bus ownership and an input to the symmetric agents. The LOCK# and BNR# signals are bi-directional signals bused among all agents. The current bus owner uses LOCK# to define an indivisible bus locked operation. BNR# is used by any bus agent to stall further request phase initiation.

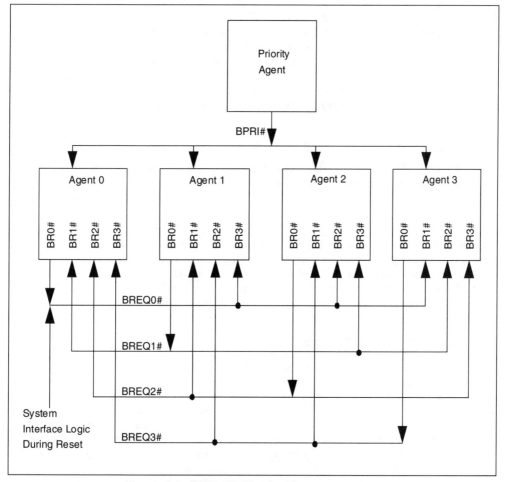

Figure 4-1. BR[3:0]# Physical Interconnection

4.1.3. Internal Bus States

In order to maintain a glueless MP interface, some bus state is distributed and must be tracked by all agents on the bus. This section describes the bus state that needs to be tracked internally by Pentium Pro processor bus agents.

4.1.3.1. SYMMETRIC ARBITRATION STATES

As described before, each symmetric agent must maintain a two-bit Agent ID and a two-bit Rotating ID to perform distributed round-robin arbitration. In addition, each symmetric agent must also maintain a symmetric ownership state bit that describes if the bus ownership is being retained by the current symmetric owner ("busy" state) or being returned to a state where no symmetric agent currently owns the bus ("idle" state). The Pentium Pro processor will enter the idle state after AERR#, BINIT# and RESET#. The notion of idle state enables a shorter, two-clock arbitration latency from bus request to its ownership. The notion of busy state enables bus parking but increases arbitration latency to a minimum of four clocks due to a handshake with the current symmetric owner. Bus parking means that the current bus owner maintains bus ownership even if it currently does not have a pending transaction. If a transaction becomes pending before that bus owner relinquishes bus ownership, it can drive the transaction without having to arbitrate for the bus. The Pentium Pro processor implements bus parking.

4.1.3.1.1. Agent ID

An agent's Agent ID is determined at reset and cannot change without the assertion of RESET#. The Agent ID is unique for every symmetric agent.

4.1.3.1.2. Rotating ID

The Rotating ID points to the agent that will be the lowest priority agent in the next arbitration event with active requests, (this is the Agent ID of the current symmetric bus owner). All symmetric agents maintain the same Rotating ID. The Rotating ID is initialized to 3 at reset. It is assigned the Agent ID of the new symmetric owner after an arbitration event so that the new owner becomes the lowest priority agent on the next arbitration event.

4.1.3.1.3. Symmetric Ownership State

The symmetric ownership state is reset to idle on an arbitration reset. The state becomes busy when any symmetric agent completes the Arbitration Phase and becomes symmetric owner. The state remains busy while the current symmetric owner retains bus ownership or transfers it to a different symmetric agent on the next arbitration event. When the state is busy, the Rotating ID is the same as the symmetric owner Agent ID. When the state is idle, the Rotating ID is the same as the last symmetric owner Agent ID. Note that the symmetric ownership state refers only to the symmetric bus owner. The priority agent can have actual physical ownership of the request bus, even while the state is busy and there is also a symmetric bus owner.

4.1.3.2. REQUEST STALL PROTOCOL

Any bus agent can stop all agents from issuing transactions via the BNR# (block next request) pin. This is typically done when the agent has one free request buffer remaining and cannot rely on the In-order Queue depth limit to sufficiently limit the number of transactions initiated on the bus. BNR# can be used to stall transactions for a user-defined amount of time, or it can be used to throttle the frequency of the transactions issued to the bus. BNR# can also be used to prevent any transactions from being issued after RESET# or BINIT# to block transactions while bus agents initialize themselves. For debugging, performance monitoring, or test purposes, an agent can assert BNR# to issue one transaction to the bus at a time (no pipelining). When stalling the bus, the stalling condition must be able to clear without requiring access to the bus.

4.1.3.2.1. Request Stall States

The request stall protocol can be described using three states: The "free" state in which transactions can be driven to the bus normally, one every 3 clocks, the "stalled" state in which no transactions are driven to the bus, and the "throttled" state in which one transaction may be driven to the bus. The throttled state is a temporary state which will transition to either free or stalled at the next sample point.

If BNR# is always active when sampled, then no transactions are driven to the bus because all agents remain in the stalled state.

To get to the free state where transactions are driven normally to the bus (a maximum of one ADS# every three clocks), BNR# must be sampled inactive on two consecutive sample points.

The existence of the throttled state enables one transaction to be sent to the bus every time BNR# is sampled deasserted. When the processor is in the throttled state, one transaction can be driven to the bus. The throttled state is a temporary state.

4.1.3.2.2. BNR# Sampling

BNR# is deasserted with RESET# and BINIT#. After RESET#, BNR# is first sampled 2 clocks after RESET# is sampled deasserted. After BINIT#, BNR# is first sampled 4 clocks after BINIT# is sampled asserted. BNR# is a wired-OR signal and must not be driven active for two consecutive clocks, if it is asserted in one clock, it must be deasserted in the next clock.

BNR# has two sampling modes. It is sampled every other clock while in the stalled or throttled state, and it is sampled in the third clock after ADS# is sampled asserted in the free state.

BNR# must be driven active only during a valid sampling window and should be deasserted in the following clock. Bus agents must ignore BNR# in the clock after a valid sampling window.

4.1.4. Arbitration Protocol Description

This section describes the arbitration protocol using examples. For reference, Section 4.1.5., "Symmetric Agent Arbitration Protocol Rules" through Section 4.1.7., "Bus Lock Protocol Rules" list the rules.

4.1.4.1. SYMMETRIC ARBITRATION OF A SINGLE AGENT AFTER RESET#

Figure 4-2 illustrates bus arbitration initiated after a reset sequence. BREQ[3:0]#, BPRI#, LOCK#, and BNR# must be deasserted during RESET#. (BREQ0# is asserted 2 clocks before RESET# is deasserted for initialization reasons as described in Section 4.1.2., "Bus Signals".) Symmetric agents can begin arbitration after BIST and MP initialization by driving the BREQ[3:0]# signals. Once ownership is obtained, the symmetric owner can park on the bus as long as no other symmetric agent is requesting it. The symmetric owner can voluntarily release the bus to idle.

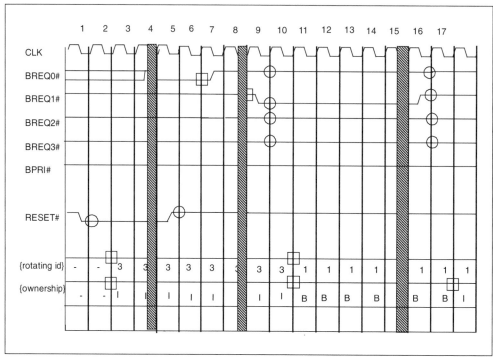

Figure 4-2. Symmetric Arbitration of a Single Agent After RESET#

RESET# is asserted in T1, which is observed by all agents in T2. This signal forces all agents to initialize their internal states and bus signals. In T3 or T4, all agents deassert their arbitration request signals BREQ[3:0]#, BPRI# and arbitration modifier signals BNR# and LOCK#. The symmetric agents reset the ownership state to idle and the Rotating ID to three (so that bus agent 0 has the highest symmetric priority after RESET# is deasserted).

In T9, after BIST and MP initialization, agent 1 asserts BREQ1# to arbitrate for the bus. In T10, all agents observe active BREQ1# and inactive BREQ[0,2,3]#. During T10, all agents determine that agent 1 is the only symmetric agent arbitrating for the bus and therefore has the highest priority. As a result, in T11, all agents update their Rotating ID to "1", the Agent ID of the new symmetric owner and its ownership state to busy, indicating that the bus is busy.

Starting from T10, agent 1 continually monitors BREQ[0,2,3]# to determine if it can park on the bus. Since BREQ[0,2,3]# are observed inactive, it continues to maintain bus ownership by keeping BREQ1# asserted.

In T16, agent 1 voluntarily deasserts BREQ1# to release bus ownership, which is observed by all agents in T17. In T18 all agents update the ownership state from busy to idle. This action reduces the arbitration latency of a new symmetric agent to two clocks on the next arbitration event.

4.1.4.2. SIGNAL DEASSERTION AFTER BUS RESET

Figure 4-3 illustrates how signals are deasserted after a bus reset. This relaxed deassertion protocol gives all bus agents time to initialize. Since agents must deassert bus signals in response to both BINIT# and RESET#, agents will respond to both reset assertions in the same fashion.

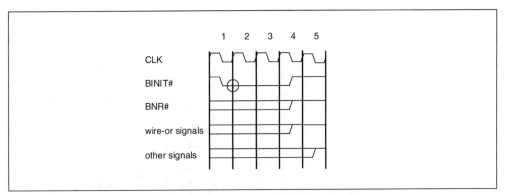

Figure 4-3. Signal Deassertion After Bus Reset

On observation of the start of the reset event, all bus signals must be deasserted as indicated in Figure 4-3. This event is the deasserted to asserted transition of RESET# or BINIT#. In T1 the first agent asserts BINIT#. In T2 all agents sample RESET# or BINIT# active. In response to observing BINIT# active in T2 any agent driving BINIT# from the first or second clock must deassert BINIT# in T4 (see Chapter 8, *Data Integrity* for details on the BINIT# protocol). Also in T4, at the latest, all agents must deassert the wired-or control signals HIT#, HITM#, AERR#, BERR# and BNR#.

In T5, BINIT#, BNR#, HIT#, HITM#, AERR# and BERR# may have invalid signal level due to wired-or glitches. T5 is the latest that an agent can deassert all other non wired-or bus signals. In T6 all signals should have a valid inactive level.

All bus signals are sampled two clocks after the end of the reset event. This event for RESET# is sampling the asserted to deasserted transition. For BINIT#, this event is the fourth clock of BINIT# assertion. BNR# must be asserted in the clock after the end of reset event, if the agent intends to block ADS#.

All bus drivers must be aware of potential wired-or glitches due to power on configuration. If a signal could be driven due to power on configuration, a driver must wait one additional cycle after the end of the reset event before the signal can be asserted for normal operation.

4.1.4.3. DELAY OF TRANSACTION GENERATION AFTER RESET

Figure 4-4 illustrates how transactions can be prevented from being issued to the bus after reset in order to give all bus agents time to initialize. Note that symmetric arbitration is not affected by the state of BNR#.

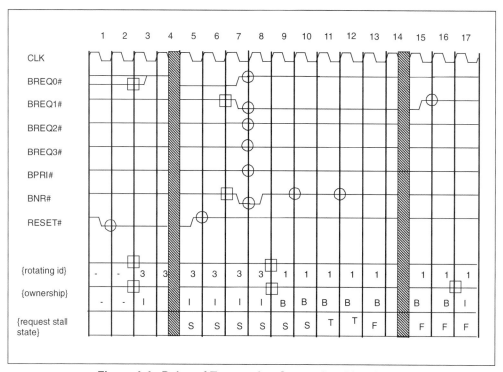

Figure 4-4. Delay of Transaction Generation After Reset

Figure 4-4 is identical to Figure 4-2 except that BNR# is sampled asserted at its first sampling point in T8. This keeps the request stall state in the stalled state(S) where no transactions are allowed to be generated. Note that this does not affect the arbitration event starting with BREQ1# assertion in T7. Agent 1 wins symmetric ownership in T8, even though no transactions may be generated.

BNR# is sampled deasserted in its next two sampling points and the request stall state transitions through the throttled state(T) in T11 to the free state(F) in T13. Transactions can be issued by agent 1 in any clock starting from T11 through T15.

4.1.4.4.   SYMMETRIC ARBITRATION WITH NO LOCK#

Figure 4-5 illustrates arbitration between two or more symmetric agents while LOCK# and BPRI# stay inactive. Because LOCK# and BPRI# remain inactive, bus ownership is determined based on a Rotating ID and bus ownership state. The symmetric agent that wins the bus releases it to the other agent as soon as possible (the Pentium Pro processor limits it to one transaction, unless the outstanding operation is locked). The symmetric agent may re-arbitrate one clock after releasing the bus. Also note that when a symmetric agent *n* issues a transaction to the bus, BREQ*n*# must stay asserted until the clock in which ADS# is asserted.

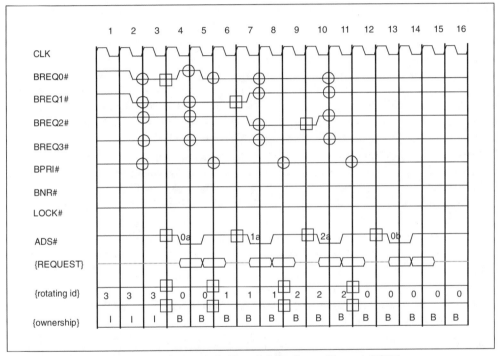

Figure 4-5. Symmetric Bus Arbitration with no LOCK#

In T1, all arbitration requests BREQ[3:0]# and BPRI# are inactive. The bus is not stalled by BNR#. The Rotating ID is 3 and bus ownership state is idle(I). Hence, the round-robin arbitration priority is 0,1,2,3.

In T2, agent 0 and agent 1 activate BREQ0# and BREQ1# respectively to arbitrate for the bus. In T3, all agents observe inactive BREQ[3:2]# and active BREQ[1:0]#. Since the Rotating ID is 3, during T3, all agents determine that agent 0 has the highest priority and is the next symmetric owner. In T4, all agents update the Rotating ID to zero and the bus ownership state to busy(B).

Since BPRI# is observed inactive in T3 and the bus is not stalled, in T4, agent 0 can begin a new Request Phase. (If BPRI# has been asserted in T3, the arbitration event, the updating of the Rotating ID, and ownership states would not have been affected. However, agent 0 would not be able to drive a transaction in T4. In T4, agent 0 initiates request phase 0a.

In response to active BREQ1# observed in T3, agent 0 deasserts BREQ0# in T4 to release bus ownership. Since it has another internal request, it immediately reasserts BREQ0# after one clock in T5.

In T5, all symmetric agents observe BREQ0# deassertion, the release of bus ownership by the current symmetric owner. During T5, all symmetric agents recognize that agent 1 now remains the only symmetric agent arbitrating for the bus. In T6, they update the Rotating ID to 1. The ownership state remains busy.

Agent 1 assumes bus ownership in T6 and generates request phase 1a in T7 (three cycles from request 0a). In response to active BREQ0# observed in T5, agent 1 deasserts BREQ1# in T7 along with the first clock of the Request Phase and releases symmetric ownership. Meanwhile, agent 2 asserts BREQ2# to arbitrate for the bus. In T8, all agents observe inactive BREQ1#, the release of ownership by the current symmetric owner. Since the Rotating ID is one, and BREQ0#, BREQ2# are active, all agents determine that agent 2 is the next symmetric owner. In T9, all agents update the Rotating ID to 2. The ownership state remains busy.

In T10, (three cycles from request 1a) agent 2 drives request 2a. In response to active BREQ0# observed in T9, agent 2 deasserts BREQ2# in T10. In T11 all agents observe inactive BREQ2# and active BREQ0#. During T11, they recognize that agent 0 is the only symmetric agent arbitrating for the bus. In T12, all agents update the Rotating ID to 0. The ownership state remains busy.

In T12, agent 0 assumes bus ownership. In T13 agent 0 initiates request 0b (three cycles from request 2a). Because no other agent has requested the bus, agent 0 parks on the bus by keeping its BREQ0# signal active.

4.1.4.5.   SYMMETRIC BUS ARBITRATION WITH NO TRANSACTION GENERATION

Figure 4-6 is a modification of Figure 4-5 to illustrate what happens if an agent n asserts BREQn#, but does not drive a transaction. Note that once bus ownership is requested by an agent by asserting its BREQn# signal, BREQn# must not be deasserted until bus ownership is gained by agent n. Bus agent n need not drive a transaction, however bus ownership must be acquired. Notice that since transaction 2a is not driven that transaction 0b can be driven sooner than it was in Figure 4-5.

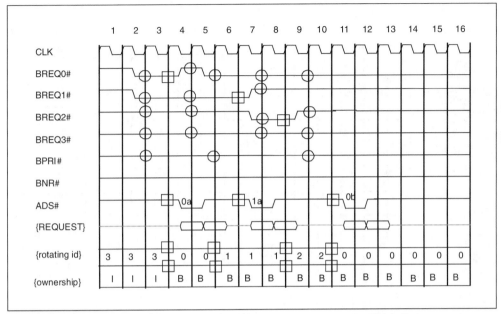

Figure 4-6. Symmetric Arbitration with no Transaction Generation

This figure is the same as Figure 4-5 up until T9.

In T9, the clock that bus agent 2 wins bus ownership, bus agent 2 deasserts BREQ2# because the need to drive the transaction was removed (for example, on the Pentium Pro processor, if a transaction is pending to writeback a replaced cache line and it gets snooped, HITM# will be asserted and the line will be written out as an implicit writeback. The pending transaction to writeback the line gets cancelled).

In T10, all agents observe an inactive BREQ2# and an active BREQ0#. During T10 they recognize that agent 0 is the only symmetric agent arbitrating for the bus. In T11, all agents update the Rotating ID to 0. The ownership remains busy and agent 0 initiates request 0b. Because no other agent has requested the bus, agent 0 parks on the bus by keeping its BREQ0# signal active.

4.1.4.6. BUS EXCHANGE AMONG SYMMETRIC AND PRIORITY AGENTS WITH NO LOCK#

Figure 4-7 illustrates bus exchange between a priority agent and two symmetric agents. A symmetric agent relinquishes physical bus ownership to a priority agent as soon as possible. A maximum of one unlocked ADS# can be generated by the current symmetric bus owner in the clock after BPRI# is asserted because BPRI# has not yet been observed. Note that the symmetric bus owner (Rotating ID) does not change due to the assertion of BPRI#. BPRI# does not affect symmetric agent arbitration, or the symmetric bus owner. Finally, note that in this example BREQ0# must remain asserted until T12 because transaction 0b has not yet been driven. An agent can not drive a transaction unless it owns the bus in the clock in which ADS# is to be driven for that transaction.

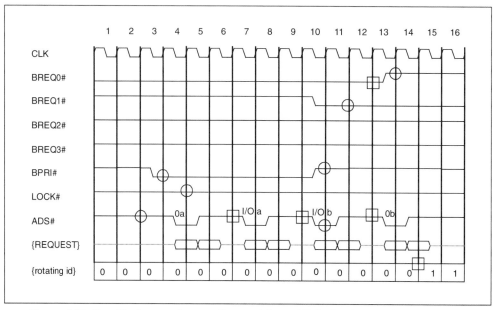

Figure 4-7. Bus Exchange Among Symmetric and Priority Agent with no LOCK#

In Figure 4-7, before T1, agent 0 owns the bus. The Rotating ID is zero, the ownership state is busy.

In T3, the priority agent asserts BPRI# to request bus ownership. In T4, agent 0, the current owner, issues its last request 0a. In T4, all symmetric agents observe BPRI# active, and guarantee no new unlocked request generation starting in T5.

In T3, the priority agent observes inactive ADS# and inactive LOCK# and determines that it may not gain request bus ownership in T5 because the current request bus owner might issue one last request in T4. In T5, the priority agent observes inactive LOCK# and determines that it owns the bus and may begin issuing requests starting in T7, four clocks from BPRI# assertion and three clocks from previous request generation.

The priority agent issues two requests, I/Oa, and I/Ob, and continues to assert BPRI# through T10. In T10, the priority agent deasserts BPRI# to release bus ownership back to the symmetric agents. In T10, agent 1 asserts BREQ1# to arbitrate for the bus.

In T11, agent 0, the current symmetric owner observes inactive BPRI# and initiates request 0b in T13 (three clocks from previous request.) In response to active BREQ1#, agent 0 deasserts BREQ0# in T13 to release symmetric ownership. In T14 all symmetric agents observe inactive BREQ0#, the release of ownership by the current symmetric owner. Since BREQ1# is the only active bus request they assign agent 1 as the next symmetric owner. In T15 symmetric agents update the Rotating ID to one the Agent ID of the new symmetric owner.

4.1.4.7. SYMMETRIC AND PRIORITY BUS EXCHANGE DURING LOCK#

Figure 4-8 illustrates an ownership request made by both a symmetric and a priority agent during an ongoing indivisible sequence by a symmetric owner. When this is the case, LOCK# takes priority over BPRI#. That is, the symmetric bus owner does not give up the bus to the priority agent while it is driving an indivisible locked operation. Note that bus agent 1 can hold bus ownership even though BPRI# is asserted. Like the BREQ[3:0]# signals, if the priority agent is going to issue a transaction, BPRI# must not be driven inactive until the clock in which ADS# is driven asserted.

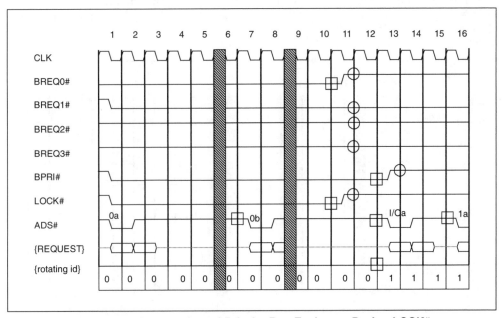

Figure 4-8. Symmetric and Priority Bus Exchange During LOCK#

Before T1, agent 0 owns the bus. In T1, agent 0 initiates the first transaction in a bus locked operation by asserting LOCK# along with request 0a. Also in T1, the priority agent and agent 1 assert BPRI# and BREQ1# respectively to arbitrate for the bus. Agent 0 does not deassert BREQ0# or LOCK# since it is in the middle of a bus locked operation.

In T7, agent 0 initiates the last transaction in the bus locked operation. At the request's successful completion the indivisible sequence is complete and agent 0 deasserts LOCK# in T11. Since BREQ1# is observed active in T10, agent 0 also deasserts BREQ0# in T11 to release symmetric ownership.

The deassertion of LOCK# is observed by the priority agent in T12 and it begins new-request generation from T13. The deassertion of BREQ0# is observed by all symmetric agents and they assign the symmetric ownership to agent 1, the agent with active bus request. In T13, all symmetric agents update the Rotating ID to one, the Agent ID of the new symmetric owner.

Since agent 1 observed active BPRI# in T12, it guarantees no new request generation beginning T13. In T13, the priority agent deasserts BPRI#. In T15, three clocks from the previous request and at least two clocks from BPRI# deassertion agent 1, the current symmetric owner issues request 1a.

4.1.4.8.   BNR# SAMPLING

This section illustrates how BNR# is sampled by all agents, and how the stall protocol is implemented. Figure 4-9 illustrates BNR# sampling as it begins after the processor is brought out of reset. Figure 4-10 illustrates how BNR# is sampled once the stall protocol state machine reaches the free state. Section 4.1.3.2., "Request Stall Protocol" may be useful as reference when reading this section.

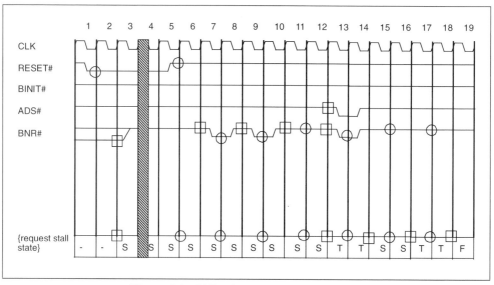

Figure 4-9. BNR# Sampling After RESET#

RESET# is asserted in T1, and observed by all agents in T2. In T3 or T4, BNR# must be deasserted and the request stall state is initialized to the stalled state.

In T5, RESET# is driven inactive, and in T6, RESET# is sampled inactive. Any agent that requires more time to initialize its bus unit logic after reset is allowed to delay transaction generation by asserting BNR# in T7. In T7, the clock after RESET# is sampled inactive, BNR# is driven to a valid level. In T8, two clocks after RESET# is sampled inactive, BNR# is sampled active, causing the processor to remain in the stalled state in T9.

Because the processor is in the stalled state, BNR# is sampled every 2 clocks. BNR# is sampled asserted again in T10, so the state remains stalled. In T12, BNR# is sampled inactive. In T13, the request stall state transitions to the throttled state. One transaction can be issued to the bus in the throttled state, so ADS# is driven active in T13. In the throttled state, BNR# continues to be sampled every other clock.

In T14, BNR# is again sampled asserted, so the state transitions to stalled in T15 and no further transactions are issued. In T16, BNR# is sampled deasserted, which causes the state machine to transition to throttled in T17. In T18, BNR is again sampled deasserted, which transitions the state machine to free in T19. BNR# is not sampled again until after ADS#, RESET#, or BINIT#. A transaction may be issued in T17 or any time after.

Once the request stall state moves into the free state, BNR# sampling no longer occurs every other clock, it occurs 3 clocks after ADS# is driven asserted. Figure 4-10 illustrates this occurrence.

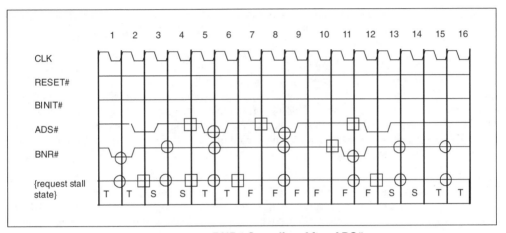

Figure 4-10. BNR# Sampling After ADS#

In T1, the request stall state is in the throttled state and a transaction is issued. BNR# is sampled every other clock. BNR# is sampled asserted in T2, so the request-stall state transitions to the stall state in T3 and no further transactions are issued. BNR# sampling continues every other clock.

In T4, BNR# is sampled deasserted, so the throttled state is entered again in T5, and a transaction is issued. In T6, BNR# is sampled deasserted again, so the request-stall state machine moves into the free state in T7. BNR# sampling changes to the 3rd clock after ADS# is sampled active.

In T8 (3 clocks after the last ADS# is driven), another Request Phase is driven. In T9, 3 clocks after the last ADS# is sampled active, BNR# is again sampled. Because BNR# is sampled deasserted, the state remains free in T10. ADS# could have been driven asserted in T11, but a transaction was not internally pending in time, so a new transaction is driven to the bus in T12.

BNR# is sampled again in T12 (3 clocks after the last ADS# was sampled active). BNR# is sampled asserted, so in T13, the request stall state transitions to the stalled state, and BNR# sampling returns to every other clock. Note that the ADS# driven in T12 is the last time a transaction can be driven to the bus after BNR# is sampled active.

In T14, BNR# is sampled deasserted so the request stall state transitions to throttled in T15. In T16, BNR# is again sampled deasserted, so the state transitions to free in T17 (not shown).

4.1.5. Symmetric Agent Arbitration Protocol Rules

4.1.5.1. RESET CONDITIONS

On observation of active RESET# or BINIT#, all BREQ[3:0]# signals must be deasserted in one or two clocks. On observation of active AERR# (with AERR# observation enabled), all BREQ[3:0]# signals must be deasserted in the next clock. All agents also re-initialize Rotating ID to three and ownership state to idle. Based on this situation, the new arbitration priority is 0,1,2,3 and there is no current symmetric owner.

When a reset condition is generated by the activation of BINIT#, BREQn# must remain deasserted until 4 clocks after BINIT# is driven inactive. The first BREQ# sample point is 4 clocks after BINIT# is sampled inactive.

When the reset condition is generated by the activation of RESET#, BREQn# as driven by symmetric agents must remain deasserted until 2 clocks after RESET# is driven inactive. The first BREQ# sample point is 2 clocks after RESET# is sampled inactive. For power-on configuration, the system interface logic must assert BREQ0# for at least two clocks before the clock in which RESET# is deasserted. BREQ0# must be deasserted by the system interface logic in the clock after RESET# is sampled deasserted. Agent 0 must delay BREQ0# assertion for a minimum of three clocks after the clock in which RESET# is deasserted to guarantee wire-or glitch free operation.

When a reset condition is generated by AERR#, all agents except for a symmetric owner that has issued the second or subsequent transaction of a bus-locked operation must keep BREQn# inactive for a minimum of four clocks. The bus owner n that has issued the second or subsequent transaction of bus locked operation must activate its BREQn# two clocks from inactive BREQn#. This approach ensures that the locked operation remains indivisible.

4.1.5.2. BUS REQUEST ASSERTION

A symmetric agent n can activate BREQn# to arbitrate for the bus provided the reset conditions described in Section 4.1.5.1., "Reset Conditions" are satisfied. Once activated, BREQn# must remain active until the agent becomes the symmetric owner. Becoming the symmetric owner is a precondition to entering the Request Phase.

4.1.5.3. OWNERSHIP FROM IDLE STATE

When the ownership state is idle, a new arbitration event begins with activation of at least one BREQ[3:0]#. During the next clock, all symmetric agents assign ownership to the highest priority symmetric agent with active bus request. In the following clock, all symmetric agents update the Rotating ID to the new symmetric owner Agent ID and the ownership state to busy. The new symmetric owner may enter the Request Phase as early as the clock the Rotating ID is updated.

4.1.5.4. OWNERSHIP FROM BUSY STATE

When the ownership state is busy, the next arbitration event begins with the deassertion of BREQ*n*# by the current symmetric owner.

4.1.5.4.1. Bus Parking and Release with a Single Bus Request

When the ownership state is busy, bus parking is an accepted mode of operation. The symmetric owner can retain ownership even if it has no pending requests, provided no other symmetric agent has an active arbitration request.

The symmetric owner "*n*" may eventually deassert BREQ*n*# to release symmetric ownership even when other requests are not active. When the owner deasserts BREQ*n*#, all agents update the ownership state to idle, but maintain the same Rotating ID.

4.1.5.4.2. Bus Exchange with Multiple Bus Requests

When the ownership state is busy, on observing at least one other BREQ*m*# active, the current symmetric owner *n* can hold the bus for back-to-back transactions by simply keeping BREQ*n*# active. This mechanism must be used for bus-lock operations and can be used for unlocked operations, with care to prevent other symmetric agents from gaining ownership. (The Pentium Pro processor limits the number of additional unlocked requests to one.)

A new arbitration event begins with deactivation of BREQ*n*#. On observing release of ownership by the current symmetric owner, all agents assign the ownership to the highest priority symmetric agent arbitrating for the bus. In the following clock, all agents update the Rotating ID to the new symmetric owner Agent ID and maintain bus ownership state as busy.

A symmetric agent *n* shall deassert BREQ*n*# for a minimum of one clock.

4.1.6. Priority Agent Arbitration Protocol Rules

4.1.6.1. RESET CONDITIONS

On observation of active RESET# or BINIT#, BPRI# must be deasserted in one or two clocks. On observation of active AERR# (with AERR# observation enabled), BPRI# must be deasserted in the next clock.

When the reset condition is generated by the activation of BINIT#, BPRI# must remain deasserted until 4 clocks after BINIT# is driven inactive. The first BPRI# sample point is 4 clocks after BINIT# is sampled inactive.

When reset condition is generated by AERR#, the priority agent must keep BPRI# inactive for a minimum of four clocks unless it has issued the second or subsequent transaction of a locked operation. The priority owner that has issued the second or subsequent transaction of a locked operation must activate its BPRI# two clocks from inactive BPRI#. This ensures that the locked operation remains indivisible.

4.1.6.2. BUS REQUEST ASSERTION

The priority agent can activate BPRI# to seek bus ownership provided the reset conditions described in Section 4.1.6.1., "Reset Conditions" are satisfied. BPRI# can be deactivated at any time.

On observing active BPRI#, all symmetric agents guarantee no new non-locked requests are generated.

4.1.6.3. BUS EXCHANGE FROM AN UNLOCKED BUS

If LOCK# is observed inactive in two clocks after BPRI# is driven asserted, the priority agent has permission to drive ADS# four clocks after BPRI# assertion. The priority agent can further reduce its arbitration latency by observing the bus protocol and determining that no other agent could drive a request. For example, Arbitration latency can be reduced by to two clocks by observing ADS# active and LOCK# inactive on the same clock BPRI# is driven asserted or it can be reduced to three clocks by observing ADS# active and LOCK# inactive in the clock after BPRI# is driven asserted.

4.1.6.4. BUS RELEASE

The priority agent can deassert BPRI# and release bus ownership in the same cycle that it generates its last request. It can keep BPRI# active even after the last request generation provided it can guarantee forward progress of the symmetric agents. When deasserted, BPRI# must stay inactive for a minimum of two clocks.

4.1.7. Bus Lock Protocol Rules

4.1.7.1. BUS OWNERSHIP EXCHANGE FROM A LOCKED BUS

The current symmetric owner *n* can retain ownership of the bus by keeping the LOCK# signal active (even if BPRI# is asserted). This mechanism is used during bus lock operations. After the lock operation is complete, the symmetric owner deasserts LOCK# and guarantees no new request generation until BPRI# is observed inactive.

On asserting BPRI#, the priority agent observes LOCK# for the next two clocks to monitor request bus activity. If the current symmetric owner is performing locked requests (LOCK# active), the priority agent must wait until LOCK# is observed inactive.

4.2. REQUEST PHASE

After completion of the Arbitration Phase, an agent is allowed to enter the Request Phase. This phase is used to initiate new transactions on the bus, and lasts for two consecutive clocks. During the first clock, the information required to snoop a transaction and start a memory access becomes available. During the next clock, complete information required for the entire transaction becomes available.

4.2.1. Bus Signals

The Request Phase bus signals are ADS#, A[35:3]#, REQa[4:0]#, REQb[4:0]#, ATTR[7:0]#, DID[7:0]#, BE[7:0]#, EXF[4:0]#, AP[1:0]#, and RP#. In addition, the LOCK# signal is driven during this phase. Request Phase signals are bused among all agents. Since information is carried during two clocks, the first clock is identified with the suffix a and the second clock is identified with the suffix b. For example, RPa# and RPb#.

4.2.2. Request Phase Protocol Description

The Request Phase occurs when a transaction is actually issued to the bus. ADS# is asserted and the transaction information is driven. Figure 4-11 shows the Request Phase of several transactions.

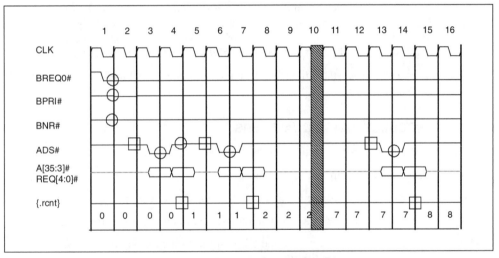

Figure 4-11. Request Generation Phase

In T1, only one bus agent (agent 0) drives a request for the bus. In T2, BREQ[3:0]#, BPRI# and BNR# are sampled and it is determined that BREQ0# becomes the bus owner in T3.

In T3, agent 0 drives a transaction by asserting ADS#. Also in T3, A[35:3]#, REQa[4:0]#, AP[1:0]# and RP# are driven valid. REQa0# indicates that the transaction is a write transaction.

In T4, the second clock of the Request Phase, the rest of the transaction information is driven out on the following signals: REQb[4:0]#, ATTR[7:0]#, DID[7:0]#, BE[7:0]#, and EXF[4:0]#. AP[1:0]#, and RP# remain valid in this clock.

When a transaction is driven to the bus, the internal state must be updated in the clock after ADS# is observed asserted. Therefore, in T5 the internal request count {rcnt} is incremented by one.

In T6, agent 0 issues another transaction, and in T8, the internal state is updated appropriately.

In the series of clocks indicated in the diagram by T10, five more transactions become outstanding (this status is indicated by the {rcnt}). In T13, the 8th transaction is issued as indicated on the bus by ADS# assertion in T13. In T15, the {rcnt} is incremented to 8, the highest possible value for {rcnt}. No additional transactions can be issued until a response is given for transaction 0.

4.2.3.   Request Phase Protocol Rules

4.2.3.1.   REQUEST GENERATION

The Request Phase is always one clock of active ADS# followed by one clock of inactive ADS#. There is always an idle clock between request phases for bus turnaround. Address, command, and parity information is transferred on the first two clocks on pins A[35:3]#, REQ[4:0]#, and AP[1:0]# and RP#. Refer to Chapter 3, *Bus Overview* for a description of which signals are driven on these pins. Although LOCK# is part of the Arbitration Phase, it is driven during the first clock of the Request Phase. AP[1:0]# and RP# are valid during a valid Request Phase.

On observation of a new request, the transaction counts including {rcnt} and {scnt} are updated with the new transaction.

4.2.3.2.   REQUEST PHASE QUALIFIERS

The Request Phase for a new transaction may be initiated when:

- The agent contains one or more pending requests.

- The agent owns the bus as described in the Arbitration Phase section.

- The internal request count state is less than the maximum number of entries in the IOQ.

- The bus is not stalled. In other words, the Request Stall state (as described in Section 4.1., "Arbitration Phase") is free or throttled.

- The preceding transaction's Request Phase is complete. In other words, ADS# is observed inactive on the previous clock.

4.3.   ERROR PHASE

Receiving agents use the Error Phase to indicate parity errors in Request Phase. Parity is checked during valid Request Phase (One clock active ADS# followed by one clock inactive ADS#) on AP[1:0]# and RP# signals.

If the request parity is enabled in the power-on configuration as described in Chapter 9, *Configuration*, then the agent checks parity in the two clocks. If transaction cancellation due to AERR# is enabled (AERR# observation) in the power-on-configuration and AERR# is observed active during Error Phase, then all agents remove the transaction from their In-order Queue, cancel subsequent transaction phases, remove bus requests, and reset their bus arbiters. Reset of the bus arbiters enables errors in the Arbitration Phase to be corrected. The transaction may be retried.

4.3.1. Bus Signals

The only signal driven in this state is AERR#. AERR# is bused among all agents.

4.4. SNOOP PHASE

In the Snoop Phase, all caching agents drive their snoop results and participate in coherency resolution. The agents generate internal snoop requests for all memory transactions. An agent is also allowed to snoop its own bus requests and participate in the Snoop Phase along with other bus agents. The Pentium Pro processor snoops its own transactions. The snoop results are driven on HIT# and HITM# signals in this phase.

In addition, during the Snoop Phase, the memory agent or I/O agent drives DEFER# to indicate whether the transaction is committed for completion immediately or if the commitment is deferred.

The results of the Snoop Phase are used to determine the final state of the cache line in all agents and which agent is responsible for completion of Data Phase and Response Phase of the current transaction.

4.4.1. Snoop Phase Bus Signals

The bus signals driven in this phase are HIT#, HITM# and DEFER#. These signals are bused among all agents. The requesting agent uses the HIT# signal to determine the permissible cache state of the line. The HITM# signal is used to indicate what agent will provide the requested data. The DEFER# signal indicates whether the transaction will be committed for completion immediately or if the commitment is deferred.

The results of combinations of HIT# and HITM# signal encodings during a valid Snoop Phase is shown in Table 4-1.

Table 4-1. HIT# and HITM# During Snoop Phase

Snoop Result	HIT#	HITM#
CLEAN	0[1]	0
MODIFIED	0	1
SHARED	1	0
STALL	1	1

NOTE:

1. 0 indicates inactive, 1 indicates active.

The CLEAN result means that at the end of the transaction, no other caching agent will retain the addressed line in its cache, and that the requesting agent can store the cache line in any state (Modified, Exclusive, Shared or Invalid).

The MODIFIED result means that the addressed line is in the modified state in an agent on the Pentium Pro processor bus. The agent that "owns" the line will writeback the line to memory. The requesting agent will pick the line off the bus as it is written back.

The SHARED result means that addressed line is valid in the cache of another agent on the Pentium Pro processor bus, but that it is not modified. The requesting agent therefore can store the cache line in the shared state only.

The STALL result means that the all agents on the Pentium Pro processor bus are not yet ready to provide a snoop result, and that the Snoop Phase will be stalled for another 2 clocks. Any agent on the bus may use the STALL state on any transaction as a stall mechanism.

4.4.2. Snoop Phase Protocol Description

This section describes the Snoop Phase using examples.

4.4.2.1. NORMAL SNOOP PHASE

Figure 4-12 illustrates a four-clock Snoop Result Phase for pipelined requests. The snoop results are driven four clocks after ADS# is asserted and at least three clocks from the Snoop Phase of a previous transaction. Note that no snoop results are stalled and the maximum request generation rate is one request every three clocks.

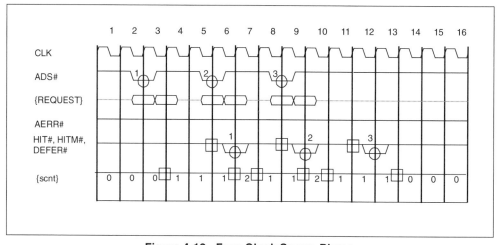

Figure 4-12. Four-Clock Snoop Phase

In T1, there are no transactions outstanding on the bus and {scnt} is 0. In T2, transaction 1 is issued. In T4, as a result of the transaction driven in T2, {scnt} is incremented.

In T5, transaction 2 is issued. In T6, which is four clocks after the corresponding ADS# in T2, the snoop results for transaction 1 are driven. In T7, {scnt} is incremented indicating that there are two transactions on the bus that have not completed the Snoop Phase. Also in T7, the snoop results for transaction 1 are observed. As a result, in T8, {scnt} is decremented.

In T8, the third transaction is issued. Two clocks later in T10, {scnt} is incremented. In T11, {scnt} is decremented because the snoop results from transaction 2 are observed in T10.

In T13, the snoop results for transaction 3 are observed and in T14 {scnt} is again decremented.

4.4.2.2.   STALLED SNOOP PHASE

Figure 4-13 illustrates how a slower snooping agent can delay the Snoop Phase if it is unable to deliver valid snoop results within four clocks after ADS# is asserted. The figure also illustrates that the snoop phase of subsequent trasactions are also stalled and occur two clocks late due to the stall of transaction one's snoop phase.

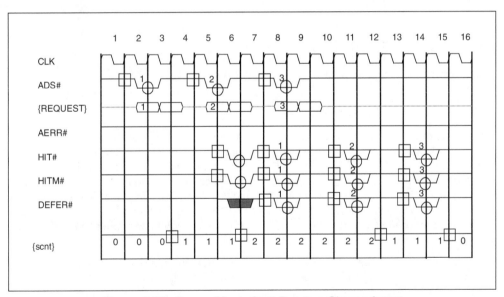

Figure 4-13. Snoop Phase Stall Due to a Slower Agent

Transactions 1, 2 and 3 are initiated with ADS# activation in T2, T5, and T8.

The Snoop Phase for transaction 1 begins in T6 four clocks from ADS#. All agents capable of driving valid snoop response in four clocks drive appropriate levels on the snoop signals HIT#, HITM#, and DEFER#. A slower agent that is unable to generate a snoop response in four clocks asserts both HIT# and HITM# together in T6 to extend the Snoop Phase. Note that if the Snoop

Phase is extended, {scnt} is not decremented. Because the Snoop Phase is extended, the value of DEFER# is a "don't care".

On observing active HIT# and HITM# in T7, all agents determine that the transaction's Snoop Phase is extended by two additional clocks through T8. In T8, the slower snooping agent is ready with valid snoop results and needs no additional Snoop Phase extensions. In T8, all agents drive valid snoop results on the snoop signals. In T9, all agents observe that HIT# and HITM# are not asserted in the same clock and determine that the valid snoop results for transaction 1 are available on the snoop signals.

The Snoop Phase for transaction 2 begins in T11, three clocks from Snoop Phase of transaction 1 or four clocks from Request Phase of transaction 2, whichever is later. Since the Snoop Phase for transaction 2 is not extended, the Snoop Phase for transaction 2 completes in one clock.

The Snoop Phase for transaction 3 begins in T14, the later of three clocks from Snoop Phase of transaction 2, and four clocks from Request Phase of transaction 3. Since the Snoop Phase for transaction 3 is not extended, the Snoop Phase for transaction 3 completes in one clock.

For the example shown, the Snoop Phase is always six clocks from the Request Phase due to the initial Snoop Phase stall from Transaction 1. However, the maximum request generation rate is still one request every three clocks.

4.4.3. Snoop Phase Protocol Rules

This section will list the Snoop Phase protocol rules for reference.

4.4.3.1. SNOOP PHASE RESULTS

During a valid Snoop Phase (as defined below), snoop results are presented on HIT#, HITM#, and DEFER# signals for one clock. If the snooping agent contains a MODIFIED copy of the cache line, then HITM# must be asserted. If the snooping agent does not assert HITM# and it plans to retain a SHARED copy of the cache line at the end of the Snoop Phase, it must assert HIT#. HIT# and HITM# are asserted together to indicate that the agent is requesting a STALL. All non-memory accesses will indicate CLEAN or STALL. DEFER# must be asserted by an addressed memory or I/O agent if the agent is unable to guarantee in-order completion of the requested transaction.

The results of the Snoop Phase require specific behavior from the addressed and snooping agents for future phases of the transaction. The agent asserting HITM# normally must writeback the modified cache line. The addressed agent must accept the writeback line from the snooping agent, merge it with any write data, and drive an implicit writeback response.

If HITM# is inactive, the agent asserting DEFER# must reply with a deferred or retry response for the transaction. Only the addressed agent can assert DEFER#. The requesting agent must not begin another order-dependent transaction until either DEFER# is sampled deasserted in the Snoop Phase, or the deferred transaction receives a successful completion via a deferred reply or a retry.

For all transactions with LOCK# inactive, HITM# active guarantees in-order completion. During unlocked transactions, HITM# overrides the assertion of DEFER#.

If DEFER# is asserted during the Snoop Phase of a locked operation, the locked operation is prematurely aborted. During the first transaction of a locked operation, if HITM# and DEFER# are active together, the transaction completes with cache line writeback and implicit writeback response, but the request agent must begin a new locked operation starting from a new Arbitration Phase (BREQn# of the requesting agent must be deasserted if a symmetric agent issued the locked operation). The assertion of DEFER# during the second or subsequent transaction of a locked operation is a protocol violation. If DEFER# is asserted and HITM# is not asserted, a Retry Response is driven in the Response Phase to force a retry of the entire locked operation.

4.4.3.2. VALID SNOOP PHASE

The Snoop Phase for a transaction begins 4 clocks after ADS# is driven asserted or 3 clocks after the snoop results of the previous transaction are driven, whichever is later.

4.4.3.3. SNOOP PHASE STALL

A slow snooping agent can request a two-clock STALL in a valid Snoop Phase by activating both HIT# and HITM#. In the case of a STALL, snoop results are sampled again 2 clocks after the previous sample point. This process continues as long as the STALL state is sampled. When stalling the bus, the stalling condition must be able to clear without requiring access to the bus.

4.4.3.4. SNOOP PHASE COMPLETION

If no STALL is requested during the valid Snoop Phase, the Snoop Phase is completed in the clock after the snoop results are driven.

4.4.3.5. SNOOP RESULTS SAMPLING

Snoop Results are sampled during the valid snoop phase. Bus agents must ignore Snoop Results in the clock after a valid sampling window.

4.5. RESPONSE PHASE

4.5.1. Response Phase Overview

A transaction enters the Response Phase when it is at the head of the In-order Queue. The agent responsible for the response is referred to as the *response agent*. The agent decoded by the address in the Request Phase determines the response agent for the transaction.

After completion of the Response Phase, the transaction is removed from the In-order Queue.

4.5.1.1. BUS SIGNALS

The Response Phase signals are TRDY#, RS[2:0]#, and RSP#. These signals are bused. RSP# provides parity support only for RS[2:0]#. The transaction response is encoded on the RS[2:0]# signals. TRDY# is only asserted for transactions with write or writeback data to transfer. The response encodings are indicated in Table 4-2.

Table 4-2. Response Phase Encodings

Response	RS2#	RS1#	RS0#
Idle	0^1	0	0
Retry	0	0	1
Deferred	0	1	0
reserved	0	1	1
Hard Failure	1	0	0
No data	1	0	1
Implicit Writeback	1	1	0
Normal Data	1	1	1

NOTE:

1. 0 indicates inactive, 1 indicates active.

There is no single response strobe signal. The response value is Idle until the response is driven. A response is driven when any one of RS[2:0]# is asserted.

4.5.2. Response Phase Protocol Description

The Response Phase is described in this section using examples. The rules for the Response Phase are listed in the next section for reference.

4.5.2.1. RESPONSE FOR A TRANSACTION WITHOUT WRITE DATA

Figure 4-14 shows several transactions that have no write or writeback data to transfer. Therefore the TRDY# signal is not asserted. The DBSY# signal is observed in this phase because if there is read data to transfer, DBSY# must be sampled inactive before the response for transaction n can be driven (this ensures that any data transfers from transaction n-1 are complete before the response is driven for transaction n).

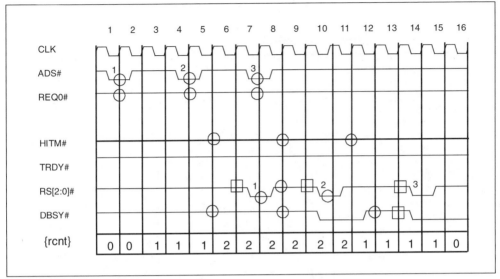

Figure 4-14. RS[2:0]# Activation with no TRDY#

Three transactions are issued in clocks T1, T4, and T7. None of these transactions have write data to transfer as indicated by the REQa0# signal.

The Snoop Phase for each transaction indicates that no implicit writeback data will be transferred and the response agent indicated by the address will provide the transaction response and the read data if there is any.

Because the transactions have no write or implicit writeback data, the TRDY# signal is not asserted.

The rcnt indicates that the In-order Queue is empty. The ADS# for transaction 1 is driven in T1. The snoop results for transaction 1 are driven four clocks later in T5 (observed in T6). Note that the Response and Data Phases for transaction n-1 have to be complete before the response for transaction n can be driven. Since transaction 1 is at the top of the IOQ and DBSY# is inactive in T6, RS[2:0]# can be driven for transaction 1 in T7, two clocks after the snoop results are driven. Transaction 1 is removed from the IOQ after T8, and transaction 2 is now at the top of the IOQ. The rcnt is not decremented in T9 because transaction 3 was issued in the same clock that transaction 1 received its response.

Transaction 2 is issued to the bus in T4 (three clocks after Transaction 1). The snoop results for transaction 2 are driven four clocks later in T8. Transaction 2 is at the top of the IOQ. RS[2:0]# for transaction 2 is driven two clocks later in T10 because DBSY# and RS[2:0]# were sampled deasserted in T9.

The response for transaction 3 cannot be driven two clocks after the snoop results are driven in T11 because DBSY# is asserted in T11. DBSY# is sampled deasserted in T13 and RS[2:0]# for transaction 3 is driven in T14.

The response driven for each of these transactions is the Normal Data Response.

4.5.2.2.   WRITE DATA TRANSACTION RESPONSE

Figure 4-15 shows a transaction with a simple request initiated data transfer. A request initiated data transfer means that the request agent issuing the transaction has write data to transfer. Note that TRDY# is always asserted after the response for transaction n-1 is driven and before the transaction response for transaction n is driven.

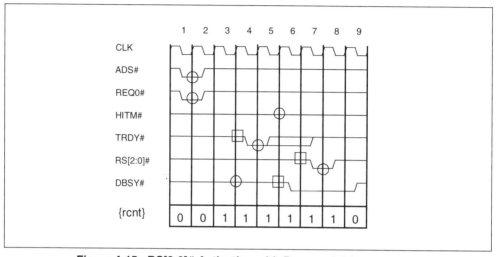

Figure 4-15. RS[2:0]# Activation with Request Initiated TRDY#

Before T1, the IOQ is empty. A write transaction as indicated by active ADS# and REQa0# is issued in T1.

Since the Response Phase for the previous transaction is complete, the Response Phase for transaction 1 can begin with the assertion of TRDY# as early as T4, 3 clocks after ADS# is asserted. In T4, DBSY# is observed inactive on the clock TRDY# is asserted and TRDY# had previously been inactive for 3 clocks, so the TRDY# agent is allowed to deassert TRDY# within one clock as a special optimization. Data is driven the clock after TRDY# is sampled and the data bus is free. TRDY# need not be deasserted until the response is driven.

The snoop results are driven in T5 and sampled in T6.

Since RS[2:0]# is deasserted in T6, TRDY# has been asserted and deasserted, and the snoop results were observed in T6, the response for the transaction is driven on RS[2:0]# in T7. Notice even if TRDY# is only asserted for one clock, the response may still be asserted when TRDY# is deasserted (assuming snoop results have been observed). Because this is a simple write transaction the response driven is the No Data Response.

4.5.2.3. IMPLICIT WRITEBACK ON A READ TRANSACTION

Figure 4-16 shows a read transaction with an implicit writeback. TRDY# is asserted in this operation because there is writeback data to transfer. Note that the implicit writeback response must be asserted exactly one clock after valid TRDY# assertion is sampled. That is, TRDY# is sampled active and DBSY# is sampled inactive.

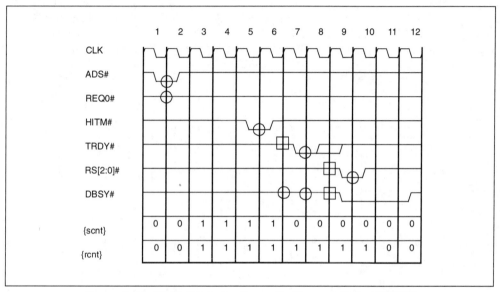

Figure 4-16. RS[2:0]# Activation with Snoop Initiated TRDY#

A transaction is issued in T1. The REQa0# pin indicates a read transaction, so TRDY# is assumed not needed for this transaction.

But snoop results observed in T6 indicate that an implicit writeback will occur (HITM# is asserted), therefore a TRDY# assertion is needed. Since the response for the previous transaction is complete, and no request initiated TRDY# assertion is needed, TRDY# for the implicit writeback is asserted in T7. (TRDY# assertion due to an implicit writeback is called a snoop initiated TRDY#.) Since DBSY# is observed inactive in T7, TRDY# can be deasserted in one clock in T8, but need not be deasserted until the response is driven on RS[2:0]#.

In T9, one clock after the observation of active TRDY# with inactive DBSY# for the implicit writeback, the Implicit Writeback Response must be driven on RS[2:0]# and the data is driven on the data bus. This makes the data transfer and response behave like both a read (for the requesting agent) and a write (for the addressed agent).

4.5.2.4. IMPLICIT WRITEBACK WITH A WRITE TRANSACTION

Figure 4-17 shows a write transaction combined with a hit to a modified line that requires an implicit writeback. This operation has two data transfers and requires two assertions of TRDY#. The first TRDY# is asserted by the receiver of the write data whenever it is ready to receive the write data. Once active TRDY# and inactive DBSY# is observed, the first TRDY# is deasserted to allow the second TRDY#. The second TRDY# is asserted by the receiver whenever it is ready to receive the writeback data. The second TRDY# may be deasserted when active TRDY# and inactive DBSY# is sampled or when the response is driven on RS[2:0]#. One clock after observation of active TRDY# (and inactive DBSY#) for the implicit writeback, the implicit writeback response is driven on RS[2:0]# at the same time data is driven for the implicit writeback.

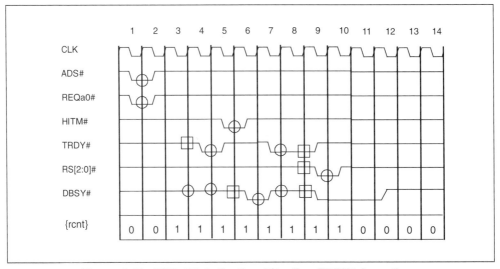

Figure 4-17. RS[2:0]# Activation After Two TRDY# Assertions

In T1, a write transaction is issued as indicated by active ADS# and REQa0#. At this point, the transaction appears to be a normal write transaction, so TRDY# is asserted 3 clocks later in T4. TRDY# is deasserted in T5. Since DBSY# was observed inactive in T4, TRDY# can be deasserted in one clock as a special optimization to allow a faster implicit writeback TRDY#.

In T5, the snoop results are driven, and in T6, they are observed. In T7, TRDY# is asserted again for the implicit writeback. TRDY# can be asserted immediately because the TRDY# for the request initiated data transfer was already deasserted.

In T9, one clock after observation of active TRDY# with inactive DBSY# for the implicit writeback, TRDY# must be deasserted and the implicit writeback response is driven on RS[2:0]#.

Since DBSY# was observed active in T7, but inactive in T8, TRDY# is deasserted in T9.

4.5.3. Response Phase Protocol Rules

4.5.3.1. REQUEST INITIATED TRDY# ASSERTION

A request initiated transaction is a transaction where the request agent has write data to transfer.

The addressed agent asserts TRDY# to indicate its ability to receive data from the request agent intending to perform a write data operation. Request initiated TRDY# for transaction "*n*" is asserted:

- when the transaction has a write data transfer,

- a minimum of 3 clocks after ADS# of transaction "*n*", and

- a minimum of 1 clock after RS[2:0]# active assertion for transaction "*n*-1". (After the response for transaction *n*-1 is driven).

4.5.3.2. SNOOP INITIATED TRDY# PROTOCOL

The response agent asserts TRDY# to indicate its ability to receive the modified cache line from a snooping agent. Snoop Initiated TRDY# for transaction "*n*" is asserted when:

- the transaction has an implicit writeback data transfer indicated in the Snoop Result Phase.

- in the case of a request initiated transfer, the request initiated TRDY# was asserted and then deasserted (TRDY# must be deasserted for at least one clock between the TRDY# for the write and the TRDY# for the implicit writeback),

- at least 1 clock has passed after RS[2:0]# active assertion for transaction "*n*-1" (after the response for transaction *n*-1 is driven).

4.5.3.3. TRDY# DEASSERTION PROTOCOL

The agent asserting TRDY# can deassert it as soon as it can ensure that TRDY# deassertion meets following conditions.

- TRDY# may be deasserted when inactive DBSY# and active TRDY# are observed for one clock.

- TRDY# can be deasserted within one clock if DBSY# was observed inactive on the clock TRDY# is asserted and the deassertion is at least three clocks from previous TRDY# deassertion.

- TRDY# does not need to be deasserted until the response on RS[2:0]# is asserted.

- TRDY# for a request initiated transfer must be deasserted to allow the TRDY# for an implicit writeback.

4.5.3.4. RS[2:0]# ENCODING

Valid response encodings are determined based on the snoop results and the following request:

- **Hard Failure** is a valid response for all transactions and indicates transaction failure. The requesting agent is required to take recovery action.

- **Implicit Writeback** is a required response when HITM# is asserted during the Snoop Phase. The snooping agent is required to transfer the modified cache line. The memory agent is required to drive the response and accept the modified cache line.

- **Deferred Response** is only allowed when DEN# is asserted in the Request Phase and DEFER# (with HITM# inactive) is asserted during Snoop Phase. With the Deferred Response, the response agent promises to complete the transaction in the future using the Deferred Reply transaction.

- **Retry Response** is only allowed when DEFER# (with HITM# inactive) is asserted during the Snoop Phase. With the Retry Response, the response agent informs the request agent that the transaction must be retried.

- **Normal Data Response** is required when the REQ[4:0]# encoding in the Request Phase requires a read data response and HITM# and DEFER# are both inactive during Snoop Phase. With the Normal Data Response, the response agent is required to transfer read data along with the response.

- **No Data Response** is required when no data will be returned by the addressed agent and DEFER# and HITM# are inactive during the Snoop Phase.

4.5.3.5. RS[2:0]#, RSP# PROTOCOL

The response signals are normally in idle state when not being driven active by any agent. The response agent asserts RS[2:0]# and RSP# for one clock to indicate the type of response used for transaction completion. In the next clock, the response agent must drive the signals inactive to the idle state.

Response for transaction "*n*" is asserted when the following are true:

- Snoop Phase for transaction "*n*" is observed.

- RS[2:0]# for transaction "*n*-1" were asserted to an active response state and then sampled inactive in the idle state (the response for transaction "n" is driven no sooner than three clocks after the response for transaction "n-1").

- If the transaction contains a write data transfer, TRDY# deassertion conditions have been met.

- If the transaction contains an implicit writeback data transfer, snoop initiated TRDY# is asserted for transaction "*n*" and TRDY# is sampled active with inactive DBSY#.

- DBSY# is observed inactive if RS[2:0]# response is Normal Data Response.

- A response that does not require the data bus (no data response, deferred response, retry response, or hard failure response) may be driven even if DBSY# is active due to a previous transaction.

On observation of active RS[2:0]# response, the Transaction Queues are updated and {rcnt} is decremented.

4.6. DATA PHASE

4.6.1. Data Phase Overview

During the Data Phase, data is transferred between different bus agents. Data transfer responsibilities are negotiated between bus agents as the transaction proceeds through various phases. Based on the Request Phase, a transaction either contains a "request-initiated" (write) data transfer, a "response-initiated" (read) data transfer, or no data transfer. On a modified hit during the Snoop Phase, a "snoop-initiated" data transfer may be added to the request or substituted from the response in place of the "response-initiated" data transfer. On a deferred completion response in the Response Phase, "response-initiated" data transfer is deferred.

4.6.1.1. BUS SIGNALS

The bus signals driven in this phase are D[63:0]#, DEP[7:0]#, DRDY#, and DBSY#.

All Data Phase signals are bused.

4.6.2. Data Phase Protocol Description

4.6.2.1. SIMPLE WRITE TRANSFER

Figure 4-18 shows a simple write transaction (request-initiated data transfer). Note that the data is transferred before the response is driven.

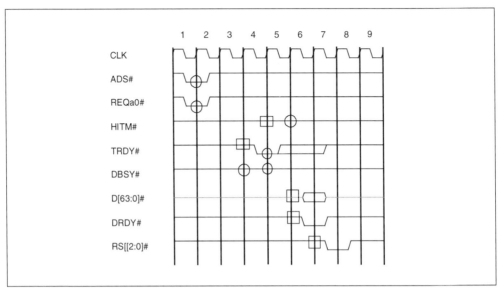

Figure 4-18. Request Initiated Data Transfer

The write transaction is driven in T1 as indicated by active ADS# and REQa0#. TRDY# is driven 3 clocks later in T4. The No Data response is driven in T7 after inactive HITM# sampled in T6 indicates no implicit writeback.

In the example, the data transfer only takes one clock, so DBSY# is not asserted.

TRDY# is observed active and DBSY# is observed inactive in T5. Therefore the data transfer can begin in T6 as indicated by DRDY# assertion. Note that since DBSY# was also observed inactive in T4, the same clock that TRDY# was asserted, TRDY# can be deasserted in T6. Refer to Section 4.5.3.3., "TRDY# Deassertion Protocol" for further details.

RS[2:0]# is driven to No Data Response in T7, two clocks after the snoop phase.

4.6.2.2. SIMPLE READ TRANSACTION

Figure 4-19 shows a simple read transaction (response-initiated data transfer). Note that the data transfer begins in the same clock that the response is driven on RS[2:0]#.

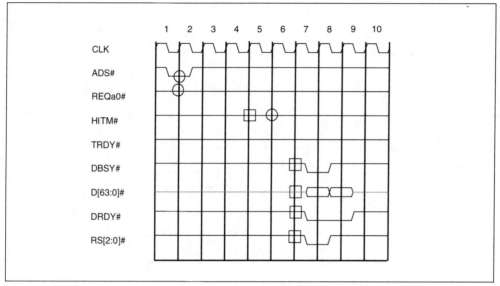

Figure 4-19. Response Initiated Data Transfer

A read transaction is driven in T1 as indicated by the ADS# and REQa0# pins. Because the transaction is a read and HITM# indicates that there will be no implicit writeback data, TRDY# is not asserted for this transaction.

The response for this transaction is driven on RS[2:0]# in T7, two clocks after the snoop results are driven in T5. For read transactions (response initiated data transfers), the data transfer must begin in the same clock that the response is driven.

4.6.2.3. IMPLICIT WRITEBACK

Figure 4-20 shows a simple implicit writeback (snoop-initiated data transfer) occurring during a read transfer transaction. Note that wait states can be added into the data transfer by the deassertion of DRDY#. Note also that the data transfer for the implicit writeback must begin on the same clock that the response is driven on RS[2:0]#.

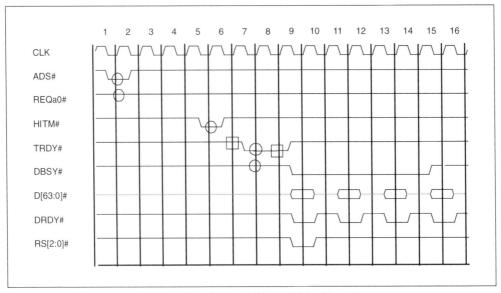

Figure 4-20. Snoop Initiated Data Transfer

A transaction is issued to the bus in T1. REQa0# indicates that the transaction does not have write data to transfer. The snoop results driven in T5 indicate that an implicit writeback will be driven.

The response agent may assert TRDY# as early as T7, the clock after the snoop results are sampled. In T8, TRDY# is sampled asserted while DBSY# is sampled deasserted. Therefore, the snoop agent begins the data transfer in T9 with the assertion of DRDY#, DBSY#, and valid data. Note, TRDY# must be deasserted in T9. Refer to Section 4.5.3.3., "TRDY# Deassertion Protocol" for further details.

DBSY# must stay active at least until the clock before the last data transfer to indicate that more data is coming. DRDY# is driven active by the snooping agent to indicate that it has driven valid data. To insert waitstates into the data transfer, DRDY# is deasserted.

The response agent must drive the response on RS[2:0]# in T9, the clock after the active TRDY# for an implicit writeback and inactive DBSY# is sampled. Note that the response must be driven in the same clock that the data transfer begins. This makes the data transfer and response behave like both a read (for the requesting agent) and a write (for the addressed agent).

4.6.2.4. FULL SPEED READ PARTIAL TRANSACTIONS

Figure 4-21 shows steady-state behavior with full speed Read Partial Transactions. DBSY# is deasserted since the single chunk is transferred immediately. Note that there are no bottlenecks to maintaining this steady-state.

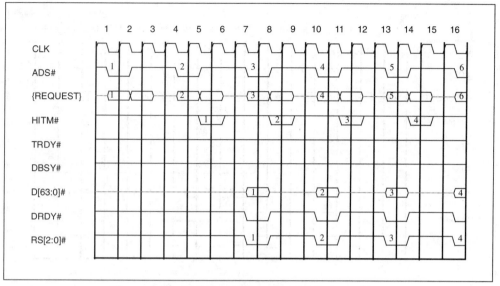

Figure 4-21. Full Speed Read Partial Transactions

4.6.2.5.   RELAXED DBSY# DEASSERTION

DBSY# may be left asserted beyond the last DRDY# assertion. The data bus is released one clock after DBSY# is deasserted, as shown in Figure 4-22. This figure also shows how the response for transaction 2 may be driven even though DBSY is still active for the Data Phase of transaction 1 because transaction 2 does not require the data bus. Because agent 1 deasserts DBSY# in T13 and it is sampled inactive by the other agents in T14, DBSY# and data are driven for transaction 3 in T15.

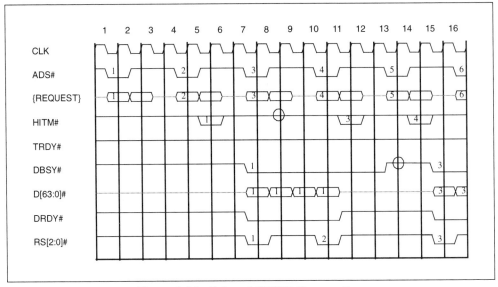

Figure 4-22. Relaxed DBSY# Deassertion

4.6.2.6.   FULL SPEED READ LINE TRANSFERS (SAME AGENT)

Figure 4-23 shows the steady-state behavior of Read Line Transactions with back-to-back read data transfers from the same agent. Consecutive data transfers may occur without a turn-around cycle only if from the same agent. Note that DBSY# must be asserted in the same clock that the response is driven on RS[2:0]# if the response is the Normal Data Response. This means that DBSY# must be deasserted before the response can be driven.

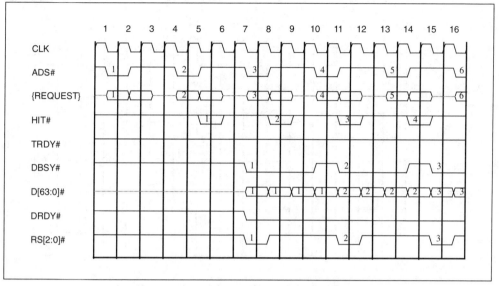

Figure 4-23. Full Speed Read Line Transactions

Read Line transactions are issued to the bus at full speed. TRDY# is not asserted because the transactions are reads and the snoop results indicate no implicit writeback data transfers.

The response and data transfers for transaction 1 occur in T7, the clock after the snoop results are sampled. The data is transferred in 4 consecutive clocks.

DBSY# is asserted for transaction 1 in T7 and remains asserted until T10, the clock before the last data transfer. A special optimization can be made because the same agent drives both data transfers. Since the response agent knows that DBSY# will be deasserted in T10 and it owns the next data transfer, it can drive the next response and data transfer in T11, one clock after DBSY# deassertion.

Note that no waitstates are inserted by the single addressed/responding agent. The back end of the bus will eventually throttle the front end in this scenario, but full bus bandwidth is attainable.

4.6.2.7. FULL SPEED WRITE PARTIAL TRANSACTIONS

Figure 4-24 shows the steady-state behavior of the bus with full speed Write Partial Transactions.

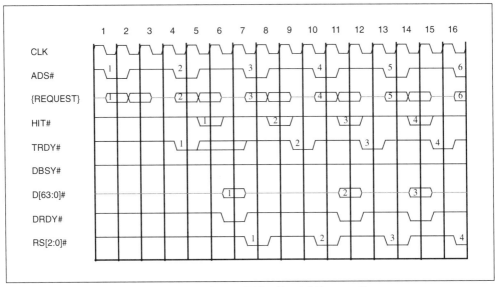

Figure 4-24. Full Speed Write Partial Transactions

In the example, the data transfer only takes one clock, so DBSY# is not asserted.

Write Partial Transactions are driven at full speed. The first transaction occurs on an idle bus and looks just like the simple write case in Figure 4-18. TRDY# is driven 3 clocks later in T4. The Normal No Data response is driven in T7 after inactive HITM# sampled in T6 indicates no implicit writeback. TRDY# is observed active and DBSY# is observed inactive in T5. Therefore the data transfer can begin in T6 as indicated by DRDY# assertion.

The TRDY# for transaction 2 must wait until the response for transaction 1 is sampled. TRDY# is asserted the cycle after RS[2:0]# is sampled. Because the snoop results for transaction 2 have been observed in T9, the response may be driven on RS[2:0]# in T10. TRDY# is sampled with DBSY# deasserted in T10 and data is driven in T11.

There are no bottlenecks to maintaining this steady state.

4.6.2.8. FULL SPEED WRITE LINE TRANSACTIONS (SAME AGENTS)

Figure 4-25 shows the steady-state behavior of the bus with full speed Write Line Transactions with data transfers from the same request agent to the same addressed agent. Data transfers may occur without a turn-around cycle only if from the same agent.

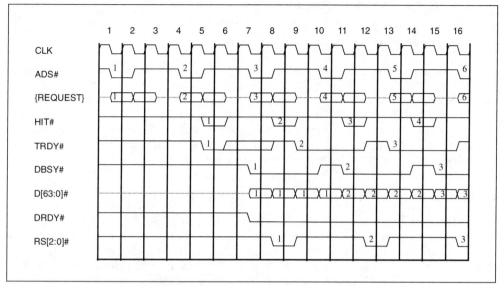

Figure 4-25. Full Speed Write Line Transactions

Write Line Transactions are driven at full speed. The first transaction occurs on an idle bus. TRDY# is delayed until T5 to arrive at steady-state quicker for this example. The Normal No Data response can be driven in T7 after inactive HITM# sampled in T6 indicates no implicit writeback (it is driven in T8 in this example). TRDY# is observed active and DBSY# is observed inactive in T6. Therefore the data transfer can begin in T7 as indicated by DRDY# assertion.

TRDY# for transaction 2 can be driven the cycle after RS[2:0]# is driven, if RS[2:0]# and TRDY# both come from the same target. A special optimization can be made when the same agent drives both request-initiated data transfers. Since in T10 the request agent is driving DB-SY# deasserted, has sampled TRDY# asserted for transaction 2, and owns the data transfer for transaction 2, it can drive the next data transfer in T11, one clock after DBSY# deassertion.

In T11, the target samples TRDY# active and DBSY# inactive and accepts the data transfer starting in T12. Because the snoop results for transaction 2 have been observed in T9, the target is free to drive the response in T12.

Note that no waitstates are inserted by the requesting agent. The back end of the bus will eventually throttle the front end in this scenario, but full bus bandwidth is attainable. The Pentium Pro processor will always insert a turn-around cycle between write data transfers.

4.6.3. Data Phase Protocol Rules

4.6.3.1. VALID DATA TRANSFER

All Data Phase bus signals; DBSY#, DRDY#, D[63:0]#, and DEP[7:0]# are driven by the agent responsible for data transfer. Multi-clock data transfers begin with assertion of DBSY# and complete with deassertion of DBSY# no sooner than one clock prior to the last data transfer. Single-clock and single-chunk data transfers are not required to assert DBSY#. The Request Phase and the Snoop Phase determine the number of valid data transfer chunks, which range from 0 - 4 chunks in the Pentium Pro processor. A valid data chunk on D[63:0]# and valid parity on DEP[7:0]# is indicated by DRDY# assertion in that clock.

4.6.3.2. REQUEST INITIATED DATA TRANSFER

When REQa0# is active during the Request Phase of the transaction, the transaction contains a request initiated data transfer. The request agent may not send any data in response to TRDY# if the transaction length is zero. Request initiated data transfer for transaction "n" begins only after transaction "n" reaches the top of the In-order Queue. On the first clock after TRDY# is observed active and DBSY# is observed inactive, the request agent may begin Valid Data Transfer (as defined above).

The request agent may also begin Valid Data Transfer on the same clock TRDY# is observed active and DBSY# is observed inactive if it can predict this event one cycle earlier. This only occurs when the request agent creates the event by driving the Valid Data Transfer for the previous transfer while the target is asserting TRDY#.

4.6.3.3. SNOOP INITIATED DATA TRANSFER

When HITM# is active during Snoop Phase of the transaction, the transaction contains snoop initiated data transfer. Snoop initiated data transfer for transaction "n" begins only after transaction "n" reaches the top of the In-order Queue and Request initiated data transfer, if any, is complete. Response Initiated Data Transfer

When HITM# is observed inactive during Snoop Phase and the Request Phase contains a request for return of read data, the transaction contains response initiated data transfer.

intel®

5

Bus Transactions
and Operations

This chapter describes in detail the bus transactions and operations supported by the Pentium Pro processor bus.

5.1. BUS TRANSACTIONS SUPPORTED

Figure 5-1 lists the different bus transactions.

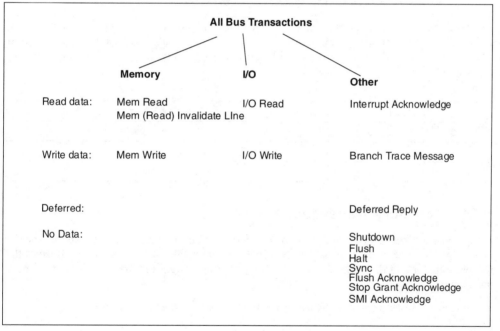

Figure 5-1. Bus Transactions

The transactions classified as read data transactions normally expect a response initiated data transfer from the agent addressed by the transaction. This is indicated by a Normal Data Response in the Response Phase of the transaction. If no bytes are enabled, then a No Data Response is returned by the addressed agent.

The transactions classified as write data transactions require request-initiated data transfer and are identified by REQa[0]#. All responses except Normal Data Response are allowed. The target asserts TRDY#. Implicit Writeback Responses may also occur and send additional snoop initiated data.

The transactions classified as deferred transactions may or may not send data in normal operation. It will return what is expected from the original transaction, unless the Snoop Result Phase indicates that data will return when not expected (HITM#).

The transactions classified as no data transactions require no data transfer. All responses except Normal Data Response and Implicit Writeback Response are allowed.

The transactions classified as memory transactions are cache-coherent and require snooping. All responses are allowed.

The transactions classified as I/O transactions are not snooped. All responses except implicit writeback are allowed.

The transactions classified as other transactions are not snooped. All responses are allowed.

5.2.   BUS TRANSACTION DESCRIPTION

This section describes each bus transaction in detail. In all tables, a "1" denotes an active level, and a "0" denotes an inactive level. Most transactions have a DSZ[1:0]# field, which is used to support agents with different data width. Currently agents with only 64 bit data width are supported.

DSZ[1:0]#		Data Bus Width
0	0	64 bit Data Bus
0	1	Reserved
1	x	Reserved

5.2.1.   Memory Transactions (see Table A-9)

An agent issues memory transactions to read or write data from memory address space. The addressed agent is the agent primarily responsible for completion of the transaction. Besides the request initiator and the addressed agent, all caching agents are required to snoop a memory transaction.

The memory transactions are indicated using the following request encodings:

REQa[4:0]#					REQb[4:0]#		
read & invalidate		0	1	W/R#=0			
rsvd		0	1	W/R#=1			
read	ASZ[1:0]#	1	x	W/R#=0	DSZ[1:0]#	rsvd	LEN[1:0]#
write		1	x	W/R#=1			

Ab[15:3]# are used to encode additional information about the transaction as follows:

Ab[15:8]#	Ab[7:3]#				
BE[7:0]#	SMMEM#	SPLCK#	rsvd	DEN#	rsvd

The ASZ[1:0]# signals are used to support agents with different memory addressing capability to coexist on the same bus. The bits indicate what address range is being addressed as shown in the table below. If a reserved range is indicated, then Snooping Agents and Responding agents must ignore this transaction.

ASZ[1:0]#		Address Range	Observing Agents
0	0	0 <= A[35:3]# < 4 GB	32 & 36 bit agents
0	1	4 GB <= A[35:3]# < 64 GB	36 bit agents
1	x	Reserved	None

The remaining three bits in the REQa[2:0]# field support identification of different types of memory transactions.

The LEN[1:0]# signals are used to indicate the length of the memory transaction. It indicates how much data will be transferred over the bus. The Pentium Pro processor will issue 0 - 8 byte and 32 byte memory transactions. Response to reserved encodings should be the largest transfer size supported.

LEN[1:0]#		Transaction Length
0	0	0 - 8 bytes
0	1	16 bytes
1	0	32 bytes
1	1	Reserved

BE[7:0]# is used in conjunction with LEN[1:0]#. If 8 bytes or more are to be transferred, then BE[7:0]# indicates that all bytes are enabled. If less than 8 bytes are to be transferred, then BE[7:0]# indicates which bytes. Transaction lengths of less than 8 bytes may have any combination of byte enables. If no bytes are enabled, then no data is transferred (in the absence of an Implicit Writeback). A zero byte-count transfer is indicated by BE[7:0]# = 00000000B and an eight or more byte transfer is indicated by BE[7:0]# = 11111111B

Zero length requests (LEN= 00B and BE = 00H) for read transactions are modeled after the Memory (Read) Invalidate transaction. Response must be No Data Response in the absence of HITM# or DEFER# assertion.

For write transactions, TRDY# assertion is required, even when no request-initiated data is being transferred. This simplifies this rare special case (Pentium Pro processor will not issue this transaction). The request agent must not assert DRDY# in response to TRDY#.

SMMEM# is asserted while the requestor is in System Management Mode (see Section 5.2.3.6.7., "SMI Acknowledge"). SPLCK# indicates an atomic split locked operation (see Section 5.3.4.1., "[Split] Bus Lock"). DEN# indicates that this transaction is deferrable (see Section 5.3.3., "Deferred Operations").

Request Initiator Responsibilities

A 32 bit address request initiator must always assert ASZ[1:0]# = 00 when making a memory transaction request and drive a valid 32 bit address on A[31:3]# pins. If parity is enabled it must also drive correct parity for A[23:3]# on AP0# and A[31:24]# on AP1#. (See Section 3.4.3., "Request Signals".)

A 36 bit address request initiator must assert ASZ[1:0]# = 01B when making a memory transaction request between 4G and 64G-1 and ASZ[1:0]# = 00B when making a memory transaction request between 0 to 4G-1. It also must drive a valid 36 bit address on A[35:2]# pins at all times. If parity is enabled it must drive correct parity for A[23:3]# on AP0# and A[35:24]# on AP1#.

A 64 bit data request initiator must always assert DSZ[1:0]# = 00B when making a memory transaction request.

All request initiators issue the required encodings on REQ[2:0]# and LEN[1:0]# pins to request the proper transaction. All reserved encodings are always driven inactive.

Addressed Agent Responsibilities

A 32 bit address memory agent must ignore all memory transaction requests besides ASZ[1:0]# = 00B. Whenever ASZ[1:0]# = 00B it must be capable of responding to the transaction.

A 36 bit address memory agent must ignore all memory transaction requests besides ASZ[1:0]# = 01 and 00. Whenever ASZ[1:0]# = 00B it must be capable of filtering the A[35:32]# signals from the address if they are not guaranteed to be in the inactive state.

A 64 bit data addressed agent must ignore the DSZ[1:0]# field. All addressed agents currently defined must obey reserved field restrictions. L3 Cache agents use ATTR[7:0]# to determine cache line allocation policy.

All addressed agents must observe the snoop results presented in the snoop phase and modify their ownerships towards transaction completion if HITM# or DEFER# is asserted by a snooping agent. These special cases are described in greater detail in later subsections of this chapter.

5.2.1.1. MEMORY READ TRANSACTIONS

REQa[2:0]#			
code read	1	D/C#=0	0
data read	1	D/C#=1	0

Memory Read Transactions perform reads of memory or memory-mapped I/O. REQa[1]# indicates whether the read is for code or data. This can be used to make cache coherency assumptions (see Chapter 7, *Cache Protocol*).

5.2.1.2. MEMORY WRITE TRANSACTIONS

REQa[2:0]#			
may not be retried	1	W/WB#=0	1
may be retried	1	W/WB#=1	1

Memory Write Transactions perform writes to memory or memory-mapped I/O. REQa[1]# indicates whether the write transaction is a writeback and may not be retried. REQa[1]# asserted indicates that the write transaction may be retried. REQa[1]# is asserted by a non-cacheable (DMA) agent to write data to memory. The Pentium Pro processor asserts REQa[1]# when writing through the cache and when evicting a full Write Combining Buffer. This transaction is snooped and can receive an Implicit Writeback Response. When REQa[1]# is deasserted, no agent may assert DEFER# to retry the transaction. A writeback caching agent must deassert REQa[1]# when writing back a modified cache line to memory. If deasserted and this transaction hits a valid line in a snooping cache, a cache coherency violation has occurred.

5.2.1.3. MEMORY (READ) INVALIDATE TRANSACTIONS

REQa[2:0]#			
Memory (Read) Invalidate	0	1	0

An agent issues a Read Invalidate Transaction to satisfy an internal cache line fill and obtain exclusive ownership of the line. All snooping agents will invalidate the line addressed by this transaction. A Read Invalidate transaction has BE[7:0]# = FFH and LEN[1:0]# = 10B. Note that if the issuing agent already has the line in the shared state, it need only invalidate the line in other caches to allow a transition to the exclusive state. In this case the requesting agent issues a zero length transaction (BE[7:0]# = 00H and LEN[1:0]# = 00) indicating that no data is required.

5.2.1.4. RESERVED MEMORY WRITE TRANSACTION

REQa[2:0]#		
Reserved Memory Write	0	1	1

This transaction is reserved, and must not be issued by any bus agents. Future bus agents may use this encoding. Current memory agents and snooping agents must treat this transaction as a Memory Write Transaction.

5.2.2. I/O Transactions

An agent issues an I/O transaction to read or write an I/O location. The addressed agent is the agent primarily responsible for completion of the I/O transaction. I/O transaction may be deferred in the snoop phase by any agent as described in the later subsection.

The I/O transactions are indicated using the following request encodings:

REQa[4:0]#					REQb[4:0]#		
read	1	0	0	0	W/R#=0			
write	1	0	0	0	W/R#=1	DSZ[1:0]#	rsvd	LEN[1:0]

Ab[15:8]#	Ab[7:3]#				
BE[7:0]#	SMMEM#	SPLCK#=0	rsvd	DEN#	rsvd

I/O transactions have similar request fields to memory transactions. However, the address space is always 64K+3 bytes[1]. Therefore, A[35:17]# will always be zero. A[16]# is zero except when the first three bytes above the 64Kbyte space are accessed (I/O wraparound). BE[7:0]# will always indicate at most 4 bytes when issued by the Pentium Pro processor.

The LEN[1:0]# signals are identical to the memory transactions, and are used to indicate the length of the I/O transaction. It indicates how much data will be transferred over the bus. Response to reserved encodings should be the largest transfer size supported.

---

[1] The Pentium® Pro processor is backwards compatible with previous implementations of the Intel Architecture I/O space. A[16]# is active whenever an I/O access is made to 4 bytes from addresses 0FFFDH, 0FFFEH, or 0FFFFH. A[16]# is also active when an I/O access is made to 2 bytes from address 0FFFFH.

LEN[1:0]#		Transaction Length
0	0	0 - 8 bytes
0	1	16 bytes
1	0	32 bytes
1	1	Reserved

BE[7:0]# is used in conjunction with LEN[1:0]#. If 8 bytes or more are to be transferred, then BE[7:0]# indicates that all bytes are enabled. If less than 8 bytes are to be transferred, then BE[7:0]# indicates which bytes. Transaction lengths of less than 8 bytes may have any combination of byte enables. If no bytes are enabled, then no data is transferred. The Pentium Pro processor will always assert 1 to 4 consecutive byte enables. I/O reads that lie within 8-byte boundaries but cross 4-byte boundaries are issued as one transaction, but I/O writes that lie within 8-byte boundaries but cross 4-byte boundaries are split into two transactions.

Zero length requests (LEN= 00B and BE = 00H) for read transactions are modeled after Memory transactions. Response must be No Data Response in the absence of DEFER# assertion.

For write transactions, TRDY# assertion is required, even though no request-initiated data is being transferred. This simplifies this rare special case (Pentium Pro processor will not issue this transaction). The request agent must not assert DRDY# in response to TRDY#.

5.2.2.1.   REQUEST INITIATOR RESPONSIBILITIES

The request initiator must assert W/R# if the transaction is an I/O Write, and must deassert W/R# signal if the transaction is an I/O Read. A 64 bit request initiator must always issue DSZ[1:0]# = 00B. The reserved fields are driven inactive.

5.2.2.2.   ADDRESSED AGENT RESPONSIBILITIES

The addressed I/O agent must ignore reserved fields. It must also ignore DSZ[1:0]#

5.2.3.   Non-memory Central Transactions

These transactions are issued by a bus agent to create special bus message. It is the responsibility of the central agent in the system to capture these transactions. All non-memory central transaction define Ab[15:8]# (BE[7:0]#) as an additional command encoding field. The central agent responds with No Data Response, RS[2:0]# = 101, for all non-memory central transactions, except for the Interrupt Acknowledge transaction which is covered in Section 5.2.3.4., "Interrupt Acknowledge Transaction".

REQa[4:0]#					REQb[4:0]#				
read	0	1	0	0	W/R#=0				
write	0	1	0	0	W/R#=1	DSZ[1:0]#	rsvd	x	x

Ab[15:8]#	Ab[7:3]#				
x	SMMEM#	SPLCK#=0	rsvd	DEN#	rsvd

These transactions drive REQa[0]#active if request initiated data is being sent. The Central Agent will then drive TRDY#.

5.2.3.1.   REQUEST INITIATOR RESPONSIBILITIES

Generate the request with valid encodings. The reserved fields are driven inactive.

5.2.3.2.   CENTRAL AGENT RESPONSIBILITIES

Generate response for all encodings including all reserved encodings. Return data as necessary

5.2.3.3.   OBSERVING AGENT RESPONSIBILITIES

Observing agents must decode the entire request field and determine if they are required to take any action. Of course, any agent may stall the Snoop Result Phase to delay completion.

5.2.3.4.   INTERRUPT ACKNOWLEDGE TRANSACTION

A processor agent issues an Interrupt Acknowledge Transaction in response to an interrupt from an 8259A or similar interrupt controller. The response agent (normally the I/O agent) must perform whatever handshaking the interrupt controller requires. For example, an I/O agent interfaced to an 8259A interrupt controller must issue two locked-interrupt-acknowledge cycles to the 8259A to process one Interrupt Acknowledge Transaction it receives from a Pentium Pro processor. The I/O agent returns the interrupt vector generated by the 8259A to the processor as a single data-cycle response on D[7:0]#. D[63:8]# are undefined. Note that the BE[7:0]# field reflects this. The address Aa[35:3]# signals are reserved and can be driven to any value.

REQa[0]#	REQb[1:0]#		Ab[15:8]#
0	0	0	01

5.2.3.5. BRANCH TRACE MESSAGE

Branch Trace Messages produce 64 bits of data. If execution tracing is enabled, an agent issues a Branch Trace Message transaction for branches taken. The address Aa[35:3]# is reserved and can be driven to any value. D[63:32]# contain the linear address of the target. D[31:0]# contain either the address of the first byte of the branch instruction or the address of the instruction immediately following the branch. If the instruction does not complete normally, then D[31:0]# will contain the address of the branch instruction itself. If the instruction completes normally, then D[31:0]# will contain the address of the instruction immediately following the branch. The BE[7:0]# field reflects that data will be valid on all bytes of the data bus. It is the responsibility of the Central Agent to assert TRDY# and the response for this transaction. If a different agent is responsible for storage, it must capture the data from the bus.

REQa[0]#	REQb[1:0]#		Ab[15:8]#
1	0	0	FF

5.2.3.6. SPECIAL TRANSACTIONS

These transactions are used to indicate to the system some rare events. The address Aa[35:3]# is undefined and can be driven to any value.

REQa[0]#	REQb[1:0]#		Ab[15:8]#
0	0	1	00-07

Special Transaction	Ab[15:8]#
NOP	0000 0000
Shutdown	0000 0001
Flush	0000 0010
Halt	0000 0011
Sync	0000 0100
Flush Acknowledge	0000 0101
Stop Clock Acknowledge	0000 0110
SMI Acknowledge	0000 0111
Reserved	all others

5.2.3.6.1. Shutdown

An agent issues a Shutdown Transaction to indicate that it has detected a severe software error that prevents further processing. The Pentium Pro processor issues a Shutdown Transaction if any other exception occurs while the processor is attempting to call the double fault handler. The internal caches remain in the same state unless a snoop hits a modified line. The following table describes how Pentium Pro processor reacts to various events while in the Shutdown state.

Event	Immediate Action	Final State
INTR	Ignore	Shutdown
NMI	NMI Handler Entry	Do not return to Shutdown on IRET
INIT#	Reset Handler	Do not return to Shutdown
RESET#	Reset Handler	Do not return to Shutdown
STPCLK#	STPCLK Acknowledge	Return to Shutdown on !STPCLK
SMI#	SMI Handler Entry	Return to Shutdown on RSM[1]
FLUSH#	FLUSH Acknowledge	Return to Shutdown Immediately
ADS#	Snoop Results	Return to Shutdown Immediately
BINIT#	MCA Handler Entry	Do not return to Shutdown
HardFail	MCA Handler Entry	Do not return to Shutdown
FRCERR	MCA Handler Entry	Do not return to Shutdown

NOTE:

1. Shutdown transaction may be reissued by the Pentium® Pro processor.

5.2.3.6.2. Flush

An agent issues a Flush Transaction to indicate that it has invalidated its internal caches *without* writing back any modified lines. If the software using the instruction requires other Pentium Pro processors to also be flushed, it must do so via APIC IPIs. The Pentium Pro processor generates this transaction on executing an INVD instruction.

5.2.3.6.3. Halt

A processor issues a Halt Transaction to indicate that it has executed the HLT instruction and stopped program execution. The following table describes how Pentium Pro processor reacts to various events while in the Halt state.

Event	Immediate Action	Final State
INTR	Interrupt Handler Entry	Do not return to Halt on IRET
NMI	NMI Handler Entry	Do not return to Halt on IRET
INIT#	Reset Handler	Do not return to Halt
RESET#	Reset Handler	Do not return to Halt
STPCLK#	STPCLK Acknowledge	Return to Halt on !STPCLK
SMI#	SMI Handler Entry	Optionally return to Halt on RSM based on a bit setting in SMRAM
FLUSH#	FLUSH Acknowledge	Return to Halt Immediately
ADS#	Snoop Results	Return to halt Immediately
BINIT#	MCA Handler Entry	Do not return to Halt
HardFail	MCA Handler Entry	Do not return to Halt
FRCERR	MCA Handler Entry	Do not return to Halt

5.2.3.6.4. Sync

An agent issues a Sync Transaction to indicate that it has written back all modified lines in its internal caches to memory and then invalidated its internal caches. If software wants to guarantee that other processors are also synchronized, it must do so via APIC IPIs. The Pentium Pro processor generates a Sync Transaction on executing a WBINVD instruction.

5.2.3.6.5. Flush Acknowledge

A caching agent issues a Flush Acknowledge Transaction when it has completed a cache sync, and flush operation in response to an earlier FLUSH# signal activation. If FLUSH# pin is bussed to N agents, the Central Agent must expect N Flush Acknowledge transactions.

5.2.3.6.6. Stop Grant Acknowledge

An agent issues a Stop Grant Acknowledge Transaction when it enters Stop Grant mode.

The agent continues to respond to RESET#, BINIT#, ADS#, and FLUSH# while in Stop Grant mode. The Pentium Pro processor powers down its caches in the Stop Grant mode to minimize its power consumption and generates a delayed snoop response on an external bus snoop request.

5.2.3.6.7. SMI Acknowledge

An agent issues an SMI Acknowledge Transaction when it enters the System Management Mode handler. SMMEM# (Ab[7]#) is first asserted at this entry point. It remains asserted for all transactions issued by the agent. An agent issues another SMI Acknowledge Transaction when it exits the System Management Mode handler. SMMEM# (Ab[7]#) is first deasserted at this exit point.

The SMI Acknowledge Transaction can be observed by the bridge agents to determine when an agent enters or exits SMM mode.

5.2.4. Deferred Reply Transaction

An agent issues a Deferred Reply Transaction to complete an earlier transaction for which the response was deferred. The Deferred Reply Transaction may return data to complete an earlier Memory Read, I/O Read, or Interrupt Acknowledge Transaction, or it may simply indicate the completion of an earlier Memory Write, I/O Write, or Invalidate Transaction (note that the data transfer for a memory write or I/O write takes place in the data phase of the earlier transaction). After being deferred, the Invalidate Transaction may have hit a modified line on another bus, which will cause the Deferred Reply Transaction to return data.

REQa[4:0]#					REQb[4:0]#				
0	0	0	0	0	x	x	x	x	x

Ab[15:8]#	Ab[7:3]#				
xx	x	SPLCK#=0	rsvd	DEN#=0	rsvd

The deferring agent is both the requesting agent and the responding agent for the Deferred Reply Transaction. The addressed agent is the agent which issued the original transaction.

5.2.4.1. REQUEST INITIATOR RESPONSIBILITIES (DEFERRING AGENT)

This transaction uses the address bus to return the Deferred ID, which was sent with the original request on DID[7:0]#. The Deferred ID is returned on address Aa[23:16]# signals. The deferring agent will not place a unique ID onto Ab[23:16]#, since DEN# is deasserted.

Aa[23:16]#	Ab[23:16]#
DID[7:0]# (original)	xx

See Section 5.3.3., "Deferred Operations" for Deferred ID generation.

The ownership transfer of a cache line transferred from the deferring agent to the original requesting agent takes place during Snoop Result Phase of this transaction. Since this transaction is not snooped, HIT# and HITM# signals are used by the requesting agent. For a Deferred Reply resulting from a Memory Read Data Line Transaction, the deferring agent must assert HIT# in the deferred reply's Snoop Result Phase if the original requesting agent should place the line in the Shared state. If the original requester does not observe HIT# active, it may place the line in Exclusive state. For a Deferred Reply resulting from a Memory Invalidate Transaction which hit a modified line on another bus, the deferring agent must echo the HITM# in the Snoop Result

Phase of the Deferred Reply (the Snoop Result Phase indicates all changes in the length of data returned).

The deferring agent may assert DEFER# in the Snoop Result Phase of the Deferred Reply to retry the original transaction.

A Deferred Reply may receive any response except a Deferred Response. The response must follow the protocol illustrated in Chapter 4, *Bus Protocol*. If a Retry Response is received, then the addressed agent will retry the original transaction.

5.2.4.2.   ADDRESSED AGENT RESPONSIBILITIES (ORIGINAL REQUESTOR)

The addressed agent is the agent which issued the original transaction. It must decode the DID[7:0]# returned on Aa[23:16]# and match it with a previously deferred transaction. At the Snoop Result Phase of the Deferred Reply, the original requestor's transaction is in the exact same state as the Snoop Result phase for a non-deferred transaction (with DEN# assumed deasserted). HIT#/HITM#/DEFER# are used as in the original transaction. It must accept any returned data and complete the original transaction as if it were not deferred. It must make the appropriate snoop state transition at the Snoop Result Phase of the Deferred Reply, and must reissue the original transaction if a Retry Response is received.

5.2.5.   Reserved Transactions

These transaction encodings are reserved. No agent should take any action when they are seen. They should be completely ignored.

REQa[4:0]#				
0	0	0	0	1
1	1	0	0	x

5.3.   BUS OPERATIONS

This section describes bus operations. A bus operation is a bus procedure that appears atomic to software even though it might not appear atomic on the bus. The operations discussed in this section are those that have multiple transactions (such as locked operations) or those that have potential multiple data transfers (implicit writebacks).

5.3.1.   Implicit Writeback Response

In response to any memory transaction, each caching agent issues an internal snoop operation. If the snoop finds the accessed line in the Modified state in a writeback cache, then the caching agent asserts HITM# in the Snoop Phase. The caching agent that asserted HITM# writes back the Modified line from its cache during snoop-initiated Data Phase. This data transfer is called an *implicit writeback.* The response for a transaction that contains an implicit writeback is the Implicit Writeback response.

5.3.1.1.   MEMORY AGENT RESPONSIBILITIES

On observing HITM# active in the Snoop Phase, the addressed memory agent remains the response agent but changes its response to an implicit writeback response.

If the transaction contains a request-initiated data transfer, it remains responsible for TRDY# assertion to indicate that the write data transfer can begin.

Since the transaction contains a snoop-initiated data transfer, (modified line writeback) the memory agent asserts a snoop initiated TRDY# once it has a free cache line buffer to receive the modified line writeback (after the TRDY# assertion and deassertion for the request initiated TRDY# is complete, if there was a request initiated data transfer).

Precisely two clocks from active TRDY# and inactive DBSY#, the Memory Agent drives the implicit writeback response synchronized with the DBSY# assertion from the snooping agent for the implicit writeback data transfer of the snoop agent.

If the snooped transaction is a write request, the memory agent is responsible for merging the write data with the writeback cache line. The memory agent then updates main memory with the latest cache line data. If the snooped transaction writes a full cache line, then there may or may not be implicit writeback data. If DBSY# is not asserted precisely two clocks from active TRDY# and inactive DBSY#, then there is no implicit writeback data.

5.3.1.2.   REQUESTING AGENT RESPONSIBILITIES

The requesting agent picks up snoop responsibility for the cache line after observing the transaction's Snoop Phase.

The requesting agent always observes the Response Phase to determine if the snoop-initiated Data Phase contains additional data beyond what was requested:

- If the original request is a Part Line Read Transaction, then the requester obtains the needed data from the first 64-bit critical chunk (as defined by the burst order described in Chapter 3, *Bus Overview*).

- If the original request is a Read Line or Read Invalidate Line Transaction, then the requester absorbs the entire line.

- If the original request is an Invalidate Line Transaction and the line is modified in another cache, then the requester updates its internal cache line with the updated cache line received in the snoop-initiated Data Phase.

- If the original Invalidate Line Transaction receives a Deferred Reply, a HITM# in the Snoop Result Phase indicates data will return, and the requesting agent updates its internal cache with the data.

5.3.2. Transferring Snoop Responsibility

A requesting agent picks up snoop responsibility for the cache line after observing a transaction's Snoop Phase. When a requesting agent accepts snoop responsibility for a cache line and immediately drops that responsibility in response to a subsequent transaction, it is allowed to use the cache line exactly once for internal use, before performing an implicit writeback.

Figure 5-2 illustrates the effect of response agent responsibility pickup on an outstanding Invalidation Transaction (Read Invalidate Line, or an Invalidate Line Transaction). It also illustrates that a cache line can be returned in response to an Invalidate Line Transaction if two competing agents request ownership of a Shared cache line simultaneously.

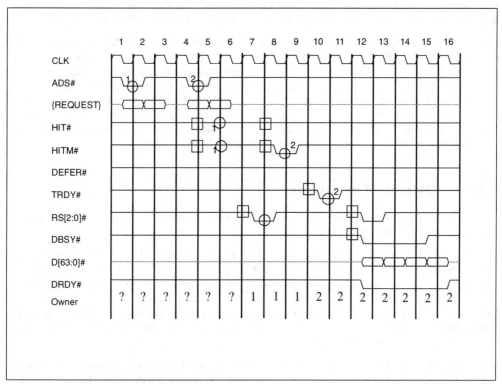

Figure 5-2. Response Responsibility Pickup Effect on an Outstanding Invalidation Transaction

In T1, the requesting agent P1 asserts ADS# and drives the {REQUEST} group to issue Invalidate Request 1. In T4, a different requesting agent, P2, asserts ADS# and intends to drive the {REQUEST} group to issue Invalidation request 2 to the same cache line. However, the snoop of Invalidate Request 1 will invalidate the shared line in P2, forcing P2 to instead issue Read Invalidate Request 2, to the same cache line.

In T5, P1 observes request 2 and notes that the request is to the same cache line for which it is expecting ownership in T6. In T6, P1 observes inactive DEFER# and confirms that the transaction has been committed for in-order completion.

If P1 changes the state of the cache line to M (as opposed to E/I), then P1 asserts HITM# in T8 to indicate that it has the cache line in the Modified state. In T8, P1 receives a successful completion response for request 1. P1 recognizes that it has promised the cache line to a different agent. It completes its internal cache line update and gets ready to return the line to P2.

In T9, the memory agent observes HITM# and asserts TRDY# in T10 in response to the HITM#. In response in T12, the memory agent asserts implicit writeback response and P1 asserts DB-SY#. From T12 to T15, P1 drives the implicit cache line data on the data bus. Agent P2 recognizes that the Read Invalidate request is given an implicit writeback response. It receives the new data associated with the cache line, updates its cache line, and then resumes operation.

Similar to this example, when an Invalidate Line Transaction receives a deferred response, the corresponding Deferred Reply Transaction may or may not contain data depending on the race condition. If the Deferred Reply Transaction does not contain data, the deferred reply agent asserts a No Data Response. If the Deferred Reply Transaction contains data, the deferred reply agent asserts HITM# in the Snoop Phase of the Deferred Reply Transaction and asserts an Implicit Writeback response. The original request initiator recognizes that a modified cache line is being returned and receives the new cache line and updates its internal storage. Memory is not updated with the Implicit Writeback data of a Deferred Reply Transaction.

5.3.3.   Deferred Operations

During the Request Phase, an agent can define Defer Enable (DEN#) to indicate if the transaction can be given Deferred Response.

When the flag is inactive, the transaction must not receive a Deferred Response. Certain transactions must always be issued with the flag inactive. Transactions in a bus-locked operation, Deferred Reply transactions, and Writeback transactions fall in this category. Transaction-latency sensitive agents may also use this feature to guarantee transaction completion within a restricted latency. In-order completion of a transaction is indicated by an inactive DEFER# signal or an active HITM# signal during the Snoop Phase, followed by normal completion or implicit writeback response in the Response Phase.

When Defer Enable (DEN#) is inactive, the transaction may be completed in-order or possibly retried, but it cannot be deferred. All transactions may be completed in order. The only transactions that may not be retried are explicit writeback transactions (REQa[2:0]# = 101B) and locked transactions subsequent to the first transaction in a locked sequence. The retry feature is available for use by any bus agent incapable of supporting Deferred Response. These transactions may either be completed in-order (DEFER# inactive or HITM# active during the Snoop Phase followed by normal completion response), or they must be retried (DEFER# active and HITM# inactive during the Snoop Phase followed by a Retry Response during the Response Phase).

When Defer Enable (DEN#) is active, the transaction may be completed in-order, or it may be retried or deferred. A deferred transaction is indicated by asserting DEFER# (with HITM# inactive) during the Snoop Phase followed by Deferred Response in the Response Phase.

For every transaction, only one agent is allowed to assert DEFER#. Normally it is the responsibility of the agent addressed by the transaction. When the addressed agent always guarantees in-order completion, the responsibility can be given to a unique third party agent who can assert DEFER# on behalf of the addressed agent. Both agents must then agree on how to complete the transaction and which agent will drive the response.

A deferred or retry response removes the transaction from the In-order Queue. On a retry response, it is the responsibility of the requesting agent to initiate the transaction repeatedly until the transaction either receives a deferred or in-order completion response. On a deferred response, the response agent must latch the Deferred ID, DID[7:0]# issued during the Request Phase. After the response agent completes the original request, it must issue a matching Deferred Reply Bus Transaction. The Deferred Reply transaction's Request Phase must begin at least one clock after the Response Phase for the original transaction. The Deferred ID, available during the original transaction's Request Phase, is used as the address in the Deferred Reply Transaction's Request Phase.

A Deferred ID contains eight bits, divided into two four-bit fields. The Deferred ID is transferred on pins Ab[23:16]# (signals DID[7:0]#) in the second clock of the original transaction's Request Phase. Ab[23:20]# contain the request agent ID, which is unique for every agent. Ab[19:16]# contains a request ID, assigned by the request agent based on its internal queue (typically a queue index). Up to sixteen different agents can allow deferred responses. Up to sixteen deferred responses can be pending for each of the sixteen agents. An agent that supports more than sixteen outstanding deferred requests can use multiple agent IDs. The Pentium Pro processor limits the number of outstanding deferred transactions to 4.

The deferred response agent uses the Deferred Reply Transaction phase to transfer completion status of the deferred transaction. The Deferred ID is driven on address Aa[23:16]# during the Deferred Reply Transaction's Request Phase. The final cache state after completion of the Deferred Reply for a Read Line Transaction is indicated by the HIT# signal. For a Deferred Reply resulting from a Memory Invalidate Transaction which hit a modified line on another bus, the deferring agent must echo the HITM# in the Snoop Result Phase of the Deferred Reply in order to return unexpected data (the Snoop Result Phase indicates all changes in the length of data returned). During the response phase, the appropriate response is driven to indicate completion status of the transaction.

Agents can use the deferred response mechanism when an operation has significantly greater latency than the normal in-order response. The deferred response mechanism can be used to implement non-blocking bridge components between the Pentium Pro processor bus and a system bus to maintain concurrency with guaranteed forward progress.

Deferred transactions enter the In-order Queue in the same way as all other transactions. ADS# for a deferred reply may be asserted no sooner than one cycle after RS[2:0]# is asserted for the original transactions that has been deferred.

5.3.3.1. RESPONSE AGENT RESPONSIBILITIES

A response agent willing to give a deferred response must maintain an internal deferred reply pool with up to *n* entries. At the time it wishes to give a deferred response, the response agent must assign an entry for the transaction in the deferred reply pool and store the Deferred ID available during the request phase of the transaction. After the transaction's Response Phase has been driven, it must become a request bus owner and initiate a Deferred Reply Transaction using the Deferred ID as the address. It must also reclaim free queue entries in the deferred reply pool.

5.3.3.2.   REQUESTING AGENT RESPONSIBILITIES

A requesting agent must assume that every outstanding transaction issued with an asserted Defer Enable (DEN#) flag in the Request Phase may receive a deferred response. Therefore, it must maintain an internal outstanding transaction queue and ID with the same size as its ability to pipeline new requests. During the Deferred Reply Transaction, it must compare the reply address with all Deferred IDs in its outstanding transaction queue. On an ID match, the requesting agent can retire the original transaction from its outstanding transaction queue and complete the operation.

Figure 5-3 illustrates a deferred response followed by the corresponding Deferred Reply for a read operation.

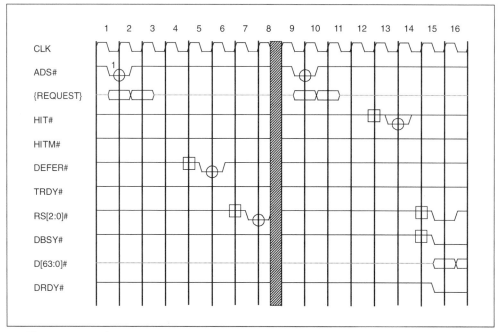

Figure 5-3. Deferred Response Followed by a Deferred Reply to a Read Operation

In T1, the requesting agent asserts ADS# and drives the {REQUEST} group to issue a Read Line request. In T5, the Snoop Phase, the addressed agent determines that the transaction cannot be completed in-order and hence asserts DEFER#. Since HITM# is observed inactive in T6, in T7 the addressed agent returns a deferred response by asserting the proper encoding on RS[2:0]#.

Before T9, the addressed response agent obtains the data required in the original request. In T9, the original response agent issues a Deferred Reply Transaction, using the value latched from the DID[7:0]# signals in the original transaction as the address. In T13, the response agent drives a valid level on the HIT# signal to indicate the final cache state of the returned line. The original requestor picks up snoop responsibility. In T15, it drives normal completion response and also begins the Data Phase.

In T10, the original requesting agent observes the Deferred Reply Transaction. It matches the DID[7:0]# to the Deferred ID stored with the original request in its outstanding transaction queue. The original requesting agent observes the final state of the returned cache line in T14. In T16, it observes the transaction response and removes the transaction from the outstanding transaction queue and the In-order Queue. This completes the entire deferred operation sequence.

5.3.4. Locked Operations

Locked operations provide a means of synchronization in a multiprocessor environment. They guarantee indivisible sequencing between multiple memory transactions.

A locked instruction is guaranteed to lock the area of memory defined by the destination operand. In addition, a lock's integrity is not affected by the memory operand's alignment.

In previous generation processors, lock semantics were implemented with a [split] bus lock. This approach, although sufficient to guarantee indivisibility, is not always necessary or efficient in a writeback caching agent. During bus lock, other agents are prevented from issuing bus transactions. In multiprocessing systems, it is desirable to reduce the data bus bandwidth demands of locked operations, so the Pentium Pro processor implements cache locks. Cache locks allow locked operations to take place in the cache without tying up the bus.

A locked operation in the Intel386 and Intel486 architecture involves an indivisible read-modify-write operation on the lock variable. Based on the memory type and alignment of the lock variable, a locked operation is carried out using one of three options:

Cache Lock. When the lock variable is in a writeback-cacheable (WB) memory range and the lock variable is contained in one cache line, the locked operation can be executed by: 1) executing any bus transactions necessary to bring the line into the Exclusive or Modified cache state, and 2) executing the locked read-modify-write sequence in the cache, placing the line in the Modified state.

[Split] Bus Lock. When the lock variable cannot use a cache lock (due to attribute conflicts) or crosses an 8-byte boundary, the locked operation is issued on the Pentium Pro processor bus. The bus is locked during the entire read-modify-write sequence to guarantee indivisibility.

Some implementations might use a bus lock or split lock even when a cache lock is allowed.

5.3.4.1.   [SPLIT] BUS LOCK

All variables that cannot be cache locked are locked using the standard [split] bus lock operation. A Pentium Pro processor [split] bus locked operation (read-modify-write or RMW) involves 1 or 2 memory read transactions followed by 1 or 2 memory write transactions to the same address. When any agent issues a RMW operation, it asserts the LOCK# signal in the Request Phase and keeps it active during the entire Lock Operation. In a split bus locked operation, the agent asserts Split Lock (SPLCK#) in the first transaction to indicate a split operation. During a RMW operation the agent always deasserts Defer Enable (DEN#) for all transactions in the operation. The first transaction of the RMW operation may have DEFER# asserted, which will retry the entire RMW operation (regardless of the response). No transaction in the RMW operation after the first read transaction may have DEFER# asserted.

The RMW Operation is successfully completed when the agent successfully completes all memory transactions. Successful completion occurs when the last transaction of the RMW operation passes its Error Phase. The requestor retains ownership of the bus by keeping LOCK# active until the last transaction successfully completes. The RMW Operation is prematurely aborted and retried if the first read transaction receives an AERR# assertion in the Error Phase or DEFER# assertion in the Snoop Phase. After a premature abortion, the agent issuing the lock operation must ignore any data returned during Data Phase, deassert LOCK#, re-arbitrate for the bus (deassert its BREQn# signal if active) and reissue the first transaction.

During the memory read transactions, if other writeback cache agents contain the variable in Modified state, they supply the data via the implicit writeback mechanism. If the lock variable is contained in Modified state inside the requestor, it performs self-snooping after the locked transaction is issued on the bus and evicts the cache line via the implicit writeback mechanism. As explained in Chapter 4, *Bus Protocol*, if DEFER# assertion is not over-ridden by HITM# assertion, the agent asserting DEFER# must drive a Retry Response in the Response Phase to force a retry. If DEFER# assertion is overridden by HITM# assertion, the responding agent drives an implicit writeback response, and the Data Phase completes with an implicit writeback from the snooping agent. In either case, the lock sequence is aborted and retried.

The entire RMW Operation fails if any one of the bus locked transactions receives a hard error/ deferred response or AERR# assertion beyond the retry limit of the agent, or if any one of the second to fourth transactions receives DEFER# assertion. These are protocol violations. As explained in Chapter 4, *Bus Protocol*, AERR# assertion causes an arbitration reset sequence. If AERR# gets asserted on the second to fourth transaction within the retry limit of the agent, the retrying agent must be guaranteed bus ownership to guarantee indivisibility of the lock operation. The bus protocol requires the retrying agent to arbitrate for the bus two clocks before all other agents.

intel

6

Range Registers

6.1.   INTRODUCTION

The Pentium Pro processor Memory Type Range Registers (MTRRs) are model specific registers specifying the types of memory occupying different physical address ranges. Some of this information was available to previous Intel processors via external bus signals (for example, KEN# and WB/WT#).

Because Pentium Pro processors on a particular Pentium Pro processor bus share the same memory address space, all Pentium Pro processors on a Pentium Pro processor bus must have identical range register contents. The Pentium Pro processor cache protocol assumes that different caching agents (different Pentium Pro processors) agree on the memory type and cache attributes of each memory line. MTRR updates are permitted only if all caches have been flushed before and after the update.

As described in following sections, the memory types affect both instruction execution and cache attributes.

6.2.   RANGE REGISTERS AND PENTIUM® PRO PROCESSOR INSTRUCTION EXECUTION

The Pentium Pro processor supports out-of-order and speculative instruction execution. Out-of-order execution enables the processor to execute an instruction even if previous instructions in the execution stream have not completed or executed. Speculative execution enables the processor to execute an instruction that may or may not be part of the execution stream (such as an instruction following a conditional branch), so long as the processor can undo the instruction's effect if it is not part of the execution stream.

Some memory types should not be accessed by out-of-order or speculative accesses. For example, loading from an address used for memory-mapped I/O can have side effects, such as clearing the loaded value from an I/O controller's buffer. Such an instruction should not be executed speculatively, but only if it is definitely part of the Pentium Pro processor's execution stream. If side effects of loads must take place in a certain sequence, then such loads should not be executed out-of-order either.

The memory types in the Pentium Pro processor's range registers can be used to block out-of-order or speculative accesses to memory ranges, in addition to controlling cache attributes. The two uses are not independent of each other; any memory type that blocks out-of-order or speculative accesses is also non-cacheable.

The Pentium Pro processor architecture defines memory types where speculative and out of order execution is safe (in other words, can be undone in case of misprediction). The same memory types are also extended to support different cacheability policies such as writeback, and writethrough. The memory types are defined for specific address ranges based on range registers. The memory types currently defined, are shown in Table 6-1. The Pentium Pro processor drives the memory type to the Pentium Pro processor bus in the second clock of the Request Phase on the ATTR[3:0]# (attribute) pins.

Table 6-1. Pentium® Pro Processor Architecture Memory Types

ATTR[7:0]# Encoding	Mnemonic	Name	Description
00000000	UC	uncacheable	Not cached. All reads and writes appear on the bus. Reads and writes can have side effects, therefore no speculative accesses are made to UC memory. UC memory is useful for memory-mapped I/O.
00000100	WC	write-combining	Reads are not cached. Writes can be delayed and combined. They are also weakly ordered resulting in substantially higher write throughput. Reading WC memory cannot have side effects and speculative reads are allowed. WC memory is useful for applications such as linear frame buffers.
00000101	WT	write-through	Cacheable memory for which all writes are written through to main memory. Writing WT memory never causes a cache fill of an invalid cache line and either invalidates or updates a valid cache line.
00000110	WP	write-protected	Cacheable memory for which reads can hit the cache and read misses cause cache fills, but writes bypass the cache entirely.
00000111	WB	writeback	Cacheable memory for which write misses allocate cache lines and writes are performed entirely in the cache whenever possible. WB memory is useful for normal memory, providing the best performance and the least bus traffic for many applications.
All others	—	Reserved	Attempting to write a reserved value into a memory type field of an MTRR signals a #GP(0) fault and does not update the MTRR.

6.3.   MEMORY TYPE DESCRIPTIONS

This section provides detailed descriptions of the Pentium Pro processor's memory types: UC, WC, WT, WP, and WB.

6.3.1.   UC Memory Type

The UC (uncacheable) memory type provides an uncacheable memory space. The processor's accesses to UC memory are executed in program order, without reordering. Accesses to other memory types can pass accesses to UC memory.

6.3.2.   WC Memory Type

The WC (write-combining) memory type provides a write-combining buffering strategy for write operations, useful for frame buffers.

Writes to WC memory can be buffered and combined in the processor's write-combining buffers (WCB). The WCBs are viewed as a special-purpose outgoing write buffers, rather than a cache.

The WCBs are written to memory to allocate a different address, or they are written to memory after leaving an interrupt, or executing a serializing, locked, or I/O instruction. There are no ordering constraints on the writing of WCBs to memory.

The Pentium Pro processor uses line size WCBs. WCB to memory writes use a single Memory Write Transaction (W/WB# = 1) of 32 bytes if all WCB bytes are valid. If all WCB bytes are not valid, the valid bytes are written to memory using a series of <= 8 byte Memory Write Transactions. Such a series of transactions can be issued in any order regardless of the program order in which the write data was generated. Therefore, WC memory is a weakly ordered memory type. A particular Memory Write Transaction can write discontiguous bytes within an 8-byte span. External hardware that supports the WC memory type must support such writes.

6.3.3.   WT Memory Type

The WT (write-through) memory type reads data in lines and caches read data, but maps all writes to the bus, while updating the cache to maintain cache coherency.

Writes directed at WT memory can be split across 32-byte and 8-byte boundaries, but are never combined.

The Pentium Pro processor implementation of writes to WT memory updates valid lines in the L1 data cache and invalidates valid lines in the L2 cache and in the L1 code cache.

6.3.4. WP Memory Type

The WP (write-protected) memory type is used for cacheable memory for which reads can hit the cache and read misses cause cache fills, while writes bypass the cache entirely. WP memory can be viewed as a combination of WT memory for reads and UC (nonexistent) memory for writes.

Note that the WP memory type only protects lines in the cache from being updated by writes. It does not protect main memory.

6.3.5. WB Memory Type

The WB (writeback) memory type is writeback memory that is cacheable in any cache. The WB memory type is processor-ordered. The WB memory type is the most cacheable and the highest performance memory type, and is recommended for all normal memory.

intel®

7

Cache Protocol

The Pentium Pro processor and Pentium Pro processor bus support a high performance cache hierarchy with complete support for cache coherency. The cache protocol supports multiple caching agents (processors) executing concurrently, writeback caching, and multiple levels of cache.

The cache protocol's goals include performance and coherency. Performance is enhanced by multiprocessor support, support for multiple cache levels, and writeback caching support. Coherency (or data consistency) guarantees that a system with multiple levels of cache and memory and multiple active agents presents a shared memory model in which no agent ever reads stale data and actions can be serialized as needed.

A *line* is the unit of caching. In the Pentium Pro processor, a line is 32 bytes of data or instructions, aligned on a 32-byte boundary in the physical address space. A line can be identified by physical address bits A[35:5].

The cache protocol associates states with lines and defines rules governing state transitions. States and state transitions depend on both Pentium Pro processor-generated activities and activities by other bus agents (including other Pentium Pro processors).

7.1. LINE STATES

Each line has a state in each cache. There are four line states, M (Modified), E (Exclusive), S (Shared), and I (Invalid). The Pentium Pro processor cache protocol belongs to a family of cache protocols called *MESI protocols*, named after the four line states. A line can have different states in different agents, though the possible combinations are constrained by the protocol. For example, a line can be Invalid in cache A and Shared in cache B.

A memory access (read or write) to a line in a cache can have different consequences depending on whether it is an *internal access*, by the Pentium Pro processor or another bus agent containing a cache, or an *external access*, by another Pentium Pro processor or some other bus agent.

The four states are defined as follows:

— **I (Invalid)**
The line is not available in this cache. An internal access to this line misses the cache and can cause the Pentium Pro processor to fetch the line into the cache from the bus (from memory or from another cache).

— **S (Shared)**
The line is in this cache, contains the same value as in memory, and can have the Shared state in other caches. Internally reading the line causes no bus activity. Internally writing the line causes a Write Invalidate Line transaction to gain ownership of the line.

- — **E (Exclusive)**
  The line is in this cache, contains the same value as in memory, and is Invalid in all other caches. Internally reading the line causes no bus activity. Internally writing the line causes no bus activity, but changes the line's state to Modified.

- — **M (Modified)**
  The line is in this cache, contains a more recent value than memory, and is Invalid in all other caches. Internally reading or writing the line causes no bus activity.

A line is *valid* in a cache if it is in the Shared, Exclusive, or Modified state.

7.2.   MEMORY TYPES, AND TRANSACTIONS

A number of bus and processor transactions can cause a line to transition from one state to another. The transaction being executed, a line's present state, snoop results, and memory range attributes combine to determine a line's new state and coherency-related bus activity (such as writebacks). This section describes the snoop result signals, memory types, and transaction types, the overall state transition diagram, and the possible final states for different bus transactions.

7.2.1.   Memory Types: WB, WT, WP, and UC

Each line has a memory type determined by the Pentium Pro processor's range registers and control registers, described in Chapter 6, *Range Registers*. For caching purposes, the memory type can be writeback (WB), write-through (WT), write-protected (WP), or un-cacheable (UC).

A WB line is cacheable and is always fetched into the cache if a miss occurs. A write to a WB line does not cause bus activity if the line is in the E or M states.

A WT line is cacheable but is not fetched into the cache on a write miss. A write to a WT line goes out on the bus. For the Pentium Pro processor, a WT hit to the L1 cache updates the L1 cache. A WT hit to L2 cache invalidates the L2 cache.

A WP line is also cacheable, but a write to it cannot modify the cache line and the write always goes out on the bus. A WP line is not fetched into the cache on a write miss. For the Pentium Pro processor, a WP hit to the L2 cache invalidates the line in the L2 cache.

An UC line is not put into the cache. A UC hit to the L1 or L2 cache invalidates the entry.

7.2.2.   Bus Operations

In this chapter, the bus transactions described in Chapter 5, *Bus Transactions and Operations* are classified into the following generic groups for ease of presentation:

BRL (Bus Read Line). A Bus Read Line transaction is a Memory Read Transaction for a full cache line. This transaction indicates that a requesting agent has had a read miss.

BRP (Bus Read Part-line). A Bus Read Part-line transaction indicates that a requesting agent issued a Memory Read Transaction for less than a full cache line.

BLR (Bus Locked Read). A Bus Locked Read transaction indicates that a requesting agent issued a bus locked Memory Read Transaction. For the Pentium Pro processor, this will be for <= 8 bytes.

BWL (Bus Write Line). A Bus Write Line transaction indicates that a requesting agent issued a Memory Write Transaction for a full cache line. This transaction indicates that a requesting agent intends to write back a Modified line or an I/O agent intends to write a line to memory.

BWP (Bus Write Part-line). A Bus Write Part-line transaction indicates that a requesting agent issued a Memory Write Transaction for less than a full cache line.

BLW (Bus Locked Write). A Bus Locked Write transaction indicates that a requesting agent issued a bus locked Memory Write Transaction. For the Pentium Pro processor, this will be for <= 8 bytes.

BRIL (Bus Read Invalidate Line). A Bus Read Invalidate Line transaction indicates that a requesting agent issued a Memory (Read) Invalidate Transaction for a full cache line. The requesting agent has had a read miss and intends to modify this line when the line is returned.

BIL (Bus Invalidate Line). A Bus Invalidate Line transaction indicates that a requesting agent issued a Memory (Read) Invalidate Transaction for 0 bytes. The requesting agent contains the line in S state and intends to modify the line. In case of a race condition, the response for this transaction can contain an implicit writeback.

Implicit Writeback: A Response to Another Transaction. An implicit writeback is not an independent bus transaction. It is a response to another transaction that requests the most up-to-date data. When an external request hits a Modified line in the local cache or buffer, an implicit writeback is performed to provide the Modified line and at the same time, update memory.

7.2.3.   Naming Convention for Transactions

The memory-access transaction names and abbreviations contain up to six components as follows:

1.   B=Bus, I=Internal, or omitted

2.   A=Any, CL=Cache Locked, L=[split] Locked

3.   R= Read, W= Write

4.   I=Invalidate, or omitted

5.   C=Code, D=Data, or omitted

6.   L=Line, P=Partial, or omitted

All cache state transitions with respect to Internal requests assume that the DEFER# signal sampled in the Snoop Result Phase is inactive. If DEFER# is sampled active and HITM# is inactive, then no cache state transition is made. If the transaction receives a deferred response, the actual cache state transition by the receiver is made during the Snoop Result Phase of the deferred reply transaction. Cache state transitions associated with "bus" requests ignore the DEFER# signal.

intel®

8

Data Integrity

The chapter has been updated from the EBS 3.0 to simplify and clarify the Data Integrity features of the Pentium Pro processor bus, as well as updating the Pentium Pro processor implementation.

The Pentium Pro processor and the Pentium Pro processor bus incorporate several advanced data integrity features to improve error detection, retry, and correction. The Pentium Pro processor bus includes parity protection for address/request signals, parity or protocol protection on most control signals, and ECC protection for data signals. The Pentium Pro processor provides the maximum possible level of error detection by incorporating functional redundancy checking (FRC) support.

The Pentium Pro processor data integrity features can be categorized as follows:

- Pentium Pro processor internal error detection

- Level 2 (L2) cache and Core-to-L2 cache-interface error detection and limited recovery

- Pentium Pro processor bus error detection and limited recovery

- Pentium Pro processor bus FRC support

In addition, the Pentium Pro processor extends the Pentium processor's data integrity features in several ways to form a machine check architecture. Several model specific registers are defined for reporting error status. Hardware corrected errors are reported to registers associated with the unit reporting the error. Unrecoverable errors cause the INT 18 machine check exception, as in the Pentium processor.

If machine check is disabled, or an error occurs in a Pentium Pro processor bus agent without the machine check architecture, the Pentium Pro processor bus defines a bus error reporting mechanism. The central agent can then be configured to invoke the exception handler via an interrupt (NMI) or soft reset (INIT#).

The terminology used in this chapter is listed below:

- Machine Check Architecture (MCA)

- Machine Check Exception (MCE)

- Machine Check Enable bit (CR4.MCE)

- Machine Check In Progress (MCIP)

8.1.   ERROR CLASSIFICATION

The Pentium Pro architecture uses the following error classification. An implementation may always choose to report an error in a more severe category to simplify its logic.

- **Recoverable error (RE):** The error can be corrected by a retry or by using ECC information. The error is logged in the MCA hardware.

- **Unrecoverable error (UE):** The error cannot be corrected, but it only affects one agent. The memory interface logic and bus pipeline are intact, and can be used to report the error via an exception handler.

- **Fatal error (FE):** The error cannot be corrected and may affect more than one agent. The memory interface logic and bus pipeline integrity may have been violated, and cannot be reliably used to report the error via an exception handler. A bus pipeline reset is required of all bus agents before operation can continue. An exception handler may then proceed.

8.2.   PENTIUM® PRO PROCESSOR BUS DATA INTEGRITY ARCHITECTURE

The Pentium Pro processor bus's major address and data paths are protected by ten check bits, providing parity or ECC. Eight ECC bits protect the data bus. Single-bit data ECC errors are automatically corrected. A two-bit parity code protects the address bus. Any address parity error on the address bus when the request is issued can be optionally retried to attempt a correction.

Two control signal groups are explicitly protected by individual parity bits: RP# and RSP#. Errors on most remaining bus signals can be detected indirectly due to a well-defined bus protocol specification that enables detection of protocol violation errors. Errors on a few bus signals cannot be detected without the use of FRC mode.

An agent is not required to support all data integrity features, as each feature is individually enabled through the power-on configuration register. See Chapter 9, *Configuration* of the Pentium Pro processor EBS 3.0.

8.2.1.   Bus Signals Protected Directly

Most Pentium Pro processor bus signals are protected by parity or ECC. Table 8-1 shows which signals protect which signals, what phases the protection is valid in, and what effect the address size (ASZ[1:0]#) has on the protected signals.

Table 8-1. Direct Bus Signal Protection

Signal	Protects	Phase	ASZ[1:0]#		ASZ[1:0]# Address range
RP#	ADS#,REQ[4:0]#	Request	x	x	-
AP[0]#	A[23:3]#	Request	x	x	-
AP[1]#	A[31:24]#	Request	0	0	0 <= Address < 4GB
	A[35:24]#	Request	0	1	4GB <= Address < 64GB
	Reserved	Request	1	x	Reserved
RSP#	RS[2:0]#	All	x	x	-
DEP[7:0]#	D[63:0]#	Data	x	x	-

- **Address/Request Bus Signals.** A parity error detected on AP[1:0]# or RP# is reported or retried based on the following options defined by the power-on configuration:

  — AERR# driver disabled.
  The agent detecting the parity error ignores it and continues normal operation. This option is normally used in power-on system initialization and system diagnostics.

  — AERR# driver enabled, AERR# observation disabled.
  The agent detecting the parity error asserts the AERR# signal during the Error Phase. This signal can be trapped by the central agent and be driven back to one of the processors as NMI.

  — AERR# driver enabled, AERR# observation enabled.
  The agent detecting the parity error asserts the AERR# signal during the Error Phase. All bus agents must observe AERR# and on the next clock reset bus arbiters and abort the erroneous transaction by removing the transaction from the In-Order Queue and cancelling all remaining phases associated with the transaction. The first n AERR#s to any request are logged by the initiator as recoverable errors. (n is an agent-determined retry limit chosen by the Pentium Pro processor to be 1.) The initiator retries the canceled request up to n more times. On a subsequent AERR# to the same request, the requesting agent reports it as a unrecoverable error.

- **Response Signals.** A parity error detected on RSP# should be reported by the agent detecting the error as a fatal error.

- **Data Transfer Signals.** The Pentium Pro processor bus can be configured with either no data-bus error checking or with ECC. If ECC is selected, single-bit errors can be corrected and double-bit errors can be detected. Corrected single-bit ECC errors are logged as recoverable errors. All other errors are reported as unrecoverable errors. The errors on read data being returned are treated by the requester as unrecoverable errors. The errors on write or writeback data are treated by the target as fatal errors.

- **Snoop Processing.** An error discovered during a snoop lookup may be treated as a recoverable error if the cache state is E,S, or I. If the cache is in the M state, the errors are treated as fatal errors. Any implementation may choose to report all snoop errors as fatal errors.

8.2.2. Bus Signals Protected Indirectly

Some bus signals are not directly protected by parity or ECC. However, they can be indirectly protected due to a requirement to follow a strict protocol. Although the Pentium Pro processor implementation does not directly detect the errors, future Pentium Pro processor generations or other bus agents can enhance error detection or correction for the bus by checking for protocol violations. Pentium Pro processor bus protocol errors are treated as fatal errors unless specifically stated otherwise.

- **Arbitration Signals BREQ[3:0]# and BPRI#.** Any arbitration error can be detected as a parity error during the Request Phase or as a Pentium Pro processor bus protocol error:

    — If two request phases occur in the same cycle (a collision), a parity error in the address is detected by all agents. All of these signals are open-drain, ensuring that no physical damage results from a collision. The error can be optionally reported to the requesting agent by asserting AERR#. (AERR# protocol can be optionally enabled for retries to reset the arbitration ID of all symmetric agents and begin re-arbitration. In this case, AERR# is treated as a recoverable error.)

    — If BREQn# is deasserted while the agent is not the bus owner, the error can be detected by all the bus agents as a Pentium Pro processor bus protocol error.

    — If Request generation occurs while the agent is not the bus owner, the error can be detected by the current bus owner. The same error can also be detected by other agents by comparing the agent ID with the current bus owner ID driven on DID[7:0]#.

    — If a non-lock driver activates BREQn# or BPRI# sooner than the fourth clock after an AERR# during a LOCK# sequence, the lock driver can detect the protocol violation error.

    — If a non-lock driver generates a request during a LOCK# sequence, the protocol violation error can be detected by the lock driver.

    — If the lock driver does not activate BREQn# two clocks after AERR# during a LOCK# sequence, the protocol violation error can be detected by all bus agents.

- **Lock Signal LOCK#.** LOCK# can only be asserted with a valid ADS# assertion. LOCK# can only be deasserted after sampling an active AERR# or DEFER# in the first locked bus transaction, or after sampling a successful completion response RS[2:0]# on the last bus locked transaction. All bus agents can detect a protocol violation on LOCK# assertion/deassertion.

- **Block Next Request Signal, BNR#.** In the BNR-free state, BNR# must be inactive when no request is being generated (ADS# inactive), or during the first three clocks of a new request generation (ADS#, ADS#+1, and ADS#+2). The following BNR# protocol errors can be detected by all agents.

    — Activation of BNR# when it must be inactive.

    — Activation of ADS# during a valid BNR# assertion request.

- **Snoop Signals, HIT#, HITM#, and DEFER#.** These signals can only be asserted during a valid snoop window. The following snoop protocol violation errors can be detected by all agents:

  — Activation of snoop signals outside of a valid snoop window.

  — HIT# asserted and HITM# deasserted for I/O, special, or ownership memory transactions.

  — HITM# assertion with HIT# deasserted for a non-memory transaction.

- **Response Signals, RS[2:0]#.** These signals can only be asserted during a valid response window. The following protocol violation errors can be detected by all agents:

  — Response is active for more than one consecutive clock or inactive for less than two consecutive clocks.

The following protocol violation errors can be detected by the transaction initiator:

  — The response does not match the request or snoop results data. The following are response protocol errors: no-data inconsistent with request, retry/deferred inconsistent with request, implicit writeback inconsistent with HITM#, deferred/retry inconsistent with DEFER#.

  — The response is activated in less than two clocks from the transaction snoop phase.

- **Data Ready Signal, DRDY#.**

  — An error in this signal can be detected by the initiator or target if the number of clocks DRDY# is active is inconsistent with the request or the snoop result.

  — The initiator can detect a protocol error if read data returns before a valid Response Phase.

  — The target can detect a protocol error if write data returns before valid TRDY#.

  — The data driver can detect a protocol error if DRDY# is asserted by the wrong agent.

  — All agents can detect a protocol error if DRDY# is active with DBSY# inactive for two consecutive clocks.

- **Data Busy Signal, DBSY#.**

  — The initiator can detect a protocol error if DBSY# is not active with response when more than one chunk of data is being returned, or DRDY# is inactive when a single data chunk is being returned.

  — The target can detect a protocol error if the proper number of chunks is not returned after TRDY# assertion.

  — The data driver (initiator, target, or snooper) can detect a protocol error if DBSY# is being driven by the wrong agent.

- **Target Ready Signal, TRDY#.**

  — TRDY# protocol violation can be detected by all agents when TRDY# assertion is detected with response assertion or when TRDY# is deasserted in less than three clocks from the previous TRDY# deassertion, or when TRDY# is deasserted even when it is required to be stretched due to DBSY# active from the previous data transfer.

  — The target can detect a TRDY# protocol error if TRDY# is asserted by the wrong agent.

  — The initiator and the target can detect a TRDY# protocol error if TRDY# is asserted for a transaction other than a write or a writeback.

  — The initiator or snooping agent can detect a TRDY# protocol error if TRDY# is not asserted two clocks prior to an Implicit Writeback Response.

- **Address Error Signal, AERR#.** An AERR# protocol violation can be detected if AERR# is asserted outside of a valid Error Phase.

- **Bus Error Signal, BERR#.** A BERR# protocol violation can be detected by all agents if BERR# is asserted for greater than four clocks. (3 clocks plus 1 clock for a wired-OR glitch)

- **Bus Initialize Signal, BINIT#.** A BINIT# protocol violation can be detected by all agents if BINIT# is asserted for greater than four clocks. (3 clocks plus 1 clock for a wired-OR glitch)

8.2.3. Unprotected Bus Signals

Errors on some Pentium Pro processor bus signals cannot be detected:

- The execution control signals CLK, RESET#, and INIT# are not protected.

- The error signals FRCERR and IERR# are not protected.

- The PC compatibility signals FERR#, IGNNE#, A20M#, and FLUSH# are not protected.

- The system support signals SMI# and STPCLK# are not protected.

8.2.4. Time-out Errors

A central agent on the bus can enhance error detection or correction by observing system-dependent time-out errors.

- **Response time-out.** If the response is not returned after a reasonable delay from the request, the central agent may provide a hard failure response to terminate the request.

- **Lock time-out.** If LOCK# is asserted for more than a reasonable number of clocks, then the central agent should provide a hard failure response. The lock time-out duration should be much longer than the response time-out duration.

- **Arbitration time-out.** If BPRI# is asserted for more than a reasonable number of clocks, then the central agent should indicate a bus protocol violation.

8.2.5. Hard-error Response

The target can assert a hard-error response in the Response Phase to a transaction that has generated an error. The central agent can also claim responsibility for a transaction after response time-out expiration and terminate the transaction with a hard error response.

On observing a hard-error response, the initiator may treat it as a unrecoverable or a fatal error.

8.2.6. Bus Error Codes

8.2.6.1. PARITY ALGORITHM

All bus parity signals use the same algorithm to compute correct parity. A correct parity signal is high if all covered signals are high, or if an even number of covered signals are low. A correct parity signal is low if an odd number of covered signals are low. Parity is computed using voltage levels, regardless of whether the covered signals are active-high or active-low. Depending on the number of covered signals, a parity signal can be viewed as providing "even" or "odd" parity; this specification does not use either term.

8.2.6.2. PENTIUM® PRO PROCESSOR BUS ECC ALGORITHM

The Pentium Pro processor bus uses an ECC code that can correct single-bit errors, detect double-bit errors, and detect all errors confined to one nibble (SEC-DED-S4ED). System designers may choose to detect all these errors, or a subset of these errors. They may also choose to use the same ECC code in L3 caches, main memory arrays, or I/O subsystem buffers.

8.3. ERROR REPORTING MECHANISM

8.3.1. MCA Hardware Log

If CR4.MCE is set, all errors are logged using the available MCA hardware.

8.3.2. MCA Software Log

If CR4.MCE is set, unrecoverable errors cause entry into the INT 18 exception handler, as in the Pentium processor. The INT 18 exception handler will not be entered if the error occurs while a machine check is in progress (MCIP). The exception handler will also not be entered by a checker of a FRC pair. The exception handler can be used to determine the exact source of the error by reading the model specific registers associated with the unit reporting the error. Internal machine check errors are aborts, as in the Pentium processor, but may be restartable in some cases.

8.3.3. IERR# Signal

The IERR# signal is asserted by a Pentium Pro processor when an unrecoverable error is not handled with the MCA software log (MCA disabled). The IERR# signal stays asserted until deasserted by the NMI handler or RESET#/INIT# resets the processor. BERR# can be configured to report IERR# assertion.

8.3.4. BERR# Signal and Protocol

BERR# is asserted to report unrecoverable errors not handled by MCA on the Pentium Pro processor bus. If bus error reporting on initiator internal errors is enabled (see Section 9.1.9., "Bus Error Driving Policy for Initiator Internal Errors"). The Pentium Pro processor asserts BERR# once when IERR# is asserted (the Pentium Pro processor also can drive BERR# immediately after a bus related unrecoverable error). If external error reporting is enabled, an external agent asserts BERR# when unrecoverable errors are found.

The BERR# protocol takes into account multiple bus agents trying to assert BERR# at the same time, as shown in Figure 8-1. Once BERR# is asserted by one bus agent, all agents ensure that it is asserted for exactly three clocks. An agent intending to assert BERR# observes BERR# to ensure that it is inactive. If the agent samples BERR# inactive in the clock it first drives BERR#, it retains BERR# active for exactly three clocks. If the agent samples BERR# active in the first clock, it drives BERR# (due to another bus agent asserting BERR# one clock prior to its assertion of BERR#, the agent retains BERR# active for exactly two clocks).

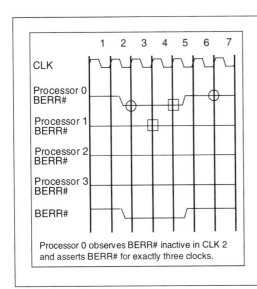
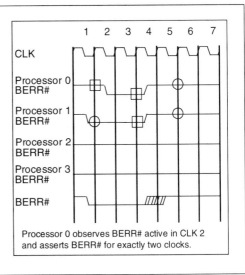

Figure 8-1. BERR# Protocol Mechanism

8.3.5.   BINIT# Signal and Protocol

BINIT# is asserted when any Pentium Pro processor agent detects a fatal error and BINIT# driver is enabled. Sampling of BINIT#, if enabled, resets all bus state, clearing a path for an exception handler (disabling of BINIT# driving/sampling is provided for power on diagnostics only). This typically causes undefined termination of all pending transactions. Therefore, it cannot be used to fully recover from the original error state. However, once the bus pipeline is reset for all Pentium Pro processor bus agents, it is possible to run an exception handler to log the error. If CR4.MCE is set, all Pentium Pro processors on the bus enter the MCE handler. If not set, IERR# to BERR# reporting should be enabled so bus error reporting can generate an interrupt (NMI) or soft reset (INIT#). The programmer-visible register state can be read by the exception handler to attempt graceful error logging.

On observation of active BINIT#, all Pentium Pro processor bus agents must do the following:

- Deassert all signals on the bus.

- Reset the arbitration IDs to the value used at power-on reset.

- Reset the transaction queues included the In-order Queue.

- Begin a new arbitration sequence for the request bus and continue.

- Return programmer-visible register state and cache state to their previous values.

The BINIT# protocol takes into account multiple bus agents trying to assert BINIT# at the same time, as shown in Figure 8-2. Once BINIT# is asserted by one bus agent, all agents ensure that it is asserted for exactly three clocks. An agent intending to assert BINIT# observes BINIT# to ensure that it is inactive. If the agent samples BINIT# inactive in the clock it first drives BINIT#, it retains BINIT# active for exactly three clocks. If the agent samples BINIT# active in the clock it first drives BINIT#, (due to another bus agent asserting BINIT# one clock prior to its assertion of BINIT#) it retains BINIT# active for exactly two clocks.

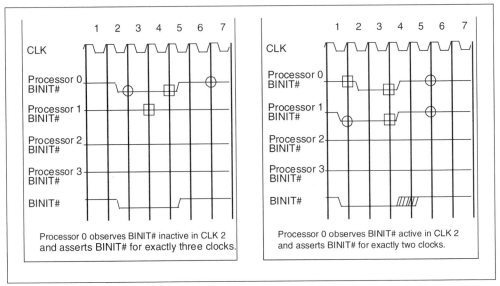

Figure 8-2. BINIT# Protocol Mechanism

8.4. PENTIUM® PRO PROCESSOR IMPLEMENTATION

Figure 8-3 shows the sources of errors within the Pentium Pro processor for each of the Pentium Pro processor error categories and the actions taken when an error occurs. The small squares indicate the configuration option enabled in the Pentium Pro processor power-on configuration Register (Chapter 9, *Configuration*, Pentium Pro processor EBS 3.0). "Log" indicates that the error is logged in the MCA registers. A down arrow indicates which Pentium Pro processor signal is asserted via the protocol for that signal. "Master" refers to an action taken by the master in a FRC pair, and "Checker" refers to an action taken by the checker in a FRC pair.

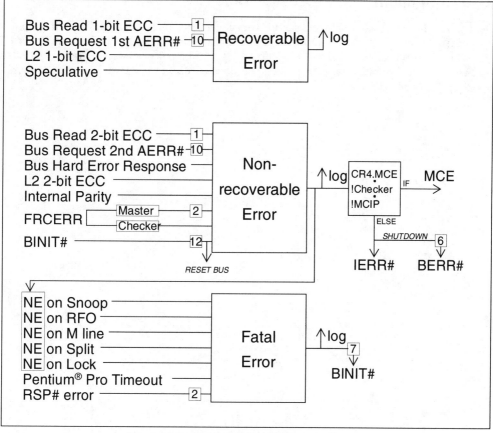

Figure 8-3. Pentium® Pro Processor Errors

8.4.1. Speculative Errors

The Pentium Pro processor may treat some errors on speculative requests as recoverable errors. The error is logged and, if the instruction is not executed, may be ignored.

8.4.2. Fatal Errors

In some circumstances, the Pentium Pro processor treats unrecoverable errors as fatal errors. This occurs for unrecoverable errors on snoops, accesses to modified data, split accesses, and locked accesses.

8.4.3. Pentium® Pro Processor Time-Out Counter

The Pentium Pro processor implements a time-out counter, which issues a fatal error if the processor is stalled for a long period of time. This mechanism is not related to the Pentium Pro processor bus time-out errors described in Section 8.2.4., "Time-out Errors". The timer is 31 bits wide and is clocked from BCLK. The processor is not considered stalled when in normal modes (e.g. Stopclock or HALT).

intel®

9

Configuration

CHAPTER 9
CONFIGURATION

This chapter describes configuration options for Pentium Pro processors and the Pentium Pro processor bus agents.

A system can contain multiple Pentium Pro processors. Processors can be used in a multiprocessor configuration, with one to four Pentium Pro processors on a single Pentium Pro processor bus. Processors can also be used in FRC configurations, with two physical processors per logical FRC unit. All Pentium Pro processors are connected to one Pentium Pro processor bus unless the description specifically states otherwise.

9.1.   DESCRIPTION

Pentium Pro processor bus agents have some configuration options which are determined by hardware, and some which are determined by software.

Pentium Pro processor bus agents sample their hardware configuration at reset, on the active-to-inactive transition of RESET#. The configuration signals (except IGNNE#, A20M# and LINT[1:0]) must be asserted 4 clocks before the active-to-inactive transition of RESET# and be deasserted two clocks after the active-to-inactive transition of RESET# (see Figure 9-1). The IGNNE#, A20M#, and LINT[1:0] signals must meet a setup time of 1ms to the active-to-inactive transition of RESET#.

The sampled information configures the Pentium Pro processor and other bus agents for subsequent operation. These configuration options cannot be changed except by another reset. All resets reconfigure the Pentium Pro processor bus agents; the bus agents not distinguish between a "warm" reset and a "power-on" reset.

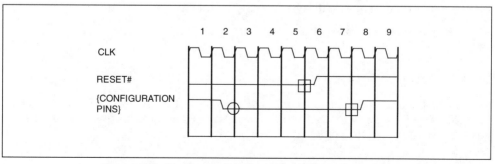

Figure 9-1. Hardware Configuration Signal Sampling

Pentium Pro processor bus agents can also be configured with some additional software configuration options. These options can be changed by writing to a power-on configuration register which all bus agents must implement. These options should be changed only after taking into account synchronization between multiple Pentium Pro processor bus agents.

Pentium Pro processor bus agents have the following configuration options:

- Output tristate {Hardware}

- Execution of the processor's built-in self-test (BIST) {Hardware}

- Data bus error-checking policy: enabled or disabled {Software}

- Response signal error-checking policy: parity disabled or parity enabled {Software}

- AERR# driving policy: enabled or disabled {Software}

- AERR# observation policy: enabled or disabled {Hardware}

- BERR# driving policy for initiator bus errors: enabled or disabled {Software}

- BERR# driving policy for target bus errors: enabled or disabled {Software}

- BERR# driving policy for initiator internal errors: enabled or disabled {Software}

- BERR# observation policy: enabled or disabled {Hardware}

- BINIT# error-driving policy: enabled or disabled {Software}

- BINIT# error-observation policy: enabled or disabled {Hardware}

- In-order Queue depth: 1 or 8 {Hardware}

- Power-on reset vector: 1M-16 or 4G-16 {Hardware}

- FRC mode: enabled or disabled {Hardware}

- APIC cluster ID: 0, 1, 2, or 3 {Hardware}

- APIC mode: enabled or disabled {Software}

- Symmetric agent arbitration ID: 0, 1, 2, or 3 {Hardware}

- Clock frequencies and ratios {Hardware}

9.1.1.   Output Tristate

The Pentium Pro processor tristates all of its outputs if the FLUSH# signal is sampled active on the RESET# signal's active-to-inactive transition. The only way to exit from Output Tristate mode is with a new activation of RESET# with inactive FLUSH#.

9.1.2. Built-in Self Test

The Pentium Pro processor executes its built-in self test (BIST) if the INIT# signal is sampled active on the RESET# signal's active-to-inactive transition. In an MP cluster based on the system architecture, the INIT# pin of different processors may or may not be bused. No software control is available to perform this function.

9.1.3. Data Bus Error Checking Policy

The Pentium Pro processor data bus error checking can be enabled or disabled. After active RESET#, data bus error checking is always disabled. Data bus error checking can be enabled under software control.

9.1.4. Response Signal Parity Error Checking Policy

The Pentium Pro processor bus supports parity protection for the response signals, RS[2:0]#. The parity checking on these signals can be enabled or disabled. After active RESET#, response signal parity checking is disabled. It can be enabled under software control.

9.1.5. AERR# Driving Policy

The Pentium Pro processor address bus supports parity protection on the Request Phase signals, Aa[35:3]#, Ab[35:3]#, ADS#, REQa[4:0]#, and REQb[3:0]#. However driving the address parity results on the AERR# pin is optional. After active RESET#, address bus parity error driving is always disabled. It may be enabled under software control.

9.1.6. AERR# Observation Policy

The AERR# input receiver is enabled if A8# is observed active on active-to-inactive transition of RESET#. No software control is available to perform this function.

9.1.7. BERR# Driving Policy for Initiator Bus Errors

A Pentium Pro processor bus agent can be enabled to drive the BERR# signal if it detects a bus error. After active RESET#, BERR# signal driving is disabled for detected errors. It may be enabled under software control.

9.1.8. BERR# Driving Policy for Target Bus Errors

A Pentium Pro processor bus agent can be enabled to drive the BERR# signal if the addressed (target) bus agent detects an error. After active RESET#, BERR# signal driving is disabled on target bus errors. It may be enabled under software control. The Pentium Pro processor does not drive BERR# on target detected bus errors. The Pentium Pro processor does support observation and machine check entrance.

9.1.9. Bus Error Driving Policy for Initiator Internal Errors

On internal errors, a Pentium Pro processor bus agent can be enabled to drive the BERR# signal. After active RESET#, BERR# signal driving is disabled on internal errors. It may be enabled under software control.

9.1.10. BERR# Observation Policy

The BERR# input receiver is enabled if A9# is observed active on the active-to-inactive transition of RESET#. The Pentium Pro processor does not support this configuration option.

9.1.11. BINIT# Driving Policy

On bus protocol violations, a Pentium Pro processor bus agent can be enabled to drive the BINIT# signal. After active RESET#, BINIT# signal driving is disabled. It may be enabled under software control. The Pentium Pro processor relies on BINIT# driving to be enabled during normal operation.

9.1.12. BINIT# Observation Policy

The BINIT# input receiver is enabled for bus initialization control if A10# is observed active on the active-to-inactive transition of RESET#. The Pentium Pro processor relies on BINIT# observation being enabled during normal operation.

9.1.13. In-order Queue Pipelining

Pentium Pro processor bus agents are configured to an In-order Queue depth of one if A7# is observed active on RESET#. Otherwise it defaults to an In-order Queue depth of eight. This function cannot be controlled by software.

9.1.14. Power-on Reset Vector

The reset vector on which the Pentium Pro processor begins execution after an active RESET# is controlled by sampling A6# on the RESET# signal's active-to-inactive transition. The reset vector for the Pentium Pro processor is 0FFFF0H (1Meg - 16) if A6# is sampled active. Otherwise, the reset vector is 0FFFFFFF0H (4Gig - 16).

9.1.15. FRC Mode Enable

Pentium Pro processor bus agents can be configured to support a mode in which FRC is disabled or a mode in which FRC is enabled. The Pentium Pro processor enters FRC enabled mode if A5# is sampled active on the active-to-inactive transition of RESET#, otherwise it enters FRC disabled mode.

9.1.16. APIC Mode

APIC may be enabled or disabled via software. For details, see the latest APIC EAS.

9.1.17. APIC Cluster ID

A Pentium Pro processor system provides common APIC bus support for up to four Pentium Pro processor-bus clusters, where each cluster contains a Pentium Pro processor bus and up to four Pentium Pro processors. The APIC cluster ID is a 2-bit value that identifies a bus cluster: 0, 1, 2, or 3. The Pentium Pro processor determines its APIC cluster ID by sampling A12# and A11# on the RESET# signal's active-to-inactive transition based on Table 9-1.

Table 9-1. APIC Cluster ID Configuration for the Pentium® Pro Processor

APIC ID	A12#	A11#
0	H[1]	H
1	H	L
2	L	H
3	L	L

NOTE:

1. L and H designate electrical levels.

9.1.18. Symmetric Agent Arbitration ID

The Pentium Pro processor bus supports symmetric distributed arbitration among one to four agents. Each Pentium Pro processor identifies its initial position in the arbitration priority queue based on an agent ID supplied at configuration. The agent ID can be 0, 1, 2, or 3. Each logical Pentium Pro processor (not a FRC master/checker pair) on a particular Pentium Pro processor bus must have a distinct agent ID.

BREQ[3:0]# bus signals are connected to the four symmetric agents in a rotating manner as shown in Table 9-2 and Figure 9-2. Every symmetric agent has one I/O pin (BR0#) and three input only pins (BR1#, BR2# and BR3#).

Table 9-2. BREQ[3:0]# Interconnect

Bus Signal	Agent ID 0 Physical Pin	Agent ID 1 Physical Pin	Agent ID 2 Physical Pin	Agent ID 3 Physical Pin
BREQ0#	BR0#	BR3#	BR2#	BR1#
BREQ1#	BR1#	BR0#	BR3#	BR2#
BREQ2#	BR2#	BR1#	BR0#	BR3#
BREQ3#	BR3#	BR2#	BR1#	BR0#

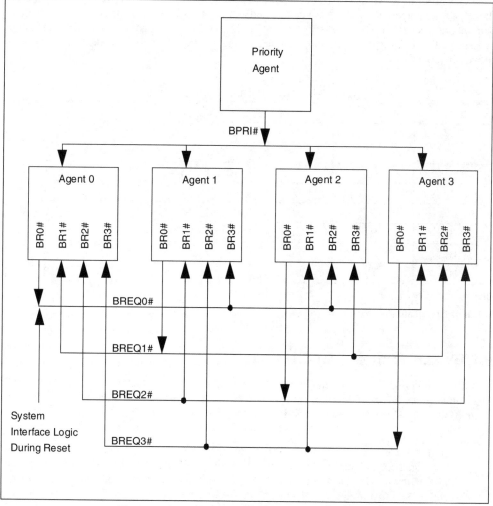

Figure 9-2. BR[3:0]# Physical Interconnection

At the RESET# signal's active-to-inactive transition, system interface logic is responsible for as-sertion of the BREQ0# bus signal. BREQ[3:1]# bus signals remain deasserted. All Pentium Pro processors sample their BR[3:1]# pins on the RESET signal's active-to-inactive transition and determine their agent ID from the sampled value.

If FRC is not enabled, then each physical processor is a logical processor. Each processor is des-ignated a non-FRC master and each processor has a distinct agent ID.

If FRC is used, then two physical processors are combined to create a single logical processor. Processors with agent ID 0 and 2 are designated as FRC-masters and use their agent ID as their parallel bus arbitration ID. Processors with agent ID 1 and 3 are designated as FRC checkers for processors 0 and 2 respectively and assume the characteristics of their respective masters as shown in Table 9-3.

Table 9-3. Arbitration ID Configuration

BR0#	BR1#	BR2#	BR3#	A5#	Arb Id
L[1]	H	H	H	H	0
H	H	H	L	L	1
H	H	L	H	H	2
H	L	H	H	H	3
L	H	H	H	L	0
H	H	H	L	L	0
H	H	L	H	L	2
H	L	H	H	L	2

NOTE:

1. L and H designate electrical levels.

9.1.19. Low Power Standby Enable

A configuration register bit which enables distribution of the core clock during AUTOHalt and Stop Grant mode has been included in the power-on configuration register. This register will support bit D26, which can be read and written by software.

— **D26=1**

In this mode when the Pentium Pro processor enters AUTOHalt or Stop Grant, it will not distribute a clock to its core units. This allows the Pentium Pro processor to reduce its standby power consumption, but large current transients are produced upon entering and exiting this mode.

— **D26=0 (Default)**

In this mode, AUTOHalt and Stop Grant will not stop internal clock distribution. The Pentium Pro processor will have higher standby power consumption, but will produce smaller current transients on entering and exiting this mode.

9.2.   CLOCK FREQUENCIES AND RATIOS

The Pentium Pro processor bus and Pentium Pro processor use a ratio clock design, in which the bus clock is multiplied by a ratio to produce the processor's internal (or "core") clock. The Pentium Pro processor begins sampling A20M# and IGNNE# on the inactive-to-active transition of RESET# to determine the core-frequency to bus-frequency relationship and immediately begins the internal PLL lock mode. On the active-to-inactive transition of RESET#, the Pentium Pro processor internally latches the inputs to allow the pins to be used for normal functionality. **Effectively, these pins must meet a large setup time (1ms) to the active-to-inactive transition of RESET#.**

Table 9-4 describes the relationship between bus frequency and core frequency. See Figure 11-10 for a list of tested ratios per product.

Table 9-4. Bus Frequency to Core Frequency Ratio Configuration[1]

Ratio of Core Freq to Bus Freq	LINT[1]	LINT[0]	IGNNE#	A20M#
2	L	L	L	L
3	L	L	H	L
4	L	L	L	H
Reserved	L	L	H	H
5/2	L	H	L	L
7/2	L	H	H	L
Reserved	L	H	L	H
Reserved	L	H	H	H
Reserved	HLLL - HHHL			
2	H	H	H	H

NOTE:

1. L and H designate electrical levels.

NOTES

If the power-on configuration information supplied on the two pins is the same for all CPUs on the Pentium Pro processor bus, the CPUs will run with identical core frequency. The system designer has the flexibility to operate different CPUs at different core frequencies by supplying a different ratio to individual CPU pins.

Intel may also introduce different bus frequency to core frequency ratios than the ones currently specified. In order to introduce ratios other than 2, 3, and 4, two additional configuration pins, LINT[1:0], are currently reserved.

9.2.1. Clock Frequencies and Ratios at Product Introduction

Only the 2X ratio is supported by the Pentium Pro 133 MHz processor. All other combinations are reserved.

9.3. SOFTWARE-PROGRAMMABLE OPTIONS

All bus agents are required to maintain some software read/writable bits in the power-on configuration register for software-configured options. This register inside the Pentium Pro processor is defined in Table 9-5.

Table 9-5. Pentium® Pro Processor Power-on Configuration Register

Feature	Pentium® Pro Processor Active Signals	Pentium Pro Processor Register Bits	Read/Write	Default
Output tristate enabled	FLUSH#	D8=1	Read	N.A.
Execute BIST	INIT#	D9=1	Read	N.A.
{rcnt], {scnt} driven during REQb# (debug mode) enabled	N.A.	D0=1	Read/Write	disabled
Data error checking enabled	N.A.	D1=1	Read/Write	disabled
Response Error checking enabled FRCERR observation enabled	N.A.	D2=1	Read/Write	disabled
AERR# driver enabled	N.A.	D3=1	Read/Write	disabled
AERR# observation enabled	A8#	D10=1	Read	N.A.
BERR# driver enabled for initiator bus requests	N.A.	D4=1	Read/Write	disabled
BERR# driver enabled for target bus requests	N.A.	Reserved	Read/Write	disabled
BERR# driver enabled for initiator internal errors.	N.A.	D6=1	Read/Write	disabled
BERR# observation enabled	A9#	Reserved	Read	N.A.
BINIT# driver enabled	N.A.	D7=1	Read/Write	disabled
BINIT# observation enabled	A10#	D12=1	Read	N.A.
In-order queue depth of 1	A7#	D13=1	Read	N.A.

Table 9-5. Pentium® Pro Processor Power-on Configuration Register (Contd.)

Feature	Pentium® Pro Processor Active Signals	Pentium Pro Processor Register Bits	Read/Write	Default
1 Mbyte power-on reset vector	A6#	D14=1	Read	N.A.
FRC Mode enabled	A5#	D15=1	Read	N.A.
APIC cluster ID	A12#,A11#	D17,D16 see Table 9-1	Read	N.A.
Reserved	A14#,A13#	D25,D19, D18	-	-
Symmetric arbitration ID	BR0#, BR1#, BR2#, BR3#, A5#	D21,D20 see Table 9-3	Read	N.A.
Clock frequency ratios	LINT[1:0], A20M#, IGNNE#	D24, D23,D22 see Table 9-4	Read	N.A.
Enable rcnt/scnt debug mode	N.A.	D0	Read/Write	disabled
Low power standby enable	N.A.	D26	Read/Write	disabled

Table 9-6. Pentium® Pro Processor Power-on Configuration Register APIC Cluster ID bit Field

APIC ID	D[17:16]
0	00
1	01
2	10
3	11

Table 9-7. Pentium® Pro Processor Power-on Configuration Register Bus Frequency to Core Frequency Ratio Bit Field

Ratio of Core Freq to Bus Freq	D[24:22]
2	000
3	001
4	010
2	011
7/2	101
5/2	111

Table 9-8. Pentium® Pro Processor Power-on Configuration Register Arbitration ID Configuration

Arb id	D[21:20]
0	00
1	01
2	10
3	11

intel®

10

Pentium® Pro Processor Test Access Port (TAP)

CHAPTER 10
PENTIUM® PRO PROCESSOR TEST
ACCESS PORT (TAP)

This chapter describes the implementation of the Pentium Pro processor test access port (TAP) logic. The Pentium Pro processor TAP complies with the IEEE 1149.1 ("JTAG") test architecture standard. Basic functionality of the 1149.1-compatible test logic is described here, but this chapter does not describe the IEEE 1149.1 standard in detail. For this information, the reader is referred to the published standard[1], and to the many books currently available on the subject.

A simplified block diagram of the Pentium Pro processor TAP is shown in Figure 10-1. The Pentium Pro processor TAP logic consists of a finite state machine controller, a serially-accessible instruction register, instruction decode logic and data registers. The set of data registers includes those described in the 1149.1 standard (the bypass register, device ID register, BIST result register, and boundary scan register).

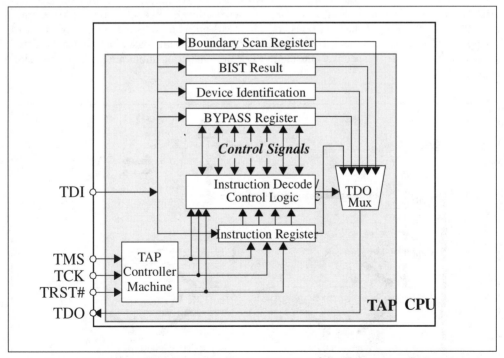

Figure 10-1. Simplified Block Diagram of Pentium® Pro Processor TAP logic

[1] ANSI/IEEE Std. 1149.1-1990 (including IEEE Std. 1149.1a-1993), "IEEE Standard Test Access Port and Boundary-Scan Architecture," IEEE Press, Piscataway NJ, 1993.

10.1. INTERFACE

The TAP logic is accessed serially through 5 dedicated pins on the Pentium Pro processor package:

- **TCK:** The TAP clock signal

- **TMS**: "Test mode select," which controls the TAP finite state machine

- **TDI**: "Test data input," which inputs test instructions and data serially

- **TRST#**: "Test reset," for TAP logic reset

- **TDO**: "Test data output," through which test output is read serially

TMS, **TDI** and **TDO** operate synchronously with **TCK** (which is independent of any other Pentium Pro processor clock). **TRST#** is an asynchronous input signal.

10.2. ACCESSING THE TAP LOGIC

The Pentium Pro processor TAP is accessed through a 1149.1-compliant TAP controller finite state machine. This finite state machine, shown in Figure 10-2, contains a reset state, a run-test/idle state, and two major branches. These branches allow access either to the TAP Instruction Register or to one of the data registers. The TMS pin is used as the controlling input to traverse this finite state machine. TAP instructions and test data are loaded serially (in the Shift-IR and Shift-DR states, respectively) using the TDI pin. State transitions are made on the rising edge of TCK.

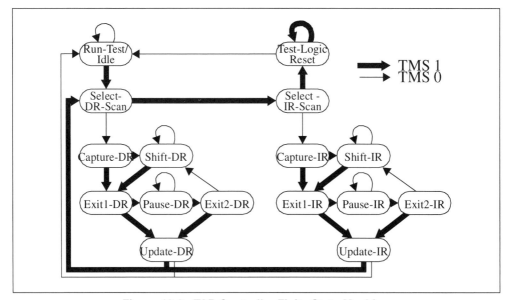

Figure 10-2. TAP Controller Finite State Machine

The following is a brief description of each of the states of the TAP controller state machine. Refer to the IEEE 1149.1 standard for detailed descriptions of the states and their operation.

- **Test-Logic-Reset**: In this state, the test logic is disabled so that normal operation of the Pentium Pro processor can continue. In this state, the instruction in the Instruction Register is forced to IDCODE. The controller is guaranteed to enter Test-Logic-Reset when the TMS input is held active for at least five clocks. The controller also enters this state immediately when TRST# is pulled active, and automatically upon power-up of the Pentium Pro processor. The TAP controller cannot leave this state as long as TRST# is held active.

- **Run-Test/Idle:** This is the idle state of the TAP controller. In this state, the contents of all test data registers retain their previous values.

- **Select-IR-Scan:** This is a temporary controller state. All registers retain their previous values.

- **Capture-IR:** In this state, the shift register contained in the Instruction Register loads a fixed value (of which the two least significant bits are "01") on the rising edge of TCK. The parallel, latched output of the Instruction Register ("current instruction") does not change.

- **Shift-IR:** The shift register contained in the Instruction Register is connected between TDI and TDO and is shifted one stage toward its serial output on each rising edge of TCK. The output arrives at TDO on the falling edge of TCK. The current instruction does not change.

- **Exit1-IR:** This is a temporary state. The current instruction does not change.

- **Pause-IR:** Allows shifting of the instruction register to be temporarily halted. The current instruction does not change.

- **Exit2-IR:** This is a temporary state. The current instruction does not change.

- **Update-IR:** The instruction which has been shifted into the Instruction Register is latched onto the parallel output of the Instruction Register on the falling edge of TCK. Once the new instruction has been latched, it remains the current instruction until the next Update-IR (or until the TAP controller state machine is reset).

- **Select-DR-Scan:** This is a temporary controller state. All registers retain their previous values.

- **Capture-DR:** In this state, the data register selected by the current instruction may capture data at its parallel inputs.

- **Shift-DR:** The Data Register connected between TDI and TDO as a result of selection by the current instruction is shifted one stage toward its serial output on each rising edge of TCK. The output arrives at TDO on the falling edge of TCK. The parallel, latched output of the selected Data Register does not change while new data is being shifted in.

- **Exit1-DR:** This is a temporary state. All registers retain their previous values.

- **Pause-DR:** Allows shifting of the selected Data Register to be temporarily halted without stopping TCK. All registers retain their previous values.

- **Exit2-DR:** This is a temporary state. All registers retain their previous values.

- **Update-DR:** Data from the shift register path is loaded into the latched parallel outputs of the selected Data Register (if applicable) on the falling edge of TCK. This (and Test-Logic-Reset) is the only state in which the latched paralleled outputs of a data register can change.

10.2.1. Accessing the Instruction Register

Figure 10-3 shows the (simplified) physical implementation of the Pentium Pro processor TAP instruction register. This register consists of a 6-bit shift register (connected between TDI and TDO), and the actual instruction register (which is loaded in parallel from the shift register). The parallel output of the TAP instruction register goes to the TAP instruction decoder, shown in Figure 10-1. This architecture conforms to the 1149.1 specification.

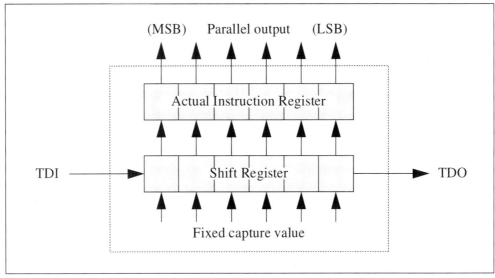

Figure 10-3. Pentium® Pro Processor TAP instruction Register

Figure 10-4 shows the operation of the TAP instruction register during the Capture-IR, Shift-IR and Update-IR states of the TAP controller. Flip-flops within the instruction register which are updated in each mode of operation are shaded. In Capture-IR, the shift register portion of the instruction register is loaded in parallel with the fixed value "000001." In Shift-IR, the shift register portion of the instruction register forms a serial data path between TDI and TDO. In Update-IR, the shift register contents are latched in parallel into the actual instruction register. Note that the only time the outputs of the actual instruction register change is during Update-IR. Therefore, a new instruction shifted into the Pentium Pro processor TAP does not take effect until the Update-IR state of the TAP controller is entered.

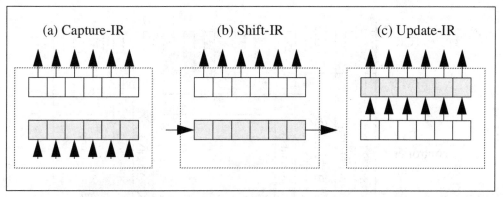

Figure 10-4. Operation of the Pentium® Pro Processor TAP Instruction Register

A timing diagram for loading the BYPASS instruction (op-code "111111") into the TAP is shown in Figure 10-5. (Note that the LSB of the TAP instruction must be shifted in first.) Vertical arrows on the figure show the specific clock edges on which the Capture-IR, Shift-IR and Update-IR actions actually take place. Capture-IR (which pre-loads the instruction shift register with "000001") and Shift-IR operate on rising edges of TCK, and Update-IR (which updates the actual instruction register) takes place on the falling edge of TCK.

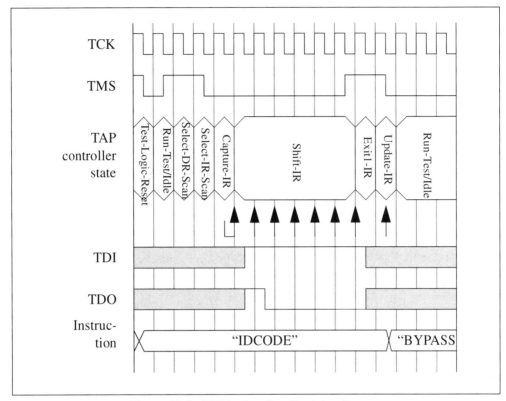

Figure 10-5. TAP Instruction Register Access

10.2.2. Accessing the Data Registers

The test data registers in the Pentium Pro processor are designed in the same way as the instruction register, with components (i.e. either the "capture" or "update" functionality) removed from the basic structure as needed. Data registers are accessed just as the instruction register is, only using the "select-DR-scan" branch of the TAP finite state machine in Figure 10-2. A specific data register is selected for access by each TAP instruction. Note that the only controller states in which data register contents actually change are Capture-DR, Shift-DR, Update-DR and Run-Test/Idle. For each of the TAP instructions described below, therefore, it is noted what operation (if any) occurs in the selected data register in each of these four states.

10.3. INSTRUCTION SET

Table 10-1 contains descriptions of the encoding and operation of the TAP instructions. There are seven 1149.1-defined instructions implemented in the Pentium Pro processor TAP. These instructions select from among four different TAP data registers – the boundary scan, BIST result, device ID, and bypass registers.

TAP instructions in the Pentium Pro processor are 6 bits long. For each listed instruction, the table shows the instruction's encoding, what happens on the Pentium Pro processor pins, which TAP data register is selected by the instruction, and the actions which occur in the selected data register in each of the controller states. A single hyphen indicates that no action is taken. Note that not all of the TAP data registers have a latched parallel output (i.e. some are only simple shift registers). For these data registers, nothing happens during the Update-DR controller state.

Table 10-1. 1149.1 Instructions in the Pentium® Pro Processor TAP

TAP Instruction	Opcode	Pentium® Pro processor pins driven from:	Data Register Selected	Action during:			
				RT/Idle	Capture-DR	Shift-DR	Update-DR
EXTEST	000000	Boundary scan	Boundary scan	-	sample all Pentium® Pro processor pins	shift data register	update data register
SAMPLE/ PRELOAD	000001	-	Boundary scan	-	sample all Pentium Pro processor pins	shift data register	update data register
IDCODE	000010	-	Device ID	-	load unique Pentium Pro processor ID code	shift data register	-
CLAMP	000100	Boundary scan	Bypass	-	reset bypass reg	shift data register	-
RUNBIST	000111	Boundary scan	Bist result	BIST starts[1]	capture BIST result	shift data register	-
HIGHZ	001000	floated	Bypass	-	reset bypass reg	shift data register	-
BYPASS	111111	-	Bypass	-	reset bypass reg	shift data register	-
Reserved	all other	rsvd	rsvd	rsvd	rsvd	rsvd	rsvd

NOTE:

1. The Pentium® Pro processor must be reset after this command.

Full details of the operation of these instructions can be found in the 1149.1 standard.

The only Pentium Pro processor TAP instruction which does not operate exactly as defined in the 1149.1 standard is RUNBIST. In the 1149.1 specification, Rule 7.9.1(b) states that: "Self-test mode(s) of operation accessed through the RUNBIST instruction shall execute only in the Run-Test/Idle controller state." In the Pentium Pro processor implementation of RUNBIST, the execution of the Pentium Pro processor BIST routine will not, however, stop if the Run-Test/Idle state is exited before BIST is complete. In all other regards, the Pentium Pro processor RUNBIST instruction operates exactly as defined in the 1149.1 specification.

Note that RUNBIST will not function when the Pentium Pro processor core clock has been stopped. All other 1149.1-defined instructions operate independently of the Pentium Pro processor core clock.

The op-codes are 1149.1-compliant, and are consistent with the Intel-standard op-code encodings and backward-compatible with the Pentium processor 1149.1 instruction op-codes.

10.4. DATA REGISTER SUMMARY

Table 10-2 gives the complete list of test data registers which can be accessed through the Pentium Pro processor TAP. The MSB of the register is connected to TDI (for writing), and the LSB of the register is connected to TDO (for reading) when that register is selected.

Table 10-2. TAP Data Registers

TAP Data Register	Size	Selected by Instructions
Bypass	1	BYPASS HIGHZ CLAMP
Device ID	32	IDCODE
BIST result	1	RUNBIST
Boundary scan	159	EXTEST SAMPLE/PRELOAD

10.4.1. Bypass Register

Provides a short path between TDI and TDO. It is loaded with a logical 0 in the Capture-DR state.

10.4.2. Device ID Register

Contains the Pentium Pro processor device identification code in the format shown in Table 10-3. The manufacturer's identification code is unique to Intel. The part number code is divided into four fields: VCC (3.3v supply), product type (an Intel Architecture compatible processor), generation (sixth generation), and model (first in the Pentium Pro processor family). The version field is used for stepping information.

Table 10-3. Device ID Register

	Version	VCC	Part Number Product Type	Part Number Generation	Part Number Model	Manufacturing ID	"1"	Entire Code
Size	4	1	6	4	5	11	1	32
Binary	xxxx	1	000001	0110	00001	00000001001	1	xxxx100000101100 0001000000010011
Hex	x	1	01	6	01	09	1	x82c1013

10.4.3. BIST Result Boundary Scan Register

Holds the results of BIST. It is loaded with a logical 0 on successful BIST completion.

10.4.4. Boundary Scan Register

Contains a cell for each defined Pentium Pro processor signal pin. The following is the bit order of the cells in the register (left to right, top to bottom). The "Reserved" cells should be left alone. PWRGOOD should never be driven low during TAP operation.

```
TDI -> CLK, PWRGOOD, Reserved, THERMTRIP#, STPCLK#, A20M#, FLUSH#,
INIT#, IGNNE#, FERR#,  FRCERR, BERR#, IERR#, A[35:3]#, AP[0:1]#,  RSP#,
SMI#, BPRI#, BNR#, BREQ[1:3]#,  REQ[4: 0]#, DEFER#, DRDY#, TRDY#,
DBSY#, HIT#, HITM#, RP#, BREQ[0]#, ADS#,  LOCK#, RS[0:2]#, AERR#,
LINT[1:0], PICD[1:0], PICCLK, BP[3:2]#, BPM[1:0]#, PREQ#, PRDY#,
RESET#, BINIT#, DEP[0:7]#, D[63:0]#, Reserved-> TDO
```

10.5. RESET BEHAVIOR

The TAP and its related hardware are reset by transitioning the TAP controller finite state machine into the Test-Logic-Reset state. Once in this state, all of the reset actions listed in Table 10-4 are performed. The TAP is completely disabled upon reset (i.e. by resetting the TAP, the Pentium Pro processor will function as though the TAP did not exist). Note that the TAP does not receive RESET#.

Table 10-4. TAP Reset Actions

TAP logic affected	TAP reset state action	Related TAP instructions
Instruction Register	Loaded with IDCODE op-code	-
Pentium® Pro processor boundary scan logic	disabled	CLAMP, HIGHZ, EXTEST
Pentium Pro processor TDO pin	tri-stated	-

The TAP can be transitioned to the Test-Logic-Reset state in any one of three ways:

- Power on the Pentium Pro processor. This automatically (asynchronously) resets the TAP controller.

- Assert the TRST# pin at any time. This asynchronously resets the TAP controller.

- Hold the TMS pin high for 5 consecutive cycles of TCK. This is guaranteed to transition the TAP controller to the Test-Logic-Reset state on a rising edge of TCK.

intel ®

11

Electrical
Specifications

11.1. THE PENTIUM® PRO PROCESSOR BUS AND V$_{REF}$

Most of the Pentium Pro processor signals use a **variation** of the low voltage GTL signaling technology (Gunning Transceiver Logic).

The Pentium Pro processor bus specification is similar to the GTL specification but has been enhanced to provide larger noise margins and reduced ringing. This is accomplished by increasing the termination voltage level and controlling the edge rates. Because this specification is different from the standard GTL specification, we will refer to the new specification as GTL+ in this document.

The GTL+ signals are open-drain and require external termination to a supply that provides the high signal level. The GTL+ inputs use differential receivers which require a reference signal (V$_{REF}$). Termination (Usually a resistor on each end of the signal trace) is used to pull the bus up to the high voltage level and to control reflections on the stub-free transmission line. V$_{REF}$ is used by the receivers to determine if a signal is a logical 0 or a logical 1. See Table 11-8 for the bus termination specifications for GTL+, and Chapter 12, *GTL+ Interface Specification* for the GTL+ Interface Specification.

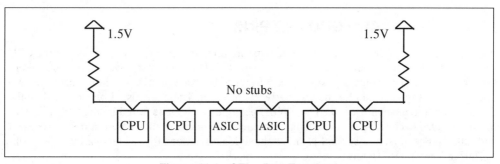

Figure 11-1. GTL+ Bus Topology

There are 8 VREF pins on the Pentium Pro processor to ensure that internal noise will not affect the performance of the I/O buffers. Pins A1, C7, S7 and Y7 (VREF[3:0]) must be tied together and pins A47, U41, AE47 and AG45 (VREF[7:4]) must be tied together. The two groups may also be tied to each other if desired.

The GTL+ bus depends on incident wave switching. Therefore timing calculations for GTL+ signals are based on *flight time* as opposed to capacitive deratings. Analog signal simulation of the Pentium Pro processor bus including trace lengths is highly recommended when designing a system with a heavily loaded GTL+ bus. See Intel's technical documents on the world wide web page (http:\\www.intel.com) to down-load the buffer models for the Pentium Pro processor in IBIS format.

11.2. POWER MANAGEMENT: STOP GRANT AND AUTO HALT

The Pentium Pro processor allows the use of Stop Grant and Auto HALT modes to immediately reduce the power consumed by the device. When enabled, these cause the clock to be stopped to most of the CPU's internal units and thus significantly reduces power consumption by the CPU as a whole.

Stop Grant is entered by asserting the STPCLK# pin of the Pentium Pro processor. When STP-CLK# is recognized by the Pentium Pro processor, it will stop execution and will not service interrupts. It will continue snooping the bus. Stop Grant power is specified assuming no snoop hits occur.

Auto HALT is a low power state entered when the Pentium Pro processor executes a halt (HLT) instruction. In this state the Pentium Pro processor behaves as if it executed a halt instruction, and it additionally powers-down most internal units. In Auto HALT, the Pentium Pro processor will recognize all interrupts and snoops. Auto HALT power is specified assuming no snoop hits or interrupts occur.

The low power standby mode of Stop Grant or Auto HALT can be defined by a configuration bit to be either the lowest power achievable by the Pentium Pro processor (Stop Grant power), or a power state in which the clock distribution is left running (Idle power). "Low power standby" *disabled* leaves the core logic running, while "Low power standby" *enabled* allows the Pentium Pro processor to enter its lowest power mode. See the EBL_CR_POWERON Model Specific Register in Appendix C of the *Pentium® Pro Family Developer's Manual, Volume 3: Operating System Writer's Guide* (Order Number 242692-001).

11.3. POWER AND GROUND PINS

As future versions of the Pentium Pro processor are released, the operating voltage of the CPU die and of the L2 Cache die may differ from each other. There are two power inputs on the Pentium Pro processor package to support the difference between the two die in the package, and one 5V pin to support a fan for the OverDrive® processor. There are also 4 pins defined on the package for voltage identification These pins specify the voltage required by the CPU die. This has been added to cleanly support voltage specification variations on the Pentium Pro processor and future processors. See Section 11.6., "Voltage Identification" for an explanation of the voltage identification (VID) pins.

Future mainstream devices will fall into two groups. Either the CPU die and the L2 Cache die will both run at the same voltage ($V_{cc}P$), or the L2 Cache die will use $V_{cc}S$ (3.3V) while the CPU die runs at another voltage on $V_{cc}P$. When the L2 Cache die is running on the same supply as the CPU die, the $V_{cc}S$ pins will consume no current. To properly support this, the system should distribute 3.3V and a selectable voltage to the Pentium Pro processor socket. Selection may be provided for by socketed regulation or by using the voltage identification pins. Note that it is possible that $V_{cc}P$ and $V_{cc}S$ are both nominally 3.3V. It should not be assumed that these will be able to use the same power supply.

For clean on-chip power distribution, the Pentium Pro processor has 76 V_{cc} (power) and 101V_{ss} (ground) inputs. The 76 V_{cc} pins are further divided to provide the different voltage levels to the device. $V_{cc}P$ inputs for the CPU die and some L2 die account for 47 of the V_{cc} pins, while

28 V$_{cc}$S inputs (3.3V) are for use by the on-package L2 Cache die of some processors. One V$_{cc}$5 pin is provided for use by the fan of the OverDrive processor. V$_{cc}$5, V$_{cc}$S and V$_{cc}$P must remain electrically separated from each other. On the circuit board, *all* V$_{cc}$P pins must be connected to a voltage island and *all* V$_{cc}$S pins must be connected to a separate voltage island (an island is a portion of a power plane that has been divided, or an entire plane). Similarly, *all* V$_{ss}$ pins must be connected to a system ground plane. See Figure 15-3 for the locations of the power and ground pins.

11.4. DECOUPLING RECOMMENDATIONS

Due to the large number of transistors and high internal clock speeds, the Pentium Pro processor can create large, short duration transient (switching) current surges that occur on internal clock edges which can cause power planes to spike above and below their nominal value if not properly controlled. The Pentium Pro processor is also capable of generating large average current swings between low and full power states, called Load-Change Transients, which can cause power planes to sag below their nominal value if bulk decoupling is not adequate. See Figure 11-2 for an example of these current fluctuations. Care must be taken in the board design to guarantee that the voltage provided to the Pentium Pro processor remains within the specifications listed in this volume. Failure to do so can result in timing violations or a reduced lifetime of the component.

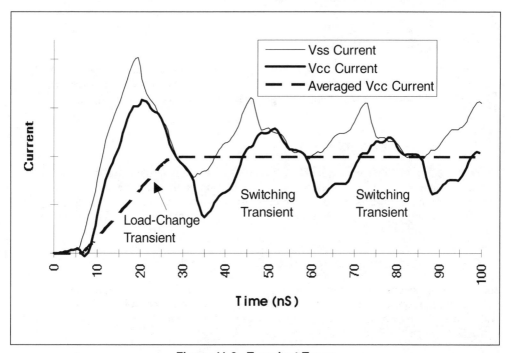

Figure 11-2. Transient Types

Adequate decoupling capacitance should be placed near the power pins of the Pentium Pro processor. Low inductance capacitors such as the 1206 package surface mount capacitors are recommended for the best high frequency electrical performance. Forty (40) 1μF 1206-style capacitors with a ±22% tolerance make a good starting point for simulations as this is our recommended decoupling when using a standard Pentium Pro processor Voltage Regulator Module. Inductance should be reduced by connecting capacitors directly to the $V_{CC}P$ and V_{SS} planes with minimal trace length between the component pads and vias to the plane. Be sure to include the effects of board inductance within the simulation. Also, when choosing the capacitors to use, bear in mind the operating temperatures they will see and the tolerance that they are rated at. Type Y5S or better are recommended (±22% tolerance over the temperature range -30°C to +85°C).

Bulk capacitance with a low Effective Series Resistance (ESR) should also be placed near the Pentium Pro processor in order to handle changes in average current between the low power and normal operating states. About 4000μF of capacitance with an ESR of 5mΩ makes a good starting point for simulations, although more capacitance may be needed to bring the ESR down to this level due to the current technology in the industry. The standard Pentium Pro processor Voltage Regulator Modules already contain this bulk capacitance. Be sure to determine what is available on the market before choosing parameters for the models. Also, include power supply response time and cable inductance in a full simulation.

See *AP-523 Pentium® Pro Processor Power Distribution Guidelines* Application Note (Order Number 242764) for power modeling for the Pentium Pro processor.

11.4.1. $V_{CC}S$ Decoupling

Decoupling of ten (10) 1μF ceramic capacitors (type Y5S or better) and a minimum of five 22μF tantalum capacitors is recommended for the $V_{CC}S$ pins. This is to handle the transients that may occur in future devices. These are not required for the processors described herein.

11.4.2. GTL+ Decoupling

Although the Pentium Pro processor GTL+ bus receives power external to the Pentium Pro processor, it should be noted that this power supply will also require the same diligent decoupling methodologies as the processor. Notice that the existence of external power entering through the I/O buffers causes V_{SS} current to be higher than the V_{CC} current as evidenced in Figure 11-2.

11.4.3. Phase Lock Loop (PLL) Decoupling

Isolated analog decoupling is required for the internal PLL. This should be equivalent to 0.1μF of ceramic capacitance. The capacitor should be type Y5R or better and should be across the PLL1 and PLL2 pins of the Pentium Pro processor. ("Y5R" implies ±15% tolerance over the temperature range -30°C to +85°C.)

11.5. BCLK CLOCK INPUT GUIDELINES

The BCLK input directly controls the operating speed of the GTL+ bus interface. All GTL+ external timing parameters are specified with respect to the rising edge of the BCLK input. Clock multiplying within the processor is provided by an internal Phase Lock Loop (PLL) which requires a constant frequency BCLK input. Therefore the BCLK frequency cannot be changed dynamically. It can however be changed when RESET# is active assuming that all reset specifications are met for the clock and the configuration signals.

The Pentium Pro processor core frequency must be configured during reset by using the A20M#, IGNNE#, LINT1/NMI, and LINT0/INTR pins. The value on these pins during RESET#, and until two clocks beyond the end of the RESET# pulse, determines the multiplier that the PLL will use for the internal core clock. See the Appendix A for the definition of these pins during reset. At all other times their functionality is defined as the compatibility signals that the pins are named after. These signals are 3.3V tolerant so that they may be driven by existing logic devices. This is important for both functions of the pins.

Supplying a bus clock multiplier this way is required in order to increase processor performance without changing the processor design, and to maintain the bus frequency such that system boards can be designed to function properly as CPU frequencies increase.

11.5.1. Setting the Core Clock to Bus Clock Ratio

Table 9-4 lists the configuration pins and the values that must be driven at reset time in order to set the core clock to bus clock ratio. Figure 11-3 shows the timing relationship required for the clock ratio signals with respect to RESET# and BCLK. CRESET# from an 82453GX is shown since its timing is useful for controlling the multiplexing function that is required for sharing the pins.

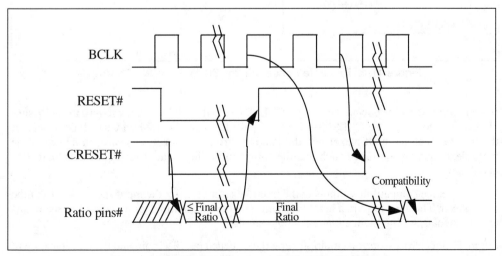

Figure 11-3. Timing Diagram of Clock Ratio Signals

Using CRESET# (CMOS reset), the circuit in Figure 11-4 can be used to share the pins. The pins of the processors are bussed together to allow any one of them to be the compatibility processor. The component used as the multiplexer must not be powered by more than 3.3V in order to meet the Pentium Pro processor's 3.3V tolerant buffer specifications. The multiplexer output current should be limited to 200mA max, in case the $V_{cc}P$ supply ever fails to the processor.

The pull-down resistors between the multiplexer and the processor (1KΩ) force a ratio of 2x into the processor in the event that the Pentium Pro processor powers up before the multiplexer and/or the chipset. This prevents the processor from ever seeing a ratio higher than the final ratio.

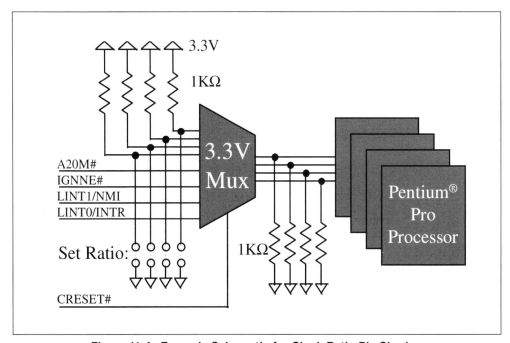

Figure 11-4. Example Schematic for Clock Ratio Pin Sharing

If the multiplexer were powered by $V_{cc}P$, CRESET# would still be unknown until the 3.3V supply came up to power the CRESET# driver. A pull-down can be used on CRESET# instead of the four between the multiplexer and the Pentium Pro processor in this case. In this case, the multiplexer must be designed such that the compatibility inputs are truly ignored as their state is unknown.

In any case, the compatibility inputs to the multiplexer must meet the input specifications of the multiplexer. This may require a level translation before the multiplexer inputs unless the inputs and the signals driving them are already compatible.

For FRC mode processors, one multiplexer will be needed per FRC pair, and the multiplexer will need to be clocked using BCLK to meet setup and hold times to the processors. This may require the use of high speed programmable logic.

11.5.2. Mixing Processors of Different Frequencies

Mixing components of different internal clock frequencies is not supported and has not been validated by Intel. One should also note when attempting to mix processors rated at different frequencies in a multi-processor system that a *common* bus clock frequency and a set of multipliers must be found that is acceptable to all processors in the system. Of course, a processor may be run at a core frequency as low as its minimum rating. Operating system support for multiprocessing with mixed frequency components should also be considered.

Note that in order to support different frequency multipliers to each processor, the design shown above would require four multiplexers.

11.6. VOLTAGE IDENTIFICATION

There are 4 Voltage Identification Pins on the Pentium Pro processor package. These pins can be used to support automatic selection of power supply voltages. These pins are not *signals* but are each either an open circuit in the package or a short circuit to V_{SS}. The opens and shorts defines the voltage required by the processor. This has been added to cleanly support voltage specification variations on future Pentium Pro processors. These pins are named VID0 through VID3 and the definition of these pins is shown in Table 11-1. A '1' in this table refers to an open pin and '0' refers to a short to ground. **The $V_{cc}P$ power supply should supply the voltage that is requested *or* disable itself.**

Table 11-1. Voltage Identification Definition[1, 2]

VID[3:0]	Voltage setting	VID[3:0]	Voltage Setting
0000	3.5	1000	2.7
0001	3.4	1001	2.6
0010	3.3	1010	2.5
0011	3.2	1011	2.4
0100	3.1	1100	2.3
0101	3.0	1101	2.2
0110	2.9	1110	2.1
0111	2.8	1111	No CPU Present

NOTES:

1. Nominal setting requiring regulation to ±5% at the Pentium® Pro processor pins under all conditions. Support not expected for 2.1V-2.3V.

2. 1= Open circuit; 0= Short to V_{SS}

Support for a wider range of VID settings will benefit the system in meeting the power requirements of future Pentium Pro processors. Note that the '1111' (or all opens) ID can be used to
detect the absence of a processor in a given socket as long as the power supply used does not
affect these lines.

To use these pins, they may need to be pulled up by an external resistor to another power source.
The power source chosen should be one that is guaranteed to be stable whenever the supply to
the voltage regulator is stable. This will prevent the possibility of the Pentium Pro processor supply running up to 3.5V in the event of a failure in the supply for the VID lines. Note that the
specification for the standard Pentium Pro processor Voltage Regulator Modules allows the use
of these signals either as TTL compatible levels or as opens and shorts. Using them as TTL compatible levels will require the use of pull-up resistors to 5V if the input voltage to the regulator
is 5V and the use of a voltage divider if the input voltage to the regulator is 12V. The resistors
chosen should not cause the current through a VID pin to exceed its specification in Table 11-3.
There must not be any other components on these signals if the VRM uses them as opens and
shorts.

11.7. JTAG CONNECTION

The Debug Port described in Section 16.2., "In-Target Probe for the Pentium® Pro Processor
(ITP)" should be at the start and end of the JTAG chain with TDI to the first component coming
from the Debug Port and TDO from the last component going to the Debug Port. The recommended pull-up value for Pentium Pro processor TDO pins is 240Ω

Due to the voltage levels supported by the Pentium Pro processor JTAG logic, it is recommended that the Pentium Pro processors and any other 3.3V components be first in the JTAG chain.
A translation buffer should be used to connect to the rest of the chain unless a 5V component
can be used next that is capable of accepting a 3.3V input. Similar considerations must be made
for TCK, TMS and TRST#. Components may need these signals buffered to match required logic levels.

In a multi-processor system, be cautious when including empty Pentium Pro processor sockets
in the scan chain. All sockets in the scan chain must have a processor installed to complete the
chain or the system must support a method to bypass the empty sockets.

See Section 16.2., "In-Target Probe for the Pentium® Pro Processor (ITP)" for full information
on placing a Debug Port in the JTAG chain.

11.8. SIGNAL GROUPS

In order to simplify the following discussion, signals have been combined into groups by buffer type. **All outputs are open drain** and require an external hi-level source provided externally by the termination or a pull-up resistor.

GTL+ input signals have differential input buffers which use V_{REF} as their reference signal. GTL+ output signals require termination to 1.5V. Later in this document, the term "GTL+ Input" refers to the GTL+ input group as well as the GTL+ I/O group when receiving. Similarly, "GTL+ Output" refers to the GTL+ output group as well as the GTL+ I/O group when driving.

The 3.3V tolerant, Clock, APIC and JTAG inputs can each be driven from ground to 3.3V. The 3.3V tolerant, APIC, and JTAG outputs can each be pulled high to as much as 3.3V. See Table 11-7 for specifications.

The groups and the signals contained within each group are shown in Table 11-2. Note that the signals ASZ[1:0]#, ATTR[7:0]#, BE[7:0]#, BREQ#[3:0], DEN#, DID[7:0]#, DSZ[1:0]#, EXF[4:0]#, LEN[1:0]#, SMMEM#, and SPLCK# are all GTL+ signals that are shared onto another pin. Therefore they do not appear in this table.

11.8.1. Asynchronous vs. Synchronous

All GTL+ signals are synchronous. All of the 3.3V tolerant signals can be applied asynchronously, except when running two processors in FRC mode. To run in FRC mode, synchronization logic is required on all signals, except PWRGOOD, going to both processors. Also note the timing requirements for PICCLK with respect to BCLK. With FRC enabled, PICCLK must be ¼X BCLK and synchronized with respect to BCLK with PICCLK lagging BCLK by at least 1 ns and no more than 5 ns.

Table 11-2. Signal Groups

Group Name	Signals
GTL+ Input	BPRI#, BR[3:1]# [1], DEFER#, RESET#, RS[2:0]#, RSP#, TRDY#
GTL+ Output	PRDY#
GTL+ I/O	A[35:3]#, ADS#, AERR#, AP[1:0]#, BERR#, BINIT#, BNR#, BP[3:2]#, BPM[1:0]#, BR0# [1], D[63:0]#, DBSY#, DEP[7:0]#, DRDY#, FRCERR, HIT#, HITM#, LOCK#, REQ[4:0]#, RP#
3.3V Tolerant Input	A20M#, FLUSH#, IGNNE#, INIT#, LINT0/INTR, LINT1/NMI, PREQ#, PWRGOOD [2], SMI#, STPCLK#
3.3V Tolerant Output	FERR#, IERR#, THERMTRIP#[3]
Clock [4]	BCLK
APIC Clock [4]	PICCLK
APIC I/O [4]	PICD[1:0]
JTAG Input [4]	TCK, TDI, TMS, TRST#
JTAG Output [4]	TDO
Power/Other [5]	CPUPRES#, PLL1, PLL2, TESTHI, TESTLO, UP#, $V_{cc}P$, $V_{cc}S$, $V_{cc}5$, VID[3:0], $V_{REF}[7:0]$, V_{SS}

NOTES:

1. The BR0# pin is the only BREQ signal that is bi-directional. The internal BREQ# signals are mapped onto BR# pins after the agent ID is determined.

2. See PWRGOOD in Section 11.9., "PWRGOOD".

3. See THERMTRIP# in Section 11.10., "THERMTRIP#".

4. These signals are tolerant to 3.3V. Use a 150Ω pull-up resistor on PIC[1:0] and 240Ω on TDO.

5. CPUPRES# is a ground pin defined to allow a designer to detect the presence of a processor in a socket. PLL1 & PLL2 are for decoupling the PLL (See Section 11.4.3., "Phase Lock Loop (PLL) Decoupling"). TESTHI pins should be tied to $V_{cc}P$. A 10K pull-up may be used. See Section 11.11., "Unused Pins". TESTLO pins should be tied to V_{SS}. A 1K pull-down may be used.See Section 11.11., "Unused Pins". UP# is an open in the Pentium® Pro processor and Vss in the OverDrive® processor See Chapter 17, *OverDrive® Processor Socket Specification*.
$V_{cc}P$ is the primary power supply.
$V_{cc}S$ is the secondary power supply used by some versions of the second level cache.
$V_{cc}5$ is unused by the Pentium Pro processor and is used by the OverDrive processor for fan-sink power.
VID[3:0] lines are described in Section 11.6., "Voltage Identification".
$V_{REF}[7:0]$ are the reference voltage pins for the GTL+ buffers.
V_{SS} is ground.

11.9. PWRGOOD

PWRGOOD is a 3.3V tolerant input. It is expected that this signal will be a *clean* indication that clocks and the 3.3V, 5V and $V_{cc}P$ supplies are stable and within their specifications. Clean implies that the signal will remain low, (capable of sinking leakage current) without glitches, from the time that the power supplies are turned on until they come within specification. The signal will then transition monotonically to a high (3.3V) state. Figure 11-5 illustrates the relationship of PWRGOOD to other system signals. PWRGOOD can be driven inactive at any time, but power and clocks must again be stable before the rising edge of PWRGOOD. It must also meet the minimum pulse width specification in Table 11-13 and be followed by a 1mS RESET# pulse.

This signal must be supplied to the Pentium Pro processor as it is used to protect internal circuits against voltage sequencing issues. Use of this signal is recommended for added reliability.

This signal does not need to be synchronized for FRC operation. It should be high throughout boundary scan testing.

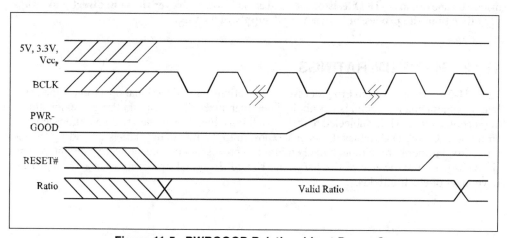

Figure 11-5. PWRGOOD Relationship at Power-On

11.10. THERMTRIP#

The Pentium Pro processor protects itself from catastrophic overheating by use of an internal thermal sensor. This sensor is set well above the normal operating temperature to ensure that there are no false trips. The processor will stop all execution when the junction temperature exceeds ~135° C. This is signaled to the system by the THERMTRIP# pin. Once activated, the signal remains latched, and the processor stopped, until RESET# goes active. There is no hysteresis built into the thermal sensor itself, so as long as the die temperature drops below the trip level, a RESET# pulse will reset the processor and execution will continue. If the temperature has not dropped beyond the trip level, the processor will continue to drive THERMTRIP# and remain stopped.

11.11. UNUSED PINS

All RESERVED pins must remain unconnected. All pins named TESTHI must be pulled up, no higher than $V_{cc}P$, and may be tied directly to $V_{cc}P$. All pins named TESTLO pulled low and may be tied directly to V_{ss}.

PICCLK must always be driven with a clock input, and the PICD[1:0] lines must each be pulled-up to 3.3V with a separate 150Ω resistor, even when the APIC will not be used.

For reliable operation, always connect unused inputs to an appropriate signal level. Unused GTL+ inputs should be pulled-up to V_{tt}. Unused active low 3.3V tolerant inputs should be connected to 3.3V with a 150Ω resistor and unused active high inputs should be connected to ground (V_{ss}). A resistor must also be used when tying bi-directional signals to power or ground. When tieing *any* signal to power or ground, a resistor will also allow for fully testing the processor after board assembly.

For unused pins, it is suggested that ~$10K\Omega$ resistors be used for pull-ups (except for PICD[1:0] discussed above), and ~$1K\Omega$ resistors be used as pull-downs. **Never tie a pin directly to a supply other than the processor's own $V_{CC}P$ supply or to V_{SS}.**

11.12. MAXIMUM RATINGS

Table 11-3 contains Pentium Pro processor stress ratings only. Functional operation at the absolute maximum and minimum is not implied nor guaranteed. The Pentium Pro processor should not receive a clock while subjected to these conditions. Functional operating conditions are given in the A.C. and D.C. tables. Extended exposure to the maximum ratings may affect device reliability. Furthermore, although the Pentium Pro processor contains protective circuitry to resist damage from static electric discharge, one should always take precautions to avoid high static voltages or electric fields.

Table 11-3. Absolute Maximum Ratings [1]

Symbol	Parameter	Min	Max	Unit	Notes
$T_{Storage}$	Storage Temperature	-65	150	°C	
T_{Bias}	Case Temperature under Bias	-65	110	°C	
$V_{cc}P(Abs)$	Primary Supply Voltage with respect to V_{SS}	-0.5	Operating Voltage + 1.4	V	2
$V_{cc}S(Abs)$	3.3V Supply Voltage with respect to V_{SS}	-0.5	4.6	V	
$V_{cc}P$-$V_{cc}S$	Primary Supply Voltage with respect to 3.3V Supply Voltage	-3.7	Operating Voltage + 0.4	V	2
V_{in}	GTL+ Buffer DC Input Voltage with respect to V_{SS}	-0.5	$V_{cc}P+$ 0.5 but Not to exceed 4.3	V	3
V_{in3}	3.3V Tolerant Buffer DC Input Voltage with respect to V_{SS}	-0.5	$V_{cc}P+$ 0.9 but Not to exceed 4.7	V	4
I_I	Max input current		200	mA	5
I_{VID}	Max VID pin current		5	mA	

NOTES:

1. Functional operation at the absolute maximum and minimum is not implied nor guaranteed.
2. Operating voltage is the voltage that the component is designed to operate at. See Table 11-4.
3. Parameter applies to the GTL+ signal groups only.
4. Parameter applies to 3.3V tolerant, APIC, and JTAG signal groups only.
5. Current may flow through the buffer ESD diodes when $V_{IH} > V_{cc}P+1.1V$, as in a power supply fault condition or while power supplies are sequencing. Thermal stress should be minimized by cycling power off if the $V_{cc}P$ supply fails.

11.13. D.C. SPECIFICATIONS

Table 11-4 through Table 11-7 list the D.C. specifications associated with the Pentium Pro processor. Specifications are valid only while meeting the processor specifications for case temperature, clock frequency and input voltages. **Care should be taken to read all notes associated with each parameter.** See Section 11.3., "Power and Ground Pins" for an explanation of voltage plans for Pentium Pro processors. See Section 17.4.1.1., "OverDrive® Processor D.C. Specifications" for OverDrive processor information and Section 11.16., "Flexible Mother-Board Recommendations" for flexible motherboard recommendations.

The D.C. specifications for the $V_{cc}P$, $V_{cc}S$ and $V_{cc}5$ supplies are listed in Table 11-4 and Table 11-5.

Table 11-4. Voltage Specification

Symbol	Parameter	Min	Typ	Max	Unit	Notes
$V_{cc}P$	Primary V_{cc}	2.945	3.1	3.255	V	@150MHz, 256K L2
		3.135	3.3	3.465	V	All other components[1]
$V_{cc}S$	Secondary V_{cc}	3.135	3.3	3.465	V	$3.3 \pm 5\%$ [2]
$V_{cc}5$	5V Supply	4.75	5.0	5.25	V	$5.0 \pm 5\%$ [3]

NOTES:

1. This is a 5% tolerance. To comply with these guidelines and the industry standard voltage regulator module specifications, the equivalent of forty (40) 1μF±22% capacitors in 1206 packages should be placed near the power pins of the processor. More specifically, at least 40μF of capacitance should exist on the power plane with less than 250pH of inductance and 4mΩ of resistance between it and the pins of the processor, assuming a regulator set point of ±1%.

2. This voltage is currently not required by the Pentium® Pro processor. The voltage is defined for future use.

3. This voltage is required for OverDrive® processor support.

Table 11-5. Power Specifications [1]

Symbol	Parameter	Min	Typ	Max	Unit	Notes
P_{Max}	Thermal Design Power		23.0 27.5 24.8 27.3 32.6	29.2 35.0 31.7 35.0 37.9	W W W W W	@ 150MHz, 256K L2 @ 166MHz, 512K L2 @ 180MHz, 256K L2 @ 200MHz, 256K L2 @ 200MHz, 512K L2 2, 3
I_{SGntP}	$V_{CC}P$ Stop Grant Current	0.3 0.3		1.0 1.2	A A	@ 150MHz, 256K L2 All other components 4, 3
I_{SGntS}	$V_{CC}S$ Stop Grant Current	0	0	0	A	All components
$I_{CC}P$	$V_{CC}P$ Current			9.9 11.2 10.1 11.2 12.4	A A A A A	@ 150MHz, 256K L2 @ 166MHz, 512K L2 @ 180MHz, 256K L2 @ 200MHz, 256K L2 @ 200MHz, 512K L2 5, 3
$I_{CC}S$	$V_{CC}S$ Current			0	A	6
$I_{CC}5$	5V Supply Current			0	A	All components
T_C	Operating Case Temperature	0		85	°C	

NOTES:

1. All power measurements taken with CMOS inputs driven to $V_{CC}P$ and to 0V.

2. Maximum values are measured at typical Vcc to take into account the thermal time constant of the package. Typical values not tested, but imply the maximum power one should see when running normal high power applications on most devices. When designing a system to the typical power level, there should be a fail-safe mechanism to guarantee control of the CPU T_C specification in case of statistical anomalies in the workload. This workload could cause a temporary rise in the maximum power.

3. **Power specifications for 512K L2 components are PRELIMINARY. Consult your local FAE.**

4. Max values measured at typical $V_{CC}P$ by asserting the STPCLK# pin or executing the HALT instruction (Auto Halt) with the EBL_CR_POWERON *Low_Power_Enable* bit set to *enabled*. See Model Specific Registers in Appendix C of the *Pentium® Pro Family Developer's Manual, Volume 3: Operating System Writer's Guide* (Order Number 242692-001). Minimum values are guaranteed by design/characterization at minimum $V_{CC}P$ in the same state.

5. Max $V_{CC}P$ current measured at max V_{CC}. All CMOS pins are driven with $V_{IH} = V_{CC}P$ and $V_{IL} = 0V$ during the execution of all Max I_{CC} and I_{CC}-Stop Grant/Auto HALT tests.

6. The L2 of the current processor will draw no current from the $V_{CC}S$ inputs. $I_{CC}S$ is 0A when the L2 die receives its power from the $V_{CC}P$ pins. See the recommended decoupling in Section 11.4.1., "VccS Decoupling".

Most of the signals on the Pentium Pro processor are in the GTL+ signal group. These signals are specified to be terminated to 1.5V. The D.C. specifications for these signals are listed in Table 11-6. Care should be taken to read all notes associated with each parameter.

Table 11-6. GTL+ Signal Groups D.C. Specifications

Symbol	Parameter	Min	Max	Unit	Notes
V_{IL}	Input Low Voltage	-0.3	V_{REF} - 0.2	V	[1] See Table 11-8
V_{IH}	Input High Voltage	V_{REF} + 0.2	$V_{CC}P$	V	[1]
V_{OL}	Output Low Voltage	0.30	0.60	V	[2]
V_{OH}	Output High Voltage	—	—	V	See V_{TT} max in Table 11-8
I_{OL}	Output Low Current	36	48	mA	[2]
I_L	Leakage Current		± 100	µA	[3]
I_{REF}	Reference Voltage Current		± 15	µA	[4]
C_{GTL+}	GTL+ Pin Capacitance		8.5	pF	[5]

NOTES:

1. V_{REF} worst case, not nominal. Noise on V_{REF} should be accounted for.
2. Parameter measured into a 25Ω resistor to 1.5V. Min. V_{OL} and max. I_{OL} are guaranteed by design/characterization.
3. $(0 \leq V_{pin} \leq V_{CC}P)$.
4. Total current for all V_{REF} pins. Section 11.1., "The Pentium® Pro Processor Bus and VREF" details the V_{REF} connections.
5. Total of I/O buffer, package parasitics and 0.5pF for a socket. Capacitance values guaranteed by design for all GTL+ buffers.

To allow compatibility with other devices, some of the signals are 3.3V tolerant and can therefore be terminated or driven to 3.3V. The D.C. specifications for these 3.3V tolerant inputs are listed in Table 11-7. Care should be taken to read all notes associated with each parameter.

Table 11-7. Non-GTL+ [1] Signal Groups D.C. Specifications

Symbol	Parameter	Min	Max	Unit	Notes
V_{IL}	Input Low Voltage	-0.3	0.8	V	

Table 11-7. Non-GTL+ [1] Signal Groups D.C. Specifications

Symbol	Parameter	Min	Max	Unit	Notes
V_{IH}	Input High Voltage	2.0	3.6	V	
V_{OL}	Output Low Voltage		0.4 0.2	V V	2 3
V_{OH}	Output High Voltage	N/A	N/A	V	All Outputs are Open-Drain
I_{OL}	Output Low Current		24	mA	
I_L	Input Leakage Current		± 100	µA	4
C_{TOL}	3.3V Tol. Pin Capacitance		10	pF	Except BCLK, TCK [5]
C_{CLK}	BCLK Input Capacitance		9	pF	5
C_{TCK}	TCK Input Capacitance		8	pF	5

NOTES:

1. Table 11-7 applies to the 3.3V tolerant, APIC, and JTAG signal groups.
2. Parameter measured at 4 mA (for use with TTL inputs).
3. Parameter guaranteed by design at 100uA (for use with CMOS inputs).
4. $(0 \leq V_{pin} \leq V_{cc}P)$.
5. Total of I/O buffer, package parasitics and 0.5pF for a socket. Capacitance values are guaranteed by design.

11.14. GTL+ BUS SPECIFICATIONS

The GTL+ bus must be routed in a daisy-chain fashion with termination resistors at each end of every signal trace. These termination resistors are placed between the ends of the signal trace and the V_{TT} voltage supply and generally are chosen to approximate the board impedance. The valid high and low levels are determined by the input buffers using a reference voltage called V_{REF}. Table 11-8 lists the nominal specifications for the GTL+ termination voltage (V_{TT}) and the GTL+ reference voltage (V_{REF}). It is important that the printed circuit board impedance be specified and held to a ±20% tolerance, and that the intrinsic trace capacitance for the GTL+ signal group traces is known. **For more details on GTL+, See Chapter 12, GTL+ Interface Specification.**

Table 11-8. GTL+ Bus D.C. Specifications

Symbol	Parameter	Min	Typical	Max	Units	Notes
V_{TT}	Bus Termination Voltage	1.35	1.5	1.65	V	± 10%
V_{REF}	Input Reference Voltage	2/3 V_{TT} -2%	2/3 V_{TT}	2/3 V_{TT} + 2%	V	± 2% [1]

NOTE:

1. V_{REF} should be created from V_{TT} by a voltage divider of 1% resistors.

11.15. A.C. SPECIFICATIONS

Table 11-9 through Table 11-16 list the A.C. specifications associated with the Pentium Pro processor. Timing Diagrams begin with Figure 11-7. The AC specifications are broken into categories. Table 11-9 and Table 11-10 contain the clock specifications, Table 11-11 and Table 11-12 contain the GTL+ specifications, Table 11-13 contains the 3.3V tolerant Signal group specifications, Table 11-14 contains timings for the reset conditions, Table 11-15 covers APIC bus timing, and Table 11-16 covers Boundary Scan timing.

All A.C. specifications for the GTL+ signal group are relative to the rising edge of the BCLK input. All GTL+ timings are referenced to V_{REF} for both "0" and "1" logic levels unless otherwise specified.

Care should be taken to read all notes associated with a particular timing parameter.

Table 11-9. Bus Clock A.C. Specifications

T#	Parameter	Min	Max	Unit	Figure	Notes
	Core Frequency	100	150	MHz		@ 150MHz
		150	166.67	MHz		@ 166MHz
		150	180	MHz		@ 180MHz
		150	200	MHz		@ 200MHz [1]
	Bus Frequency	50.00	66.67	MHz		All Frequencies [1]
T1:	BCLK Period	15	20	ns	11-7	All Frequencies
T2:	BCLK Period Stability		300	ps		[2], [3]
T3:	BCLK High Time	4		ns	11-7	@ >2.0V, [2]
T4:	BCLK Low Time	4		ns	11-7	@ <0.8V, [2]
T5:	BCLK Rise Time	0.3	1.5	ns	11-7	(0.8V - 2.0V), [2]
T6:	BCLK Fall Time	0.3	1.5	ns	11-7	(2.0V- 0.8V), [2]

NOTES:

1. The internal core clock frequency is derived from the bus clock. A clock ratio must be driven into the Pentium® Pro processor on the signals LINT[1:0], A20M# and IGNNE# at reset. See the descriptions for these signals in Appendix A. See Table 11-10 for a list of tested ratios per product.

2. Not 100% tested. Guaranteed by design/characterization.

3. Measured on rising edge of adjacent BCLKs at 1.5V.
   The jitter present must be accounted for as a component of BCLK skew between devices.
   Clock jitter is measured from one rising edge of the clock signal to the next rising edge at 1.5V. To remain within the clock jitter specifications, all clock periods must be within 300ps of the ideal clock period for a given frequency. For example, a 66.67 MHz clock with a nominal period of 15ns, must not have any single clock period that is greater than 15.3ns or less than 14.7ns.

Table 11-10. Supported Clock Ratios[1]

PART:	2X	5/2X	3X	7/2X	4X
150MHz	X	X	X		
166MHz		X	X		
180MHz		X	X		
200MHz		X	X		X

NOTE:

1. Only those indicated here are tested during the manufacturing test process.

Table 11-11. GTL+ Signal Groups A.C. Specifications

R_L = 25Ω terminated to 1.5V, V_{REF} = 1.0V					
T# Parameter	Min	Max	Unit	Figure	Notes
T7A: GTL+ Output Valid Delay H→L	0.55 0.80	4.4 4.4	ns ns	11-8	@ 150MHz, 256K L2 All other components 1, 2
T7B: GTL+ Output Valid Delay L→H	0.55 0.80	3.9 3.9	ns ns	11-8	@ 150MHz, 256K L2 All other components 1
T8: GTL+ Input Setup Time	2.2		ns	11-9	3, 4, 5
T9: GTL+ Input Hold Time	0.45 0.70		ns ns	11-9	@ 150MHz, 256K L2 All other components 5
T10: RESET# Pulse Width	1		ms	11-12 11-13	6

NOTES:

1. Valid delay timings for these signals are specified into an idealized 25Ω resistor to 1.5V with V_{REF} at 1.0V. Minimum values guaranteed by design. See Figure 12-11 for the actual test configuration.

2. **GTL+ timing specifications for 166MHz and higher components are PRELIMINARY. Consult your local FAE.**

3. A minimum of 3 clocks must be guaranteed between 2 active-to-inactive transitions of TRDY#.

4. RESET# can be asserted (active) asynchronously, but must be deasserted synchronously.

5. Specification takes into account a 0.3V/ns edge rate and the allowable V_{REF} variation. Guaranteed by design.

6. After V_{CC}, V_{TT}, V_{REF}, BCLK and the clock ratio become stable.

Table 11-12. GTL+ Signal Groups Ringback Tolerance

T#	Parameter	Min	Unit	Figure	Notes
α:	Overshoot	0.55	mV	11-10	1
τ:	Minimum Time at High	1.5	ns	11-10	1
ρ:	Amplitude of Ringback	-100	mV	11-10	1
δ:	Duration of Squarewave Ringback	N/A	ns	11-10	1
φ:	Final Settling Voltage	100	mV	11-10	1

NOTE:

1. Specified for an edge rate of 0.3-0.8V/ns. See Section 12.1.3.1., "Ringback Tolerance" for the definition of these terms. See Figure 12-3 and Figure 12-4 for the generic waveforms. All values determined by design/characterization.

Table 11-13. 3.3V Tolerant Signal Groups A.C. Specifications

T#	Parameter	Min	Max	Unit	Figure	Notes
T11:	3.3V Tolerant Output Valid Delay	1	8	ns	11-8	1
T12:	3.3V Tolerant Input Setup Time	5		ns	11-9	2, 3, 4, 5
T13:	3.3V Tolerant Input Hold Time	1.5		ns	11-9	
T14:	3.3V Tolerant Input Pulse Width, except PWRGOOD	2		BCLKs	11-8	Active and Inactive states
T15:	PWRGOOD Inactive Pulse Width	10		BCLKs	11-8 11-13	6

NOTES:

1. Valid delay timings for these signals are specified into 150Ω to 3.3V. See Figure 11-6 for a capacitive derating curve.

2. These inputs may be driven asynchronously. However, to guarantee recognition on a specific clock, the setup and hold times with respect to BCLK must be met.

3. These signals must be driven synchronously in FRC mode.

4. A20M#, IGNNE#, INIT# and FLUSH# can be asynchronous inputs, but to guarantee recognition of these signals following a synchronizing instruction such as an I/O write instruction, they must be valid with active RS[2:0]# signals of the corresponding synchronizing bus transaction.

5. INTR and NMI are only valid in APIC disable mode. LINT[1:0]# are only valid in APIC enabled mode.

6. When driven inactive, or after Power, V_{REF}, BCLK, and the ratio signals are stable.

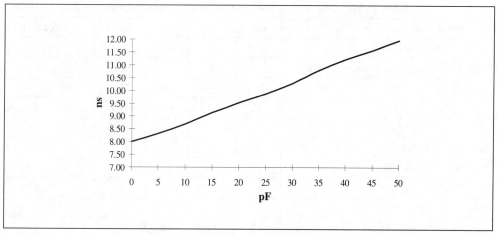

Figure 11-6. 3.3V Tolerant Group Derating Curve

Table 11-14. Reset Conditions A.C. Specifications

T#	Parameter	Min	Max	Unit	Figure	Notes
T16:	Reset Configuration Signals (A[14:5]#, BR0#, FLUSH#, INIT#) Setup Time	4		BCLKs	11-12	Before deassertion of RESET#
T17:	Reset Configuration Signals (A[14:5]#, BR0#, FLUSH#, INIT#) Hold Time	2	20	BCLKs	11-12	After clock that deasserts RESET#
T18:	Reset Configuration Signals (A20M#, IGNNE#, LINT[1:0]#) Setup Time	1		ms	11-12	Before deassertion of RESET#
T19:	Reset Configuration Signals (A20M#, IGNNE#, LINT[1:0]#) Delay Time		5	BCLKs	11-12	After assertion of RESET# [1]
T20:	Reset Configuration Signals (A20M#, IGNNE#, LINT[1:0]#) Hold Time	2	20	BCLKs	11-12 11-13	After clock that deasserts RESET#

NOTE:

1. For a reset, the clock ratio defined by these signals must be a safe value (their final or lower multiplier) within this delay unless PWRGOOD is being driven inactive.

Table 11-15. APIC Clock and APIC I/O A.C. Specifications

T# Parameter	Min	Max	Unit	Figure	Notes
T21A: PICCLK Frequency	2	33.3	MHz		
T21B: FRC Mode BCLK to PICCLK offset	1	5	ns	11-11	1
T22: PICCLK Period	30	500	ns	11-7	
T23: PICCLK High Time	12		ns	11-7	
T24: PICCLK Low Time	12		ns	11-7	
T25: PICCLK Rise Time	1	5	ns	11-7	
T26: PICCLK Fall Time	1	5	ns	11-7	
T27: PICD[1:0] Setup Time	8		ns	11-9	2
T28: PICD[1:0] Hold Time	2		ns	11-9	2
T29: PICD[1:0] Valid Delay	2.1	10	ns	11-8	2, 3, 4

NOTES:

1. With FRC enabled, PICCLK must be ¼X BCLK and synchronized with respect to BCLK with PICCLK lagging BCLK by at least 1 ns and no more than 5 ns.

2. Referenced to PICCLK Rising Edge.

3. For open drain signals, Valid Delay is synonymous with Float Delay.

4. Valid delay timings for these signals are specified into 150Ω to 3.3V.

Table 11-16. Boundary Scan Interface A.C. Specifications

T#	Parameter	Min	Max	Unit	Figure	Notes
T30:	TCK Frequency	—	16	MHz		
T31:	TCK Period	62.5	—	ns	11-7	
T32:	TCK High Time	25		ns	11-7	@2.0V, [1]
T33:	TCK Low Time	25		ns	11-7	@0.8V, [1]
T34:	TCK Rise Time		5	ns	11-7	(0.8V-2.0V), [1, 2]
T35:	TCK Fall Time		5	ns	11-7	(2.0V-0.8V), [1, 2]
T36:	TRST# Pulse Width	40		ns	11-15	[1], Asynchronous
T37:	TDI, TMS Setup Time	5		ns	11-14	[3]
T38:	TDI, TMS Hold Time	14		ns	11-14	[3]
T39:	TDO Valid Delay	1	10	ns	11-14	[4, 5]
T40:	TDO Float Delay		25	ns	11-14	[1, 4, 5]
T41:	All Non-Test Outputs Valid Delay	2	25	ns	11-14	[4, 6, 7]
T42:	All Non-Test Outputs Float Delay		25	ns	11-14	[1, 4, 6, 7]
T43:	All Non-Test Inputs Setup Time	5		ns	11-14	[3, 6, 7]
T44:	All Non-Test Inputs Hold Time	13		ns	11-14	[3, 6, 7]

NOTES:

1. Not 100% tested. Guaranteed by design/characterization.
2. 1ns can be added to the maximum TCK rise and fall times for every 1MHz below 16MHz.
3. Referenced to TCK rising edge.
4. Referenced to TCK falling edge.
5. Valid delay timing for this signal is specified into 150Ω terminated to 3.3V.
6. Non-Test Outputs and Inputs are the normal output or input signals (besides TCK, TRST#, TDI, TDO and TMS). These timings correspond to the response of these signals due to boundary scan operations. PWRGOOD should be driven high throughout boundary scan testing.
7. During Debug Port operation, use the normal specified timings rather than the boundary scan timings.

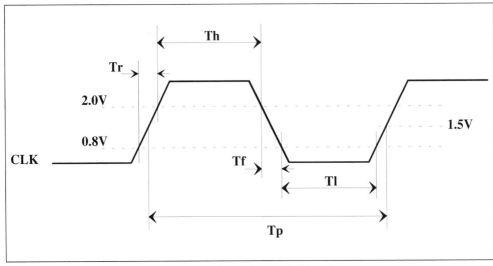

Figure 11-7. Generic Clock Waveform

T_r = Rise Time
T_f = Fall Time
T_h = High Time
T_l = Low Time
T_p = Period

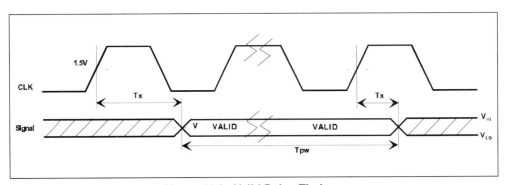

Figure 11-8. Valid Delay Timings

Tx = Valid Delay
Tpw = Pulse Width
V = 1.0V for GTL+ signal group; 1.5V for 3.3V Tolerant, APIC, and JTAG signal groups
V_{HI} = GTL+ signals must achieve a DC high level of at least 1.2V.
V_{LO} = GTL+ signals must achieve a DC low level of at most 0.8V.

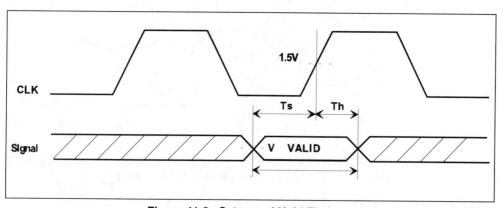

Figure 11-9. Setup and Hold Timings

T_s = Setup Time
T_h = Hold Time
V = 1.0V for GTL+ signal group; 1.5V for 3.3V Tolerant, APIC and JTAG signal groups

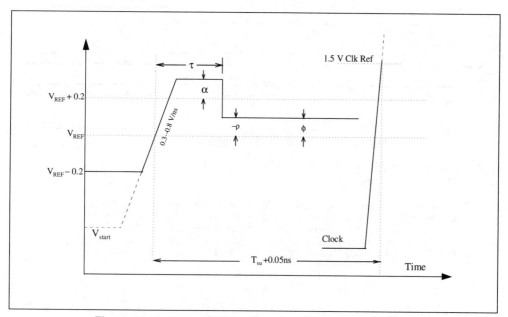

Figure 11-10. Lo to Hi GTL+ Receiver Ringback Tolerance

The Hi to Low Case is analogous.
α = Overshoot
τ = Minimum Time at High
ρ = Amplitude of Ringback
ϕ = Final Settling Voltage

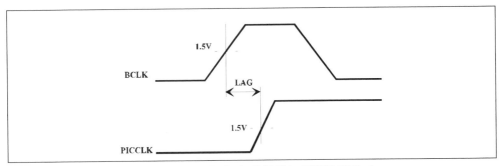

Figure 11-11. FRC Mode BCLK to PICCLK Timing

LAG = T21 (FRC Mode BCLK to PICCLK offset)

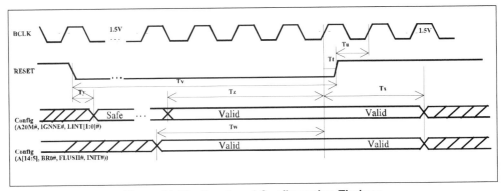

Figure 11-12. Reset and Configuration Timings

Tt = T9 (GTL+ Input Hold Time)
Tu = T8 (GTL+ Input Setup Time)
Tv = T10 (RESET# Pulse Width)
Tw = T16 (Reset Configuration Signals (A[14:5]#, BR0#, FLUSH#, INIT#) Setup Time)
Tx = T17 (Reset Configuration Signals (A[14:5]#, BR0#, FLUSH#, INIT#) Hold Time)
       T20 (Reset Configuration Signals (A20M#, IGNNE#, LINT[1:0]#) Hold Time)
Ty = T19 (Reset Configuration Signals (A20M#, IGNNE#, LINT[1:0]#) Delay Time)
Tz = T18 (Reset Configuration Signals (A20M#, IGNNE#, LINT[1:0]#) Setup Time)

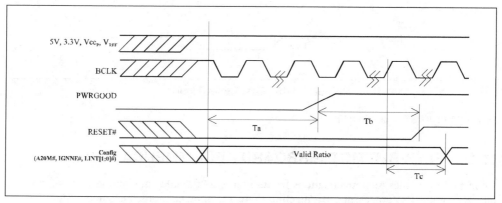

Figure 11-13. Power-On Reset and Configuration Timings

Ta = T15 (PWRGOOD Inactive Pulse Width)
Tb = T10 (RESET# Pulse Width)
Tc = T20 (Reset Configuration Signals (A20M#, IGNNE#, LINT[1:0]#) Hold Time)

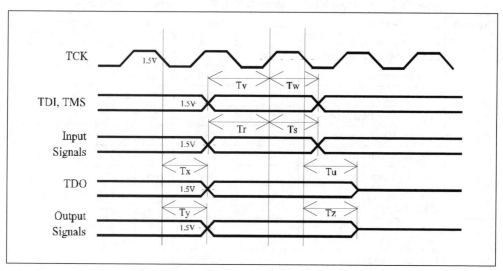

Figure 11-14. Test Timings (Boundary Scan)

Tr = T43 (All Non-Test Inputs Setup Time)
Ts = T44 (All Non-Test Inputs Hold Time)
Tu = T40 (TDO Float Delay)
Tv = T37 (TDI, TMS Setup Time)
Tw = T38 (TDI, TMS Hold Time)
Tx = T39 (TDO Valid Delay)
Ty = T41 (All Non-Test Outputs Valid Delay)
Tz = T42 (All Non-Test Outputs Float Delay)

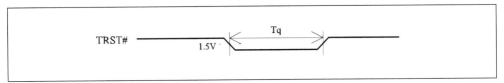

Figure 11-15. Test Reset Timing

Tq   =   T36 (TRST# Pulse Width)

11.16. FLEXIBLE MOTHERBOARD RECOMMENDATIONS

Table 11-17 provides recommendations for designing a "flexible" motherboard for supporting future Pentium Pro processors. By meeting these recommendations, the same system design should be able to support all standard Pentium Pro processors. If the voltage regulator module is socketed using Header 8, a smaller range of support is required by the voltage regulator module. See Section 17.2.3., "OverDrive® Voltage Regulator Module Definition" for information on Header 8. **These values are preliminary!**

Table 11-17. Flexible Motherboard (FMB) Power Recommendations [1]

Symbol	Parameter	Low end	High end	Unit	Notes
$V_{CC}P$	Full FMB Primary V_{CC} Socketed VRM Primary Vcc	2.4 3.1	3.5 3.5	V V	5% tolerance over range
$V_{CC}S$	FMB Secondary V_{CC}	3.3	3.3	V	5% tolerance
$V_{CC}5$	FMB 5V V_{CC}	5.0	5.0	V	5% tolerance
P_{Max}	FMB Thermal Design power		45	W	
Icc_P	Full FMB $V_{CC}P$ Current	0.3	14.5	A	
Icc_S	FMB $V_{CC}S$ Current	0	3.0	A	
Icc_5	FMB $V_{CC}5$ Current		340	mA	
C_P	High Frequency $V_{CC}P$ Decoupling		40	µF	40 1µF 1206 packages
C_S	High Frequency $V_{CC}S$ Decoupling		10	µF	10 1µF 1206 packages
T_C	FMB Operating Case Temperature		85	°C	

NOTE:

1. Values are per processor and are solely recommendations.

The use of a zero-insertion force socket for the processor and the voltage regulator module is recommended. One should also make every attempt to leave margin in the system where possible.

intel®

12

GTL+ Interface
Specification

CHAPTER 12
GTL+ INTERFACE SPECIFICATION

This section defines the new open-drain bus called GTL+. The primary target audience is designers developing systems using GTL+ devices such as the Pentium Pro processor and the 82450 PCIset. This specification will also be useful for I/O buffer designers developing an I/O cell and package to be used on a GTL+ bus.

This specification is an enhancement to the GTL (Gunning Transceiver Logic) specification. The enhancements were made to allow the interconnect of up to eight devices operating at 66.6 MHz and higher using manufacturing techniques that are standard in the microprocessor industry. The specification enhancements over standard GTL provide better noise margins and reduced ringing. Since this specification is different from the GTL specification, it is referred to as GTL+.

The GTL+ specification defines an open-drain bus with external pull-up resistors providing termination to a termination voltage (V_{TT}). The specification includes a maximum driver output low voltage (V_{OL}) value, output driver edge rate requirements, example AC timings, maximum bus agent loading (capacitance and package stub length), and a receiver threshold (V_{REF}) that is proportional to the termination voltage.

The specification is given in two parts. The first, is the system specification which describes the system environment. The second, is the actual I/O specification, which describes the AC and DC characteristics for an I/O transceiver.

Note that some of the critical distances, such as routing length, are given in electrical length (time) instead of physical length (distance). This is because the system design is dependent on the propagation time of the signal on a printed circuit board trace rather than just the length of the trace. Different PCB materials, package materials and system construction result in different signal propagation velocities. Therefore a given physical length does not correspond to a fixed electrical length. The distance (time) calculation up to the designer.

12.1. SYSTEM SPECIFICATION

Figure 12-1 shows a typical system that a GTL+ device would be placed into. The typical system is shown with two terminations and multiple transceiver agents connected to the bus. The receivers have differential inputs connected to a reference voltage, V_{REF} which is generated externally by a voltage divider. Typically, one voltage divider exists at each component. Here one is shown for the entire network.

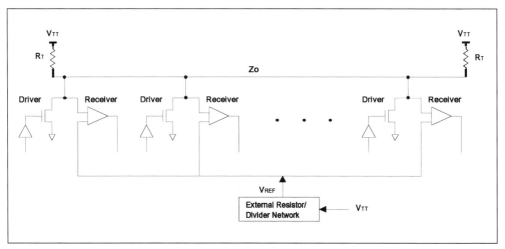

Figure 12-1. Example Terminated Bus with GTL+ Transceivers

12.1.1. System DC Parameters

The following system DC parameters apply to Figure 12-1.

Table 12-1. System DC Parameters

Symbol	Parameter	Value	Tolerance	Notes
V_{TT}	Termination Voltage	1.5V	±10%	
V_{REF}	Input Reference Voltage	2/3 V_{TT}	±2%	1
R_T	Termination Resistance	Z_{EFF} (nominal)	See Note	2, 3
Z_{EFF}	Effective (Loaded) Network Impedance	45-65Ω		4

NOTES:

1. This ±2% tolerance is in addition to the ±10% tolerance of V_{TT}, and could be caused by such factors as voltage divider inaccuracy.

2. $Z_{EFF} = Z_0(\text{nominal}) / (1+Cd/Co)^{1/2}$

   Z_0 = Nominal board impedance; recommended to be 65Ω ±10%. Z_0 is a function of the trace cross-section, the distance to the reference plane(s), the dielectric constant, ε_r, of the PCB material and the dielectric constant of the solder-mask/air for micro-strip traces.

   Co = Total intrinsic nominal trace capacitance between the first and last bus agents, excluding the termination resistor tails. Co is a function of Z_0 and ε_r. For Z_0= 65Ω and ε_r = 4.3, Co is approximately 2.66 pF/in times the network length (first agent to last agent).

   Cd = Sum of the Capacitance of all devices and PCB stubs (if any) attached to the net,
   = PCB Stub Capacitance +Socket Capacitance +Package Stub Capacitance +Die Capacitance.

3. To reduce cost, a system would usually employ one value of R_T for all its GTL+ nets, irrespective of the Z_{EFF} of individual nets. The designer may start with the average value of Z_{EFF} in the system. The value of R_T may be adjusted to balance the Hi-to-Lo and Lo-to-Hi noise margins. Increasing the value of R_T tends to slow the rising edge, increasing rising flight time, decreasing the Lo-to-Hi noise margin, and increasing the Hi-to-Lo noise margin by lowering V_{OL}. R_T can be decreased for the opposite effects.

   R_T affects GTL+ rising edge rates and the "apparent clock-to-out" time of a driver in a net as follows: A large R_T causes the standing current in the net to be low when the (open drain) driver is low (on). As the driver switches off, the small current is turned off, launching a relatively small positive-going wave down the net. After a few trips back and forth between the driver and the terminations (undergoing reflections at intervening agents in the meantime) the net voltage finally climbs to V_{TT}. Because the wave launched initially is relatively small in amplitude (than it would have been had R_T been smaller and the standing current larger), the overall rising edge climbs toward V_{TT} at a slower rate. Notice that this effect causes an increase in flight time, and has no influence on the true clock-to-out timing of the driver into the standard 25Ω test load.

4. Z_{EFF} of all 8-load nets must remain between 45-65Ω under all conditions, including variations in Z_0, Cd, temperature, V_{CC}, etc.

12.1.2. Topological Guidelines

The board routing should use layout design rules consistent with high-speed digital design (i.e. minimize trace length and number of vias, minimize trace-to-trace coupling, maintain consistent impedance over the length of a net, maintain consistent impedance from one net to another, ensure sufficient power to ground plane bypassing, etc.). In addition, the signal routing should be done in a *Daisy Chain* topology (such as shown in Figure 12-1) without any significant stubs. Table 12-2 describes, more completely, some of these guidelines. Note that the critical distances are measured in electrical length (propagation time) instead of physical length.

Table 12-2. System Topological Guidelines

Symbol	Parameter
Maximum Trace Length	To meet a specific Clock cycle time, the maximum trace length between any two agents must be restricted. The flight time (defined later) must be less than or equal to the maximum amount of time which leaves enough time within one clock cycle for the remaining system parameters such as driver clock-out delay (T_{CO}), receiver setup time (T_{SU}), clock jitter and clock skew.
Maximum Stub Length	All signals should use a Daisy Chain routing (i.e. no stubs). It is acknowledged that the package of each device on the net imposes a stub, and that a practical layout using PQFP parts may require SHORT stubs, so a truly stubless network is impossible to achieve, but any stub on the network (including the device package) should be no greater than 250 ps in electrical length.
Distributed Loads	Minimum spacing lengths are determined by hold time requirements and clock skew. Maintaining 3" ±30% inter-agent spacing minimizes the variation in noise margins between the various networks, and can provide a significant improvement for the networks. This is only a guideline.

12.1.3. System AC Parameters: Signal Quality

The system AC parameters fall into two categories, Signal Quality and Flight Time. Acceptable signal quality must be maintained over all operating conditions to ensure reliable operation. Signal Quality is defined by three parameters: Overshoot/ Undershoot, Settling Limit, and Ringback. These parameters are illustrated in Figure 12-2 and are described in Table 12-3.

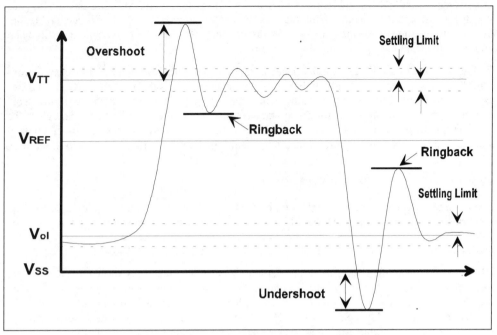

Figure 12-2. Receiver Waveform Showing Signal Quality Parameters

Table 12-3. Specifications for Signal Quality

Symbol	Parameter	Specification
Maximum Signal Overshoot/Undershoot	Maximum Absolute voltage a signal extends above V_{TT} or below V_{SS} (simulated w/o protection diodes).	0.3V (guideline)
Settling Limit	The maximum amount of ringing, at the receiving chip pad, a signal must be limited to before its next transition. This signal should be within 10% of the signal swing to its final value, when either in its high state or low state.	±10% of $(V_{OH}-V_{OL})$ (guideline)
Maximum Signal Ringback (Nominal)	The maximum amount of ringing allowed for a signal at a receiving chip pad within the receiving chips setup and hold time window before the next clock. This value is dependent upon the specific receiver design. (Normally ringing within the setup and hold windows must not come within 200 mV of V_{REF} although specific devices may allow more ringing and loosen this specification. See Section 12.1.3.1., "Ringback Tolerance" for more details.)	V_{REF} ±200 mV

The overshoot/undershoot guideline is provided to limit signals transitioning beyond V_{CC} or V_{SS} due to fast signal edge rates. Violating the overshoot/undershoot guideline is acceptable, but since excessive ringback is the harmful effect associated with overshoot/undershoot it will make satisfying the ringback specification very difficult.

Violations of the Settling Limit guideline are acceptable if simulations of 5 to 10 successive transitions do not show the amplitude of the ringing increasing in the subsequent transitions. If a signal has not settled close to its final value before the next logic transition, then the timing delay to V_{REF} of the succeeding transition may vary slightly due to the stored reactive energy in the net inherited from the previous transition. This is akin to 'eye' patterns in communication systems caused by inter-symbol interference. The resulting effect is a slight variation in flight time.

12.1.3.1.   RINGBACK TOLERANCE

The nominal maximum ringback tolerated by GTL+ receivers is stated in Table 12-3, namely: no closer to V_{REF} than a ± 200 mV overdrive zone. This requirement is usually necessary to guarantee that a receiver meets its specified minimum setup time (T_{SU}), since setup time usually degrades as the magnitude of overdrive beyond the switching threshold (V_{REF}) is reduced.

Exceptions to the nominal overdrive requirement can be made when it is known that a particular receiver's setup time (as specified by its manufacturer) is *relatively* insensitive (less than 0.05 ns impact) to well-controlled ringing into the overdrive zone or even to brief re-crossing of the switching threshold, V_{REF}. Such "ringback-tolerant" receivers give the system designer more design freedom, and, if not exploited, at least help maintain high system reliability.

To characterize ringback tolerance, employ the idealized Lo-to-Hi input signal shown in Figure 12-3. The corresponding waveform for a Hi-to-Lo transition is shown in Figure 12-4. The object of ringback characterization is to determine the range of values for the different parameters shown on the diagram, which would maintain receiver setup time and correct logic functionality.

These parameters are defined as follows:

τ *is the minimum time that the input must spend, after crossing V_{REF} at the High level, before it can ring back, having overshot $V_{IN\_HIGH\_MIN}$ by at least α, while ρ, δ, and ϕ (defined below) are at some preset values, all without increasing T_{SU} by more than 0.05 ns.* Analogously for Hi-to-Lo transitions.

It is expected that the larger the overshoot α, the smaller the amount of time, τ, needed to maintain setup time to within +0.05 ns of the nominal value. For a given value of α, it is likely that τ will be the longest for the slowest input edge rate of 0.3V/ns. Furthermore, there may be some dependence between t and lower starting voltages than $V_{REF} -0.2V$ (for Lo-to-Hi transitions) for the reason described later in the Section on receiver characterization. Analogously for Hi-Lo transitions.

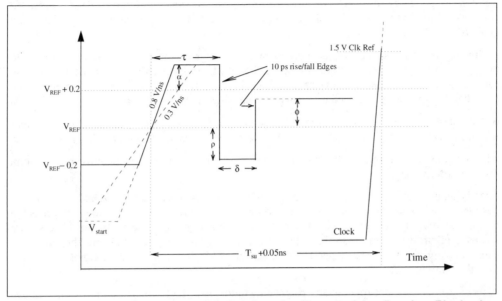

Figure 12-3. Standard Input Lo-to-Hi Waveform for Characterizing Receiver Ringback Tolerance

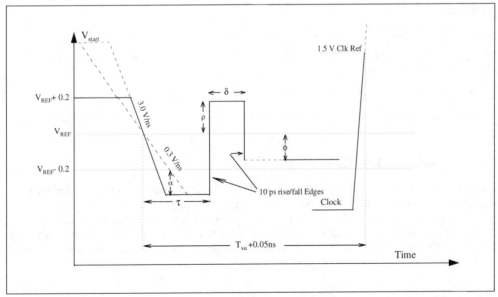

Figure 12-4. Standard Input Hi-to-Lo Waveform for Characterizing Receiver Ringback Tolerance

ρ & δ *are respectively, the amplitude and duration of square-wave ringback, below the threshold voltage (V_{REF}), that the receiver can tolerate without increasing T_{SU} by more than 0.05 ns for a given pair of (α, τ) values.*

If, for any reason, the receiver cannot tolerate any ringback across the reference threshold (V_{REF}), then ρ would be a negative number, and δ may be infinite. Otherwise, expect an inverse (or near-inverse) relationship between ρ and δ, where the more the ringback, the shorter is the time that the ringback is allowed to last without causing the receiver to detect it.

ϕ *is the final minimum settling voltage, relative to the reference threshold (V_{REF}), that the input should return to after ringback to guarantee a valid logic state at the internal flip-flop input.*

ϕ is a function of the input amplifier gain, its differential mode offset, and its intrinsic maximum level of differential noise.

Specifying the values of α, τ, ρ, δ, and ϕ is the responsibility of the receiver vendor. The system designer should guarantee that all signals arriving at such a receiver remain in the permissible region specified by the vendor parameters as they correspond to those of the idealized square waves of Figure 12-3 and Figure 12-4. For instance, a signal with ringback inside the box delineated by ρ and δ can have a τ equal to or longer than the minimum, and an α equal to or larger than the minimum also.

A receiver that does not tolerate any ringback would show the following values for the above parameters:

$\alpha \geq 0V$, $\tau \geq$ Tsu, $\rho = -200$ mV, $\delta =$ undefined, $\phi = 200$ mV.

A receiver which tolerates 50 mV of ringback would show the following values for the above parameters:

$\alpha \geq 0V$, $\tau =$ data sheet, $\rho = -150$ mV, $\delta =$ data sheet, $\phi \geq$ tens of mV (data sheet).

Finally, a receiver which tolerates ringback across the switching threshold would show the following values for the above parameters:

$\alpha \geq 0$ V, $\tau =$ data sheet, $\rho \geq 0$ mV (data sheet), $\delta =$ data sheet, $\phi \geq$ tens of mV.

where δ would usually be a brief amount of time, yielding a pulse (or "blip") beyond V_{REF}.

12.1.4. AC Parameters: Flight Time

Signal Propagation Delay is the time between when a signal appears at a driver pin and the time it arrives at a receiver pin. *Flight Time* is often used interchangeably with Signal Propagation Delay but it is actually quite different. Flight time is a term in the timing equation that includes the signal propagation delay, any effects the system has on the T_{CO} of the driver, plus any adjustments to the signal at the receiver needed to guarantee the T_{SU} of the receiver. More precisely, *Flight Time* is defined to be:

The time difference between when a signal at the **input pin** of a receiving agent (adjusted to meet the receiver manufacturer's conditions required for AC specifications) crosses V_{REF}, and the time that the **output pin** of the driving agent crosses V_{REF} **were it driving the test load** used by the manufacturer to specify that driver's AC timings.

An example of the simplest Flight Time measurement is shown in Figure 12-5. The receiver specification assumes that the signal maintains an edge rate greater than or equal to 0.3V/ns at the *receiver chip pad* in the overdrive region from V_{REF} to V_{REF} +200 mV for a rising edge and that there are no signal quality violations after the input crosses V_{REF} at the *pad*. The Flight Time measurement is similar for a simple Hi-to-Lo transition. Notice that timing is measured at the driver and receiver *pins* while signal integrity is observed at the receiver chip *pad*. When signal integrity at the pad violates the guidelines of this specification, and adjustments need to be made to flight time, the adjusted flight time obtained at the chip pad can be assumed to have been obtained at the package pin, usually with a small timing error penalty.

The 0.3V/ns edge rate will be addressed later in this document, since it is related to the conditions used to specify a GTL+ receiver's minimum setup time. What is meant by edge rate is neither instantaneous, nor strictly average. Rather, it can best be described for a rising edge -- by imagining an 0.3V/ns line crossing V_{REF} at the same moment that the signal crosses it, and extending to V_{REF} +200 mV, with the signal staying ahead (earlier in time) of that line at all times, until it reaches V_{REF} +200 mV. Such a requirement would always yield signals with an average edge rate >0.3V/ns, but which could have instantaneous slopes that are lower or higher than 0.3V/ns, as long as they do not cause a crossing of the inclined line.

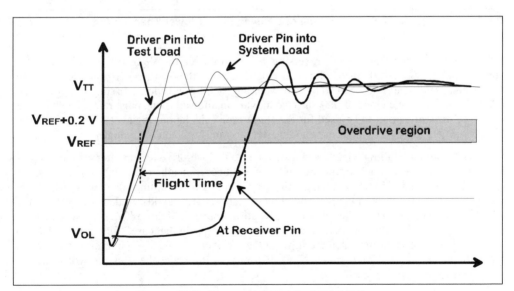

Figure 12-5. Measuring Nominal Flight Time

If either the rising or falling edge is slower than 0.3V/ns through the overdrive region beyond V_{REF} (i.e., does not always stay ahead of an 0.3V/ns line), then the flight time for a rising edge is determined by extrapolating back from the signal crossing of V_{REF} +200 mV to V_{REF} using an 0.3V/ns slope as indicated in Figure 12-6.

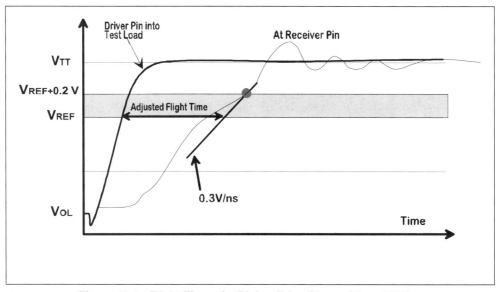

Figure 12-6. Flight Time of a Rising Edge Slower Than 0.3V/ns

If the signal is not monotonic while traversing the overdrive region (V_{REF} to V_{REF} +200 mV rising, or V_{REF} to V_{REF} - 200 mV falling), or rings back into the overdrive region after crossing V_{REF}, then flight time is determined by extrapolating back from the last crossing of $V_{REF} \pm 200$ mV using a line with a slope of 0.8V/ns (the maximum allowed rising edge rate). This yields a new V_{REF} crossing point to be used for the flight time calculation. Figure 12-7 represents the situation where the signal is non-monotonic after crossing V_{REF} on the rising edge.

Figure 12-8 shows a falling edge that rings back into the overdrive region after crossing V_{REF}, and the 0.8V/ns line used to extrapolate flight time. Since strict adherence to the edge rate specification is not required for Hi-to-Lo transitions, and some drivers' falling edges are substantially faster than 0.8V/ns --at both the fast and slow corners--, care should be taken when using the 0.8V/ns extrapolation. The extrapolation is invalid whenever it yields a V_{REF} crossing that occurs earlier than when the signal's actual edge crosses V_{REF}. In that case, flight time is defined to be the longer of: the time when the input at the receiver crosses V_{REF} initially, or when the line extrapolated (at 0.8V/ns) crosses V_{REF}. Figure 12-8 illustrates the situation where the extrapolated value would be used.

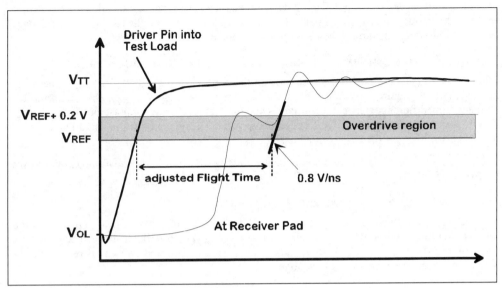

Figure 12-7. Extrapolated Flight Time of a Non-Monotonic Rising Edge

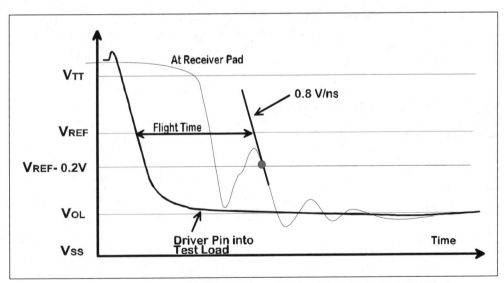

Figure 12-8. Extrapolated Flight Time of a Non-Monotonic Falling Edge

The maximum acceptable Flight Time is determined on a net-by-net basis, and is usually different for each unique driver-receiver pair. The maximum acceptable Flight Time can be calculated using the following equation (known as the setup time equation):

$$T_{FLIGHT-MAX} \leq T_{PERIOD-MIN} - (T_{CO-MAX} + T_{SU-MIN} + T_{CLK\_SKEW-MAX} + T_{CLK\_JITTER-MAX})$$

Where, T_{CO-MAX} is the maximum clock-to-out delay of a driving agent, T_{SU-MIN} is the minimum setup time required by a receiver on the same net, $T_{CLK\_SKEW-MAX}$ is the maximum anticipated time difference between the driver's and the receiver's clock inputs, and $T_{CLK\_JITTER-MAX}$ is maximum anticipated edge-to-edge phase jitter. The above equation should be checked for all pairs of devices on all nets of a bus.

The minimum acceptable Flight Time is determined by the following equation (known as the hold time equation):

$$T_{HOLD-MIN} \leq T_{FLIGHT-MIN} + T_{CO-MIN} - T_{CLK\_SKEW-MAX}$$

Where, T_{CO-MIN} is the minimum clock-to-out delay of the driving agent, $T_{HOLD-MIN}$ is the minimum hold time required by the receiver, and $T_{CLK\_SKEW-MAX}$ is defined above. The Hold time equation is independent of clock jitter, since data is released by the driver and is required to be held at the receiver on the same clock edge.

12.2.   GENERAL GTL+ I/O BUFFER SPECIFICATION

This specification identifies the key parameters for the driver, receiver, and package that must be met to operate in the system environment described in the previous section. All specifications must be met over all possible operating conditions including temperature, voltage, and semiconductor process. *This information is included for designers of components for a GTL+ bus.*

12.2.1.   I/O Buffer DC Specification

Table 12-4 contains the I/O Buffer DC parameters.

Table 12-4. I/O Buffer DC Parameters

Symbol	Parameter	Min	Max	Units	Notes
V_{OL}	Driver Output Low Voltage		0.600	V	1
V_{IH}	Receiver Input High Voltage	$V_{REF} + 0.2$		V	2
V_{IL}	Receiver Input Low Voltage		$V_{REF} - 0.2$	V	2
V_{ILC}	Input Leakage Current		10	μA	3
C_{IN}, C_{O}	Total Input/Output Capacitance		10	pF	4

NOTES:

1. Measured into a 25Ω test load tied to V_{TT} = 1.5 V, as shown in Figure 12-11.

2. V_{REF} = 2/3 V_{TT}. (V_{TT} = 1.5 V ±10%), V_{REF} has an additional tolerance of ± 2%.

3. This parameter is for inputs without internal pull-ups or pull downs and $0 \leq V_{IN} \leq V_{TT}$.

4. Total capacitance, as seen from the attachment node on the network, which includes traces on the PCB, IC socket, component package, driver/receiver capacitance, and ESD structure capacitance.

12.2.2.   I/O Buffer AC Specification

Table 12-5 contains the I/O Buffer AC parameters.

Table 12-5. I/O Buffer AC Parameters

Symbol	Parameter	Min	Max	Units	Figure	Notes
dV/dt_{EDGE}	Output Signal Edge Rate, rise	0.3	0.8	V/ns		1, 2, 3
dV/dt_{EDGE}	Output Signal Edge Rate, fall	0.3	-0.8	V/ns		1, 2, 3
T_{CO}	Output Clock to Data Time		no spec	ns	Figure 12-12	4, 5
T_{SU}	Input Setup Time		no spec	ns	Figure 12-13 Figure 12-14	4, 6
T_{HOLD}	Input Hold Time		no spec	ns		4, 6

NOTES:

1. This is the maximum instantaneous dV/dt over the entire transition range (Hi-to-Lo or Lo-to-Hi) as measured at the driver's output *pin* while driving the Ref8N network, with the driver and its package model located near the center of the network (see Section 12.4., "Ref8N Network").

2. These are design targets. The acceptance of the buffer is also based on the resultant signal quality. In addition to edge rate, the shape of the rising edge can also have a significant effect on the buffer's performance, therefore the driver must also meet the signal quality criteria in the next section. For example, a rising linear ramp of at 0.8V/ns will generally produce worse signal quality (more ringback) than an edge that rolls off as it approaches V_{TT} even though it might have exceeded that rate earlier. Hi-to-Lo edge rates may exceed this specification and produce acceptable results with a corresponding reduction in V_{OL}. For instance, a buffer with a falling edge rate larger than 1.5V/ns can been deemed acceptable because it produced a V_{OL} less than 500 mV. Lo-to-Hi edges must meet both signal quality and maximum edge rate specifications.

3. The minimum edge rate is a design target, and slower edge rates can be acceptable, although there is a timing impact associated with them in the form of an increase in flight time, since the signal at the receiver will no longer meet the required conditions for T_{SU}. Refer to Section 12.1.4., "AC Parameters: Flight Time" on computing flight time for more details on the effects of edge rates slower than 0.3V/ns.

4. These values are not specific to this specification, they are dependent on the location of the driver along a network and the system requirements such as the number of agents, the distances between agents, the construction of the PCB (Z_0, ϵr, trace width, trace type, connectors), the sockets being used, if any, and the value of the termination resistors. Good targets for components to be used in an 8-load 66.6 MHz system would be: T_{CO_MAX} = 4.5 ns, T_{CO_MIN} = 1 ns, T_{SU} = 2.5 ns, and T_{HD} = 0.

5. This value is specified at the output pin of the device. T_{CO} should be measured at the test probe point shown in the Figure 12-11, but the delay caused by the 50Ω transmission line must be subtracted from the measurement to achieve an accurate value for Tco at the output pin of the device. For simulation purposes, the tester load can be represented as a single 25Ω termination resistor connected directly to the pin of the device.

6. See Section 12.2.3., "Determining Clock-To-Out, Setup and Hold" for a description of the procedure for determining the receiver's minimum required setup and hold times.

12.2.2.1.   OUTPUT DRIVER ACCEPTANCE CRITERIA

Although Section 12.1.4., "AC Parameters: Flight Time" describes ways of amending flight time to a receiver when the edge rate is lower than the requirements shown in Table 12-5, or when there is excessive ringing, it is still preferable to avoid slow edge rates or excessive ringing through good driver and system design, hence the criteria presented in this section.

As mentioned in note 2 of the previous section, the criteria for acceptance of an output driver relate to the edge rate and the signal quality for the Lo-to-Hi transition, and primarily to the signal quality for the Hi-to-Lo transition when the device, with its targeted package, is simulated into the Ref8n network (Figure 12-15). The edge rate portion of the AC specification is a good initial target, but is insufficient for guaranteeing acceptable performance.

Since Ref8N is not the worst case network, and is expected to be modeled without many real system effects (e.g., inter-trace crosstalk, DC & AC losses), the required signal quality is slightly different than that specified in Section 12.1.3., "System AC Parameters: Signal Quality" of this document.

The signal quality criterion for an acceptable driver design is that the signals produced by the driver (at its fastest corner) at all Ref8N receiver pads must remain outside of the shaded areas shown in Figure 12-9. Simulations must be performed at both device and operating extremes: fast process corner at high V_{CC} and low temperature, and slow process corner at low V_{CC} and high temperature, for both the rising and falling edges. The clock frequency should be at the desired maximum (e.g. 66.6 MHz, or higher), and the simulation results should be analyzed both from a quiescent start (i.e., first cycle in a simulation), and when preceded by at least one previous transition (i.e. subsequent simulation cycles).

The boundaries of the keep-out area for the Lo-to-Hi transition are formed by a vertical line at the start of the receiver setup window (a distance T_{SU}' from the next clock edge), an 0.3V/ns ramp line passing through the intersection between the V_{REF} +100 mV level (the 100 mV is assumed extra noise) and the beginning of the setup window, a horizontal line at V_{REF} +300 mV (which covers 200 mV of specified overdrive, and the 100 mV margin for extra noise coupled to the waveform), and finally a vertical line behind the Clock at THD'. The keep-out zone for the Hi-to-Lo transition uses analogous boundaries in the other direction. Raising V_{REF} by 100 mV is assumed to be equivalent to having 100 mV of extra noise coupled to the waveform giving it more downward ringback, such coupled noise could come from a variety of sources such as trace-to-trace PCB coupling.

T_{SU}' is the receiver's setup time plus board clock driver and clock distribution skew and jitter, plus an additional number that is inherited from the driver's internal timings (to be described next). Since the I/O buffer designer will most likely be simulating the driver circuit alone, certain delays that add to T_{CO}, such as: on-chip clock phase shift, clock distribution skew, and jitter, plus other data latch or JTAG delays would be missing. It is easier if these numbers are added to T_{SU}, yielding T_{SU}' making the driver simulation simpler. For example, assume T_{SU} to be 2.8 ns, PCB clock generation and distribution skew plus jitter to be 1 ns, and unmodeled delays in the driver to be typically about 0.8 ns, this yields a total T_{SU}' = 4.6 ns.

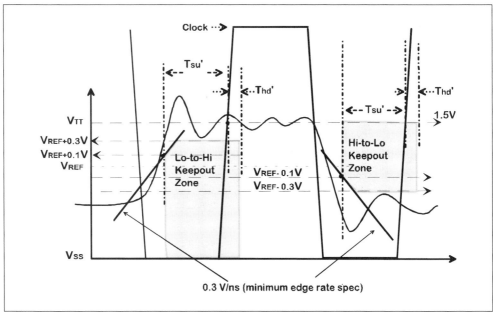

Figure 12-9. Acceptable Driver Signal Quality

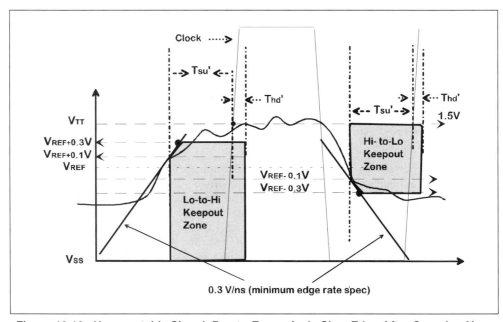

Figure 12-10. Unacceptable Signal, Due to Excessively Slow Edge After Crossing V$_{REF}$

T_{HD}' is the receiver's hold time plus board clock driver and clock distribution skew *minus* the driver's on-chip clock phase shift, clock distribution skew, and jitter, plus other data latch or JTAG delays (assuming these driver numbers are not included in the driver circuit simulation, as was done for setup in the above paragraph). Note that T_{HD}' may end up being a negative number, i.e. ahead of the clock, rather than after it. That would be acceptable, since that is equivalent to shifting the driver output later in time had these extra delays been added to the driver as opposed to setup and hold.

When using Ref8N to validate a driver design, it is recommended that all relevant combinations of driver and receiver locations be checked.

As with other buffer technologies, such as TTL or CMOS, any given buffer design is not guaranteed to always meet the requirements of all possible system and network topologies. Meeting the acceptance criteria listed in this document helps ensure the I/O buffer can be used in a variety of GTL+ applications, but it is the system designer's responsibility to examine the performance of the buffer in the specific application to ensure that all GTL+ networks meet the signal quality requirements.

12.2.3.   Determining Clock-To-Out, Setup and Hold

This section describes how to determine setup, hold and clock to out timings.

12.2.3.1.   CLOCK-TO-OUTPUT TIME, T_{CO}

T_{CO} is measured using the test load in Figure 12-11, and is the delay from the 1.5 V crossing point of the clock signal at the clock input *pin* of the device, to the V_{REF} crossing point of the output signal at the output *pin* of the device. For simulation purposes, the test load can be replaced by its electrical equivalent, which is a single 25Ω resistor connected directly to the package pin and terminated to 1.5V.

In a production test environment, it is nearly impossible to measure T_{CO} directly at the output pin of the device, instead, the test is performed a finite distance away from the pin and compensated for the finite distance. The test load circuit shown in Figure 12-11 takes this into account by making this finite distance a 50-Ω transmission line. To get the exact timings at the output pin, the propagation delay along the transmission line must be subtracted from the measured value at the probe point.

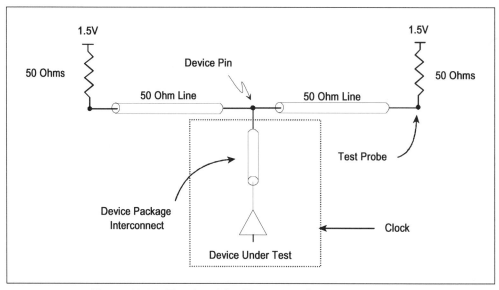

Figure 12-11. Test Load for Measuring Output AC Timings

T_{CO} measurement for a Lo-to-Hi signal transition is shown in Figure 12-12. The T_{CO} measurement for Hi-to-Lo transitions is similar.

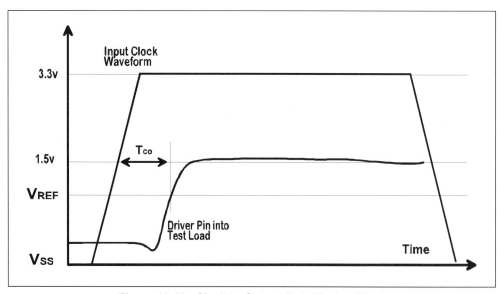

Figure 12-12. Clock to Output Data Timing (T_{CO})

12.2.3.2. MINIMUM SETUP AND HOLD TIMES

Setup time for GTL+ (T_{SU}) is defined as:

> The minimum time from the input signal pin crossing of V_{REF} to the clock pin of the receiver crossing the 1.5 V level, which guarantees that the input buffer has captured **new** data at the input pin, given an infinite hold time.

Strictly speaking, setup time must be determined when the input barely meets minimum hold time (see definition of hold time below). However, for current GTL+ systems, hold time should be met well beyond the minimum required in cases where setup is critical. This is because setup is critical when the receiver is far removed from the driver. In such cases, the signal will be held at the receiver for a long time after the clock, since the change needs a long time to propagate from the driver to the receiver.

The recommended procedure for the I/O buffer designer to extract T_{SU} is outlined below. If one employs additional steps, it would be beneficial that any such extra steps be documented with the results of this receiver characterization:

- The full receiver circuit must be used, comprising the input differential amplifier, any shaping logic gates, and the edge-triggered (or pulse-triggered) flip-flop. The output of the flip-flop must be monitored.

- The receiver's Lo-to-Hi setup time should be determined using a nominal input waveform like the one shown in Figure 12-13 (solid line). The Lo-to-Hi input starts at $V_{IN\_LOW\_MAX}$ (V_{REF} - 200 mV) and goes to $V_{IN\_HIGH\_MIN} = V_{REF}$ +200 mV, at a slow edge rate of 0.3V/ns, with the process, temperature, voltage, and $V_{REF\_INTERNAL}$ of the receiver set to the worst (longest T_{SU}) corner values. Here, V_{REF} is the external (system) reference voltage at the device pin. Due to tolerance in V_{TT} (1.5V, ±10%) and the voltage divider generating system V_{REF} from V_{TT} (±2%), V_{REF} can shift around 1 V by a maximum of ±122 mV. When determining setup time, the internal reference voltage $V_{REF\_INTERNAL}$ (at the reference gate of the diff. amp.) must be set to the value which yields the longest setup time. Here, $V_{REF\_INTERNAL} = V_{REF} \pm (122$ mV $+V_{NOISE})$. Where, V_{NOISE} is the net maximum differential noise amplitude on the component's internal V_{REF} distribution bus (at the amplifier's reference input gate) comprising noise picked up by the connection from the V_{REF} package pin to the input of the amp.

- Analogously, for the setup time of Hi-to-Lo transitions (Figure 12-14), the input starts at $V_{IN\_HIGH\_MIN} = V_{REF}$ +200 mV and drops to $V_{IN\_LOW\_MAX} = V_{REF}$ - 200 mV at the rate of 0.3V/ns.

- For both the 0.3V/ns edge rate and faster edge rates (up to 0.8V/ns for Lo-to-Hi, and 3V/ns for Hi-to-Lo —dashed lines in Figure 12-13 and Figure 12-14), one must ensure that lower starting voltages of the input swing (V_{START} in the range 'V_{REF}-200 mV' to 0.5 V for Lo-to-Hi transitions, and 1.5 V to 'V_{REF}+200 mV' for Hi-to-Lo transitions —dashed lines in Figure 12-13 and Figure 12-14) do not require T_{SU} to be made longer. This step is needed since a lower starting voltage may cause the input differential amplifier to require more time to switch, due to having been in deeper saturation in the initial state.

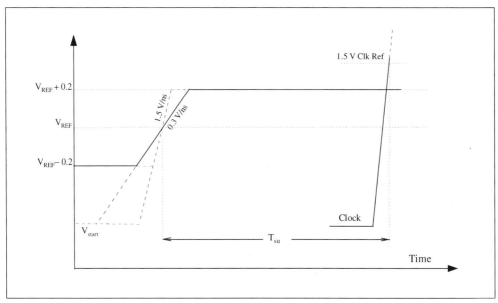

Figure 12-13. Standard Input Lo-to-Hi Waveform for Characterizing Receiver Setup Time

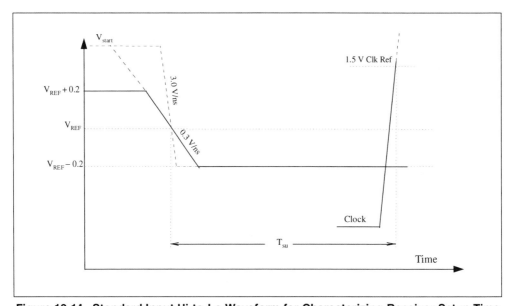

Figure 12-14. Standard Input Hi-to-Lo Waveform for Characterizing Receiver Setup Time

Hold time for GTL+, T_{HOLD}, is defined as:

> The minimum time from the clock pin of the receivers crossing of the 1.5 V level to the receiver input signal pin crossing of V_{REF}, which guarantees that the input buffer has captured **new** data at the receiver input signal pin, given an infinite setup time.

Strictly speaking, hold time must be determined when the input barely meets minimum setup time (see definition of setup time above). However, for current GTL+ systems, setup time is expected to be met, well beyond the minimum required in cases where hold is critical. This is because hold is critical when the receiver is very close to the driver. In such cases, the signal will arrive at the receiver shortly after the clock, hence meeting setup time with comfortable margin.

The recommended procedure for extracting T_{HOLD} is outlined below. If one employs additional steps, it would be beneficial that any such extra steps be documented with the results of this receiver characterization:

- The full receiver circuit must be used, comprising the input differential amplifier, any shaping logic gates, and the edge-triggered (or pulse-triggered) flip-flop. The output of the flip-flop must be monitored.

- The receiver's Lo-to-Hi hold time should be determined using a nominal input waveform that starts at $V_{IN\_LOW\_MAX}$ (V_{REF} - 200 mV) and goes to V_{TT}, at a fast edge rate of 0.8V/ns, with the process, temperature, voltage, and $V_{REF\_INTERNAL}$ of the receiver set to the fastest (or best) corner values (yielding the longest T_{HOLD}). Here, V_{REF} is the external (system) reference voltage at the device pin. Due to tolerance in V_{TT} (1.5V, ±10%) and the voltage divider generating system V_{REF} from V_{TT} (±2%), V_{REF} can shift around 1V by a maximum of ±122 mV. When determining hold time, the internal reference voltage $V_{REF\_INTERNAL}$ (at the reference gate of the diff. amp.) must be set to the value which yields the worst case hold time. Here, $V_{REF\_INTERNAL} = V_{REF} \pm (122 \text{ mV} + V_{NOISE})$. Where, V_{NOISE} is the net maximum differential noise amplitude on the component's internal V_{REF} distribution bus (at the amplifier's reference input gate) comprising noise picked up by the connection from the V_{REF} package pin to the input of the amp.

- Analogously, for the hold time of Hi-to-Lo transitions, the input starts at $V_{IN\_HIGH\_MIN} = V_{REF}$ +200 mV and drops to < 0.5 V at the rate of 3V/ns.

12.2.3.3. RECEIVER RINGBACK TOLERANCE

Refer to Section 12.1.3.1., "Ringback Tolerance" for a complete description of the definitions and methodology for determining receiver ringback tolerance.

12.2.4. System-Based Calculation of Required Input and Output Timings

Below are two sample calculations. The first determines T_{CO-MAX} and T_{SU-MIN}, while the second determines $T_{HOLD-MIN}$. These equations can be used for any system by replacing the assumptions listed below, with the actual system constraints.

12.2.4.1. CALCULATING TARGET T_{CO-MAX}, AND T_{SU-MIN}

T_{CO-MAX} and T_{SU-MIN} can be calculated from the Setup Time equation given earlier in Section 12.1.4., "AC Parameters: Flight Time":

$$T_{FLIGHT-MAX} \leq T_{PERIOD-MIN} - (T_{CO-MAX} + T_{SU-MIN} + T_{CLK\_SKEW-MAX} + T_{CLK\_JITTER-MAX})$$

As an example, for two identical agents located on opposite ends of a network with a flight time of 7.3 ns, and the other assumptions listed below, the following calculations for T_{CO-MAX} and T_{SU-MIN} can be done:

Assumptions:

$T_{PERIOD-MIN}$	15 ns	(66.6 MHz)
$T_{FLIGHT-MAX}$	7.3 ns	(given flight time)
$T_{CLK\_SKEW-MAX}$	0.7 ns	(0.5ns for clock driver)
		(0.2 ns for board skew)
$T_{CLK\_JITTER-MAX}$	0.2 ns	(Clock phase error)
T_{CO-MAX}	?? ns	(Clock to output data time)
T_{SU-MIN}	?? ns	(Required input setup time)

Calculation

$$7.3 \leq 15 - (T_{CO-MAX} + T_{SU-MIN} + 0.7 + 0.2)$$

$$T_{CO-MAX} + T_{SU-MIN} \leq 6.8 \text{ ns}$$

The time remaining for T_{CO-MAX} and T_{SU-MIN} can be split ~60/40% (recommendation). Therefore, in this example, T_{CO-MAX} would be 4.0 ns, and T_{SU-MIN} 2.8 ns.

NOTE

This a numerical example, and does not necessarily apply to any particular device.

Off-end agents will have less distance to the farthest receiver, and therefore will have shorter flight times. T_{CO} values longer than the example above do not necessarily preclude high-frequency (e.g. 66.6 MHz) operation, but will result in placement constraints for the device, such as being required to be placed in the middle of the daisy-chain bus.

12.2.5. Calculating Target $T_{HOLD-MIN}$

To calculate the longest possible minimum required hold time target value, assume that T_{CO-MIN} is one fourth of T_{CO-MAX}, and use the hold time equation given earlier. Note that Clock Jitter is not a part of the equation, since data is released by the driver and must be held at the receiver relative to the same clock edge:

$$T_{HOLD-MIN} \leq T_{FLIGHT-MIN} + T_{CO-MIN} - T_{CLK\_SKEW-MAX}$$

Assumptions

T_{CO-MAX}	4.0 ns	(Max clock to data time)
T_{CO-MIN}	1.0 ns	(Assumed ¼ of max)
$T_{CLK\_SKEW-MAX}$	0.7 ns	(Driver to receiver skew)
$T_{FLIGHT-MIN}$	0.1 ns	(Min of 0.5" at 0.2 ns/inch)
$T_{HOLD-MIN}$	?? ns	(Minimum signal hold time)

Calculation

$$T_{HOLD-MIN} \leq 0.1 + 1.0 - 0.7$$

$$T_{HOLD-MIN} \leq 0.4 \text{ ns}$$

NOTE

This a numerical example, and does not necessarily apply to any particular device.

12.3. PACKAGE SPECIFICATION

This information is also included for designers of components for a GTL+ bus. The package that the I/O transceiver will be placed into must adhere to two critical parameters. They are package trace length, (the electrical distance from the pin to the die), and package capacitance. The specifications for package trace length and package capacitance are not explicit, but are implied by the system and I/O buffer specifications.

12.3.1. Package Trace Length

The System specification requires that all signals be routed in a daisy chain fashion, and that no stub in the network exceed 250 ps in electrical length. The stub includes any printed circuit board (PCB) routing to the pin of the package from the 'Daisy Chain' net, as well as a socket if necessary, and the trace length of the package interconnect (i.e. the electrical length from the pin, through the package, across a bond wire if necessary, and to the die). For example, for a PGA package, which allows PCB routing both to and from a pin and is soldered to the PCB, the maximum package trace length cannot exceed 250 ps. If the PGA package is socketed, the maximum package trace length would be ~225 ps since a typical PGA socket is around 25 ps in electrical length. For a QFP package, which typically requires a short stub on the PCB from the pad landing to a via (~50 ps), the package lead frame length should be less than ~200 ps.

12.3.2. Package Capacitance

The maximum package pin capacitance is a function of the Input/Output capacitance of the I/O transceiver. The I/O Buffer specification requires the total of the package capacitance, output driver, input receiver and ESD structures, as seen from the pin, to be less than 10 pF. Thus, the larger the I/O transceiver capacitance, the smaller the allowable package capacitance.

12.4. REF8N NETWORK

The Ref8N network shown in Figure 12-15, which represents an eight-node reference network (hence the name Ref8N), is used to characterize I/O drivers' behavior into a known environment. This network is not a worst case, but a representative sample of a typical system environment. A SPICE deck of the network is also given.

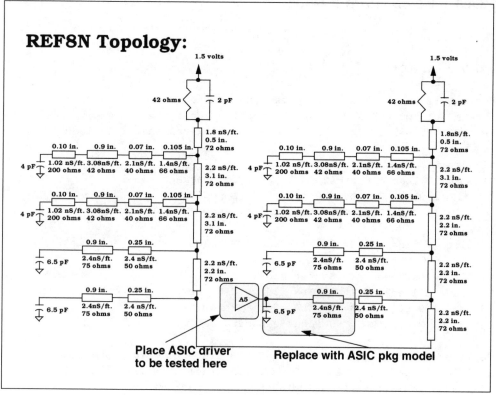

Figure 12-15. Ref8N Topology

12.4.1. Ref8N HSPICE Netlist

```
$REF8N, Rev 1.1

Vpu vpu GND DC(vtt)

rterm PU1 vpu (R=42)$ Pull-up termination resistance
crterm PU1 vpu 2PF $ Pull-up termination capacitance
TPU PU1 0 line1 0 Z0=72 TD=.075NS$ PCB link terminator to load 1

X1 line1 load1 socket$ Socket model
T1 load1 0 load1a 0 Z0=42 TD=230PS $ CPU package model
T2 load1a 0 CPU_1 0 Z0=200 TD=8.5PS$ Bondwire
CCPU_1 CPU_1 0 4PF $ CPU input capacitance

T3 line1 0 line2 0 Z0=72 TD=568PS$ PCB trace between packages

x2 line2 load2 socket$ Socket model
T4 load2 0 load2a 0 Z0=42 TD= 230ps$ CPU worst case package
T5 load2a 0 p6_2 0 Z0=200 TD=8.5ps $ Bondwire
CCPU_2 p6_2 0 4pf  $ CPU input capacitance

T6 line2 0 line3 0 Z0=72 TD=568ps$ PCB trace between packages
T7 line3 0 load3 0 Z0=50 TD=50ps $ PCB trace from via to landing pad
T8 load3 0 asic_1 0 Z0=75 TD=180PS $ ASIC package
CASIC_1 asic_1 0 6.5PF$ ASIC input capacitance (die C)

T9 line3 0 line4 0 Z0=72 TD=403PS$ PCB trace between packages
T10 line4 0 load4 0 Z0=50 TD=50PS$ PCB trace from via to landing pad
T11 load4 0 asic_2 0 Z0=75 TD=180PS$ ASIC package
CASIC_2 asic_2 0 6.5PF$ ASIC input capacitance (die C)

T12 line4 0 line5 0 Z0=72 TD=403PS$ PCB trace between packages
T13 line5 0 load5 0 Z0=50 TD=50PS$ PCB trace from via to landing pad
T14 load5 0 asic_3 0 Z0=75 TD=180PS$ Replace these 2 lines
CASIC_3 asic_3 0 6.5PF$ with the equivalent model
                $ for your package. (This model
                $ should include the package
                $ pin, package trace, bond wire and
                $ any die capacitance that is not
                $ already included in your driver
                $ model.)
```

```
T15 line5 0 line6 0 Z0=72 TD=403PS$ PCB trace between packages
T16 line6 0 load6 0 Z0=50 TD=50PS$ PCB trace from via to landing pad
T17 load6 0 asic_4 0 Z0=75 TD=180PS$ ASIC package
CASIC_4 asic_4 0 6.5PF$ ASIC input capacitance

T18 line6 0 line7 0 Z0=72 TD=403PS $ PCB trace between packages
X3 line7 load7 socket$ Socket model
T19 load7 0 load7a 0 Z0=42 TD=230PS$ CPU worst case package
T20 load7a 0 p6_3 0 Z0=200 TD=8.5PS$ Bondwire
CCPU_3 p6_3 0 4PF  $ CPU input capacitance

T21 line7 0 line8 0 Z0=72 TD=568PS $ PCB trace between packages
X4 line8 load8 socket $ Socket model
T22 load8 0 load8a 0 Z0=42 TD=230PS$ CPU worst case package
T23 load8a 0 p6_4 0 Z0=200 TD=8.5PS$ Bondwire
CCPU_4 p6_4 0 4PF  $ CPU input capacitance

T24 line8 0 R_TERM 0 Z0=72 TD=75PS$ PCB trace to termination resistor
Rterm1 R_TERM vpu (R=42)$ Pull-up termination resistance
CRTERM1 R_TERM vpu (C=2PF)$ Pull-up termination capacitance

Rout bond asic_3.001

.subckt socket in out$ Socket model
TX out 0 jim 0 Z0=40 TD=12.25PS
ty jim 0 in 0 Z0=66 TD=12.25ps
.ENDS
```

intel ®

13

3.3V Tolerant Signal Quality Specifications

The signals that are 3.3V tolerant should also meet signal quality specifications to guarantee that the components read data properly and to ensure that incoming signals do not affect the long term reliability of the component. There are three signal quality parameters defined for the 3.3V tolerant signals. They are Overshoot/Undershoot, Ringback and Settling Limit. All three signal quality parameters are shown in Figure 13-1. The *Pentium® Pro Processor I/O Buffer Models—IBIS Format* (on world wide web page www.intel.com) contain models for simulating 3.3V tolerant signal distribution.

13.1. OVERSHOOT/UNDERSHOOT GUIDELINES

Overshoot (or undershoot) is the absolute value of the maximum voltage allowed above the nominal high voltage or below V_{SS}. The overshoot/undershoot guideline limits transitions beyond $V_{CC}P$ or V_{SS} due to the fast signal edge rates. See Figure 13-1. The processor can be damaged by repeated overshoot events on 3.3V tolerant buffers if the charge is large enough (i.e. if the overshoot is great enough). However, excessive ringback is the dominant harmful effect resulting from overshoot or undershoot (i.e. violating the overshoot/undershoot guideline will make satisfying the ringback specification difficult). The **overshoot/undershoot guideline is 0.8V** and assumes the absence of diodes on the input. These guidelines should be verified in simulations **without the on-chip ESD protection diodes present** because the diodes will begin clamping the 3.3V tolerant signals beginning at approximately 1.5V above $V_{CC}P$ and 0.5V below V_{SS}. If signals are not reaching the clamping voltage, then this is not an issue. A system should not rely on the diodes for overshoot/undershoot protection as this will negatively affect the life of the components and make meeting the ringback specification very difficult.

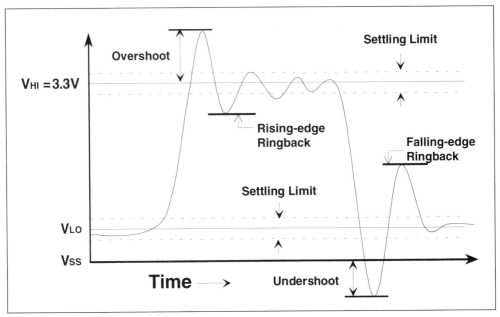

Figure 13-1. 3.3V Tolerant Signal Overshoot/Undershoot and Ringback

13.2. RINGBACK SPECIFICATION

Ringback refers to the amount of reflection seen after a signal has undergone a transition. The ringback specification is *the voltage that the signal rings back to after achieving its farthest excursion*. See Figure 13-1 for an illustration of ringback. Excessive ringback can cause false signal detection or extend the propagation delay. The ringback specification applies to the input pin of each receiving agent. Violations of the signal Ringback specification are not allowed under any circumstances.

Ringback can be simulated with or without the input protection diodes that can be added to the input buffer model. However, signals that reach the clamping voltage should be evaluated further. See Table 13-1 for the signal ringback specifications for Non-GTL+ signals.

Table 13-1. Signal Ringback Specifications

Transition	Maximum Ringback (with input diodes present)
0→1	2.5V
1→0	0.8V

13.3.   SETTLING LIMIT GUIDELINE

A Settling Limit defines the maximum amount of ringing at the receiving pin that a signal must be limited to before its next transition. The amount allowed is 10% of the total signal swing (V_{HI}-V_{LO}) above and below its final value. A signal should be within the settling limits of its final value, when either in its high state of low state, before it transitions again.

Signals that are not within their settling limit before transitioning are at risk of unwanted oscillations which could jeopardize signal integrity. Simulations to verify Settling Limit may be done either with or without the input protection diodes present. Violation of the Settling Limit guideline is acceptable if simulations of 5-10 successive transitions do not show the amplitude of the ringing increasing in the subsequent transitions.

intel

14

Thermal
Specifications

CHAPTER 14
THERMAL SPECIFICATIONS

Table 11-5 specifies the Pentium Pro processor power dissipation. It is highly recommended that systems be designed to dissipate at least **40W** per processor to allow the same design to accommodate higher frequency or otherwise enhanced members of the Pentium Pro family.

14.1.   THERMAL PARAMETERS

This section defines the terms used for Pentium Pro processor thermal analysis.

14.1.1.   Ambient Temperature

Ambient temperature, T_A, is the temperature of the ambient air surrounding the package. In a system environment, ambient temperature is the temperature of the air upstream from the package and in its close vicinity; or in an active cooling system, it is the inlet air to the active cooling device.

14.1.2.   Case Temperature

To ensure functionality and reliability, the Pentium Pro processor is specified for proper operation when T_C (case temperature) is within the specified range in Table 11-5. Special care is required when measuring the case temperature to ensure an accurate temperature measurement. Thermocouples are often used to measure T_C. Before any temperature measurements, the thermocouples must be calibrated. When measuring the temperature of a surface which is at a different temperature from the surrounding ambient air, errors could be introduced in the measurements if not handled properly. The measurement errors could be due to having a poor thermal contact between the thermocouple junction and the surface, heat loss by radiation, or by conduction through thermocouple leads. To minimize the measurement errors, the following approach is recommended:

- Use a 35 gauge K-type thermocouple or equivalent.

- Attach the thermocouple bead or junction to the package top surface at a location corresponding to the center of the Pentium Pro processor die. (Location A in Figure 14-1) Using the center of the Pentium Pro processor die gives a more accurate measurement and less variation as the boundary condition changes.

- Attach the thermocouple bead or junction at a 90° angle by an adhesive bond (such as thermal grease or heat-tolerant tape) to the package top surface as shown in Figure 14-2. When a heat sink is attached, a hole should be drilled through the heat sink to allow probing the Pentium Pro processor package above the center of the processor die. The hole diameter should be no larger than 0.150."

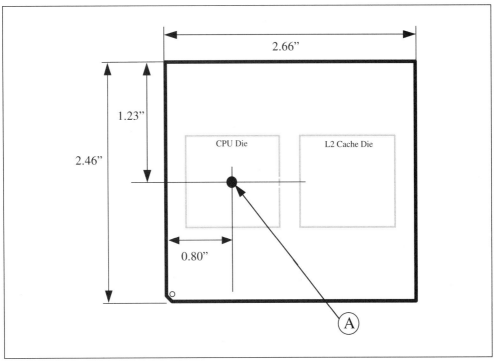

Figure 14-1. Location of Case Temperature Measurement (Top-Side View)

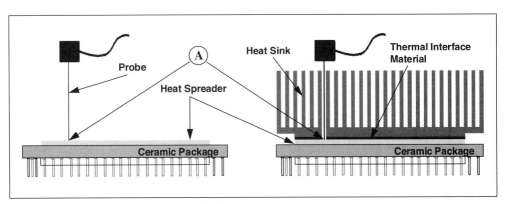

Figure 14-2. Thermocouple Placement

14.1.3. Thermal Resistance

The thermal resistance value for the case-to-ambient, Θ_{CA}, is used as a measure of the cooling solution's thermal performance. Θ_{CA} is comprised of the case-to-sink thermal resistance, Θ_{CS}, and the sink-to-ambient thermal resistance, Θ_{SA}. Θ_{CS} is a measure of the thermal resistance along the heat flow path from the top of the IC package to the bottom of the thermal cooling solution. This value is strongly dependent on the material, conductivity, and thickness of the thermal interface used. Θ_{SA} is a measure of the thermal resistance from the top of the cooling solution to the local ambient air. Θ_{SA} values depend on the material, thermal conductivity, and geometry of the thermal cooling solution as well as on the airflow rates.

The parameters are defined by the following relationships (See also Figure 14-3):

$$\Theta_{CA} = (T_C - T_A) / P_D$$
$$\Theta_{CA} = \Theta_{CS} + \Theta_{SA}$$

Where:

Θ_{CA} = Case-to-Ambient thermal resistance ($^\circ$C/W)
Θ_{CS} = Case-to-Sink thermal resistance ($^\circ$C/W)
Θ_{SA} = Sink-to-Ambient thermal resistance ($^\circ$C/W)
T_C = Case temperature at the defined location ($^\circ$C)
T_A = Ambient temperature ($^\circ$C)
P_D = Device power dissipation (W)

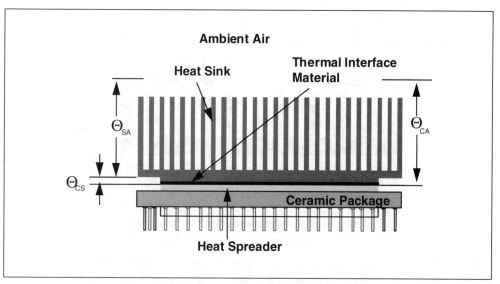

Figure 14-3. Thermal Resistance Relationships

14.2. THERMAL ANALYSIS

Table 14-1 below lists the case-to-ambient thermal resistances of the Pentium Pro processor for different air flow rates and heat sink heights.

Table 14-1. Case-To-Ambient Thermal Resistance

	Θ_{CA} [°C/W] vs. Airflow [Linear Feet per Minute] and Heat Sink Height[1]					
Airflow (LFM):	**100**	**200**	**400**	**600**	**800**	**1000**
With 0.5" Heat Sink [2]	—	3.16	2.04	1.66	1.41	1.29
With 1.0" Heat Sink [2]	2.55	1.66	1.08	0.94	0.80	0.76
With 1.5" Heat Sink [2]	1.66	1.31	0.90	0.78	0.71	0.67
With 2.0" Heat Sink [2]	1.47	1.23	0.87	0.75	0.69	0.65

NOTES:

1. All data taken at sea level. For altitudes above sea level, it is recommended that a derating factor of 1°C/1000 feet be used.

2. Heat Sink: 2.235" square omni-directional pin, aluminum heat sink with a pin thickness of 0.085", a pin spacing of 0.13" and a base thickness of 0.15". See Figure 14-4. A thin layer of thermal grease (Thermoset TC208 with thermal conductivity of 1.2W/m-°K) was used as the interface material between the heat sink and the package.

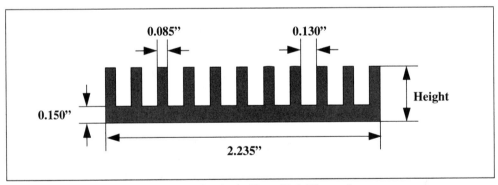

Figure 14-4. Analysis Heat Sink Dimensions

Table 14-2 shows the T_A required given a 29.2W processor (150 MHz, 256K cache), and a T_C of 85°C. Table 14-3 shows the T_A required assuming a 40W processor. Table 14-2 and Table 14-3 were produced by using the relationships of Section 14.1.3., "Thermal Resistance" and the data of Table 14-1.

Table 14-2. Ambient Temperatures Required at Heat Sink for 29.2W and 85° Case

Airflow (LFM):	T_A vs. Airflow [Linear Feet per Minute] and Heat Sink Height[1]					
	100	200	400	600	800	1000
With 0.5" Heat Sink [2]	—	-8	25	36	43	47
With 1.0" Heat Sink [2]	10	36	53	57	61	62
With 1.5" Heat Sink [2]	36	46	58	62	64	65
With 2.0" Heat Sink [2]	42	49	59	63	64	66

NOTES:

1. At sea level. See Table 14-1.
2. Heat sink design as in Table 14-1.

Table 14-3. Ambient Temperatures Required at Heat Sink for 40W and 85° Case

Airflow (LFM):	T_A vs. Airflow [Linear Feet per Minute] and Heat Sink Height[1]					
	100	200	400	600	800	1000
With 0.5" Heat Sink [2]	—	—	3	18	28	33
With 1.0" Heat Sink [2]	—	18	41	47	53	54
With 1.5" Heat Sink [2]	18	32	49	53	56	58
With 2.0" Heat Sink [2]	26	35	50	55	57	59

NOTES:

1. At sea level. See Table 14-1.
2. Heat sink design as in Table 14-1.

intel®

15

Mechanical
Specifications

CHAPTER 15
MECHANICAL SPECIFICATIONS

The Pentium Pro processor is packaged in a modified staggered 387 pin ceramic pin grid array (SPGA) with a gold plated Copper-Tungsten (CuW) heat spreader on top. Mechanical specifications and the pin assignments follow.

15.1. DIMENSIONS

The mechanical specifications are provided in Table 15-1. Figure 15-1 shows the bottom and side views with package dimensions for the Pentium Pro processor and Figure 15-2 shows the top view with dimensions. Figure 15-3 is the top view of the Pentium Pro processor with $V_{CC}P$, $V_{CC}S$, $V_{CC}5$ and V_{SS} locations shown. **Be sure to read Chapter 17,** *OverDrive® Processor Socket Specification* **for the mechanical constraints for the OverDrive processor. Also, investigate the tools that will be used for debug before laying out the system. Intel's tools are described in Chapter 16,** *Tools*.

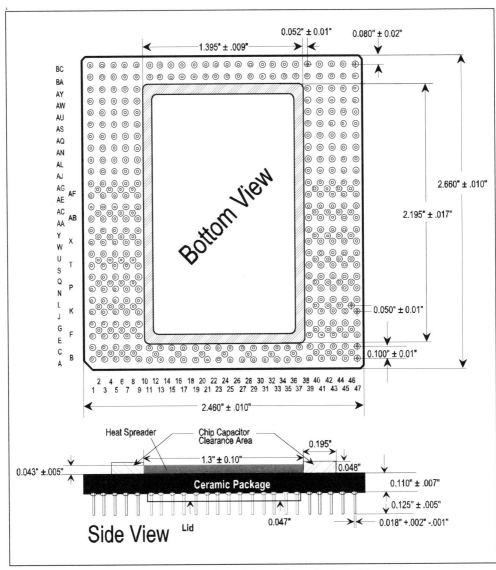

Figure 15-1. Package Dimensions-Bottom View

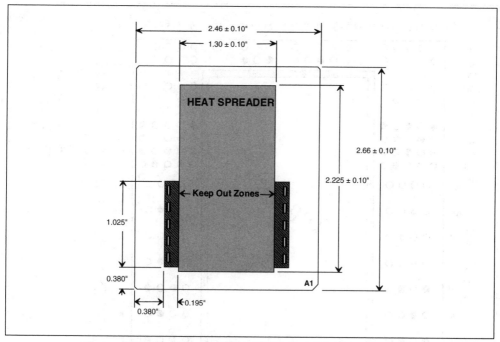

Figure 15-2. Top View of Keep Out Zones and Heat Spreader

Table 15-1. Pentium® Pro Processor Package

Parameter	Value
Package Type	PGA
Total Pins	387
Pin Array	Modified Staggered
Package Size	2.66" x 2.46" (7.76cm x 6.25cm)
Heat Spreader Size	2.225" x 1.3" x 0.04" (5.65cm x 3.3cm x 0.1cm)
Weight	90 grams

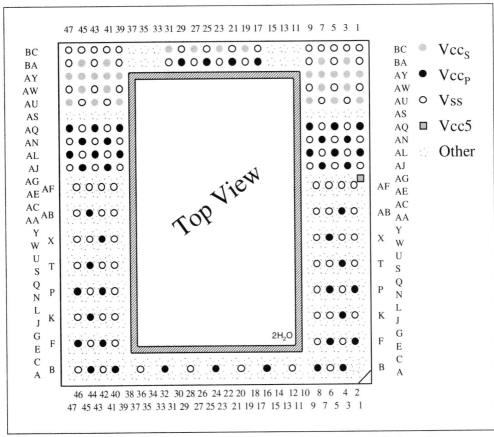

Figure 15-3. Pentium® Pro Processor Top View with Power Pin Locations

15.2. PINOUT

Table 15-2 is the pin listing in pin number order. Table 15-3 is the pin listing in pin name order. Please see Section 11.8., "Signal Groups" to determine a signal's I/O type. Bus signals are described in Appendix A and the other pins are described in Chapter 11, *Electrical Specifications* and in Table 11-2.

Table 15-2. Pin Listing in Pin # Order

Pin #	Signal Name	Pin #	Signal Name	Pin #	Signal Name
A1	VREF0	B32	VCCP	E7	A33#
A3	STPCLK#	B36	VSS	E9	A34#
A5	TCK	B40	VCCP	E39	D22#
A7	TRST#	B42	VSS	E41	D23#
A9	IGNNE#	B44	VCCP	E43	D25#
A11	A20M#	B46	VSS	E45	D24#
A13	TDI	C1	A35#	E47	D26#
A15	FLUSH#	C3	IERR#	F2	VCCP
A17	THERMTRIP#	C5	BERR#	F4	VSS
A19	BCLK	C7	VREF1	F6	VCCP
A21	RESERVED	C9	FRCERR	F8	VSS
A23	TESTHI	C11	INIT#	F40	VSS
A25	TESTHI	C13	TDO	F42	VCCP
A27	D1#	C15	TMS	F44	VSS
A29	D3#	C17	FERR#	F46	VCCP
A31	D5#	C19	PLL1	G1	A22#
A33	D8#	C21	TESTLO	G3	A24#
A35	D9#	C23	PLL2	G5	A27#
A37	D14#	C25	D0#	G7	A26#
A39	D10#	C27	D2#	G9	A31#
A41	D11#	C29	D4#	G39	D27#
A43	D13#	C31	D6#	G41	D29#
A45	D16#	C33	D7#	G43	D30#
A47	VREF4	C35	D12#	G45	D28#
B2	CPUPRES#	C37	D15#	G47	D31#
B4	VCCP	C39	D17#	J1	A19#
B6	VSS	C41	D20#	J3	A21#
B8	VCCP	C43	D18#	J5	A20#
B12	VSS	C45	D19#	J7	A23#
B16	VCCP	C47	D21#	J9	A28#
B20	VSS	E1	A29#	J39	D32#
B24	VCCP	E3	A30#	J41	D35#
B28	VSS	E5	A32#	J43	D38#

Table 15-2. Pin Listing in Pin # Order (Contd.)

Pin #	Signal Name	Pin #	Signal Name	Pin #	Signal Name
J45	D33#	P8	VSS	U1	AP0#
J47	D34#	P40	VSS	U3	RSP#
K2	VSS	P42	VCCP	U5	BPRI#
K4	VCCP	P44	VSS	U7	BNR#
K6	VSS	P46	VCCP	U9	BR3#
K8	VSS	Q1	A9#	U39	DEP7#
K40	VSS	Q3	A7#	U41	VREF6
K42	VSS	Q5	A5#	U43	D60#
K44	VCCP	Q7	A8#	U45	D56#
K46	VSS	Q9	A10#	U47	D55#
L1	RESERVED	Q39	D51#	W1	SMI#
L3	A16#	Q41	D52#	W3	BR1#
L5	A15#	Q43	D49#	W5	REQ4#
L7	A18#	Q45	D48#	W7	REQ1#
L9	A25#	Q47	D46#	W9	REQ0#
L39	D37#	S1	A6#	W39	DEP2#
L41	D40#	S3	A4#	W41	DEP4#
L43	D43#	S5	A3#	W43	D63#
L45	D36#	S7	VREF2	W45	D61#
L47	D39#	S9	AP1#	W47	D58#
N1	A12#	S39	D59#	X2	VSS
N3	A14#	S41	D57#	X4	VSS
N5	A11#	S43	D54#	X6	VCCP
N7	A13#	S45	D53#	X8	VSS
N9	A17#	S47	D50#	X40	VSS
N39	D44#	T2	VSS	X42	VCCP
N41	D45#	T4	VCCP	X44	VSS
N43	D47#	T6	VSS	X46	VSS
N45	D42#	T8	VSS	Y1	REQ3#
N47	D41#	T40	VSS	Y3	REQ2#
P2	VCCP	T42	VSS	Y5	DEFER#
P4	VSS	T44	VCCP	Y7	VREF3
P6	VCCP	T46	VSS	Y9	TRDY#

Table 15-2. Pin Listing in Pin # Order (Contd.)

Pin #	Signal Name	Pin #	Signal Name	Pin #	Signal Name
Y39	PRDY#	AE1	RESERVED	AJ39	VSS
Y41	RESET#	AE3	ADS#	AJ41	VCCP
Y43	DEP1#	AE5	RS1#	AJ43	VSS
Y45	DEP6#	AE7	RS2#	AJ45	VCCP
Y47	D62#	AE9	AERR#	AJ47	VSS
AA1	BR2#	AE39	TESTHI	AL1	VCCP
AA3	DRDY#	AE41	PICD1	AL3	VSS
AA5	DBSY#	AE43	BP2#	AL5	VCCP
AA7	HITM#	AE45	RESERVED	AL7	VSS
AA9	LOCK#	AE47	VREF5	AL9	VCCP
AA39	BPM1#	AF2	VSS	AL39	VCCP
AA41	PICD0	AF4	VSS	AL41	VSS
AA43	PICCLK	AF6	VSS	AL43	VCCP
AA45	PREQ#	AF8	VSS	AL45	VSS
AA47	DEP5#	AF40	VSS	AL47	VCCP
AB2	VSS	AF42	VSS	AN1	VSS
AB4	VCCP	AF44	VSS	AN3	VCCP
AB6	VSS	AF46	VSS	AN5	VSS
AB8	VSS	AG1	VCC5	AN7	VCCP
AB40	VSS	AG3	UP#	AN9	VSS
AB42	VSS	AG5	RESERVED	AN39	VSS
AB44	VCCP	AG7	PWRGOOD	AN41	VCCP
AB46	VSS	AG9	RESERVED	AN43	VSS
AC1	RESERVED	AG39	RESERVED	AN45	VCCP
AC3	HIT#	AG41	LINT1/NMI	AN47	VSS
AC5	BR0#	AG43	LINT0/INTR	AQ1	VCCP
AC7	RP#	AG45	VREF7	AQ3	VSS
AC9	RS0#	AG47	RESERVED	AQ5	VCCP
AC39	BP3#	AJ1	VSS	AQ7	VSS
AC41	BPM0#	AJ3	VCCP	AQ9	VCCP
AC43	BINIT#	AJ5	VSS	AQ39	VCCP
AC45	DEP0#	AJ7	VCCP	AQ41	VSS
AC47	DEP3#	AJ9	VSS	AQ43	VCCP

Table 15-2. Pin Listing in Pin # Order (Contd.)

Pin #	Signal Name	Pin #	Signal Name	Pin #	Signal Name
AQ45	VSS	AW45	VCCS	BA37	TESTLO
AQ47	VCCP	AW47	VSS	BA39	VSS
AS1	VID0	AY1	VCCS	BA41	VCCS
AS3	VID1	AY3	VCCS	BA43	VSS
AS5	VID2	AY5	VCCS	BA45	VCCS
AS7	VID3	AY7	VCCS	BA47	VSS
AS9	RESERVED	AY9	VCCS	BC1	VSS
AS39	TESTLO	AY39	VCCS	BC3	VSS
AS41	TESTLO	AY41	VCCS	BC5	VSS
AS43	TESTLO	AY43	VCCS	BC7	VSS
AS45	TESTLO	AY45	VCCS	BC9	VSS
AS47	RESERVED	AY47	VCCS	BC11	RESERVED
AU1	VCCS	BA1	VSS	BC13	TESTLO
AU3	VSS	BA3	VCCS	BC15	TESTLO
AU5	VCCS	BA5	VSS	BC17	VSS
AU7	VSS	BA7	VCCS	BC19	VCCS
AU9	VCCS	BA9	VSS	BC21	VSS
AU39	VCCS	BA11	RESERVED	BC23	VCCS
AU41	VSS	BA13	TESTLO	BC25	VSS
AU43	VCCS	BA15	TESTLO	BC27	VCCS
AU45	VSS	BA17	VCCP	BC29	VSS
AU47	VCCS	BA19	VSS	BC31	VCCS
AW1	VSS	BA21	VCCP	BC33	TESTLO
AW3	VCCS	BA23	VSS	BC35	RESERVED
AW5	VSS	BA25	VCCP	BC37	TESTLO
AW7	VCCS	BA27	VSS	BC39	VSS
AW9	VSS	BA29	VCCP	BC41	VSS
AW39	VSS	BA31	VSS	BC43	VSS
AW41	VCCS	BA33	TESTLO	BC45	VSS
AW43	VSS	BA35	RESERVED	BC47	VSS

Table 15-3. Pin Listing in Alphabetic Order

Signal Name	Pin #	Signal Name	Pin #	Signal Name	Pin #
A3#	S5	A35#	C1	D14#	A37
A4#	S3	ADS#	AE3	D15#	C37
A5#	Q5	AERR#	AE9	D16#	A45
A6#	S1	AP0#	U1	D17#	C39
A7#	Q3	AP1#	S9	D18#	C43
A8#	Q7	BCLK	A19	D19#	C45
A9#	Q1	BERR#	C5	D20#	C41
A10#	Q9	BINIT#	AC43	D21#	C47
A11#	N5	BNR#	U7	D22#	E39
A12#	N1	BP2#	AE43	D23#	E41
A13#	N7	BP3#	AC39	D24#	E45
A14#	N3	BPM0#	AC41	D25#	E43
A15#	L5	BPM1#	AA39	D26#	E47
A16#	L3	BPRI#	U5	D27#	G39
A17#	N9	BR0#	AC5	D28#	G45
A18#	L7	BR1#	W3	D29#	G41
A19#	J1	BR2#	AA1	D30#	G43
A20#	J5	BR3#	U9	D31#	G47
A20M#	A11	CPUPRES#	B2	D32#	J39
A21#	J3	D0#	C25	D33#	J45
A22#	G1	D1#	A27	D34#	J47
A23#	J7	D2#	C27	D35#	J41
A24#	G3	D3#	A29	D36#	L45
A25#	L9	D4#	C29	D37#	L39
A26#	G7	D5#	A31	D38#	J43
A27#	G5	D6#	C31	D39#	L47
A28#	J9	D7#	C33	D40#	L41
A29#	E1	D8#	A33	D41#	N47
A30#	E3	D9#	A35	D42#	N45
A31#	G9	D10#	A39	D43#	L43
A32#	E5	D11#	A41	D44#	N39
A33#	E7	D12#	C35	D45#	N41
A34#	E9	D13#	A43	D46#	Q47

Table 15-3. Pin Listing in Alphabetic Order (Contd.)

Signal Name	Pin #	Signal Name	Pin #	Signal Name	Pin #
D47#	N43	IERR#	C3	RESERVED	BC35
D48#	Q45	IGNNE#	A9	RESET#	Y41
D49#	Q43	INIT#	C11	RP#	AC7
D50#	S47	LINT0/INTR	AG43	RS0#	AC9
D51#	Q39	LINT1/NMI	AG41	RS1#	AE5
D52#	Q41	LOCK#	AA9	RS2#	AE7
D53#	S45	PICCLK	AA43	RSP#	U3
D54#	S43	PICD0	AA41	SMI#	W1
D55#	U47	PICD1	AE41	STPCLK#	A3
D56#	U45	PLL1	C19	TCK	A5
D57#	S41	PLL2	C23	TDI	A13
D58#	W47	PRDY#	Y39	TDO	C13
D59#	S39	PREQ#	AA45	TESTHI	A23
D60#	U43	PWRGOOD	AG7	TESTHI	A25
D61#	W45	REQ0#	W9	TESTHI	AE39
D62#	Y47	REQ1#	W7	TESTLO	C21
D63#	W43	REQ2#	Y3	TESTLO	AS39
DBSY#	AA5	REQ3#	Y1	TESTLO	AS41
DEFER#	Y5	REQ4#	W5	TESTLO	AS43
DEP0#	AC45	RESERVED	A21	TESTLO	AS45
DEP1#	Y43	RESERVED	L1	TESTLO	BA13
DEP2#	W39	RESERVED	AC1	TESTLO	BA15
DEP3#	AC47	RESERVED	AE1	TESTLO	BA33
DEP4#	W41	RESERVED	AE45	TESTLO	BA37
DEP5#	AA47	RESERVED	AG5	TESTLO	BC13
DEP6#	Y45	RESERVED	AG9	TESTLO	BC15
DEP7#	U39	RESERVED	AG39	TESTLO	BC33
DRDY#	AA3	RESERVED	AG47	TESTLO	BC37
FERR#	C17	RESERVED	AS9	THERMTRIP#	A17
FLUSH#	A15	RESERVED	AS47	TMS	C15
FRCERR	C9	RESERVED	BA11	TRDY#	Y9
HIT#	AC3	RESERVED	BA35	TRST#	A7
HITM#	AA7	RESERVED	BC11	UP#	AG3

Table 15-3. Pin Listing in Alphabetic Order (Contd.)

Signal Name	Pin #	Signal Name	Pin #	Signal Name	Pin #
VCC5	AG1	VCCP	AL47	VCCS	AY45
VCCP	B4	VCCP	AN3	VCCS	AY47
VCCP	B8	VCCP	AN7	VCCS	BA3
VCCP	B16	VCCP	AN41	VCCS	BA7
VCCP	B24	VCCP	AN45	VCCS	BA41
VCCP	B32	VCCP	AQ1	VCCS	BA45
VCCP	B40	VCCP	AQ5	VCCS	BC19
VCCP	B44	VCCP	AQ9	VCCS	BC23
VCCP	F2	VCCP	AQ39	VCCS	BC27
VCCP	F6	VCCP	AQ43	VCCS	BC31
VCCP	F42	VCCP	AQ47	VID0	AS1
VCCP	F46	VCCP	BA17	VID1	AS3
VCCP	K4	VCCP	BA21	VID2	AS5
VCCP	K44	VCCP	BA25	VID3	AS7
VCCP	P2	VCCP	BA29	VREF0	A1
VCCP	P6	VCCS	AU1	VREF1	C7
VCCP	P42	VCCS	AU5	VREF2	S7
VCCP	P46	VCCS	AU9	VREF3	Y7
VCCP	T4	VCCS	AU39	VREF4	A47
VCCP	T44	VCCS	AU43	VREF5	AE47
VCCP	X6	VCCS	AU47	VREF6	U41
VCCP	X42	VCCS	AW3	VREF7	AG45
VCCP	AB4	VCCS	AW7	VSS	B6
VCCP	AB44	VCCS	AW41	VSS	B12
VCCP	AJ3	VCCS	AW45	VSS	B20
VCCP	AJ7	VCCS	AY1	VSS	B28
VCCP	AJ41	VCCS	AY3	VSS	B36
VCCP	AJ45	VCCS	AY5	VSS	B42
VCCP	AL1	VCCS	AY7	VSS	B46
VCCP	AL5	VCCS	AY9	VSS	F4
VCCP	AL9	VCCS	AY39	VSS	F8
VCCP	AL39	VCCS	AY41	VSS	F40
VCCP	AL43	VCCS	AY43	VSS	F44

Table 15-3. Pin Listing in Alphabetic Order (Contd.)

Signal Name	Pin #	Signal Name	Pin #	Signal Name	Pin #
VSS	K2	VSS	AF6	VSS	AW1
VSS	K6	VSS	AF8	VSS	AW5
VSS	K8	VSS	AF40	VSS	AW9
VSS	K40	VSS	AF42	VSS	AW39
VSS	K42	VSS	AF44	VSS	AW43
VSS	K46	VSS	AF46	VSS	AW47
VSS	P4	VSS	AJ1	VSS	BA1
VSS	P8	VSS	AJ5	VSS	BA5
VSS	P40	VSS	AJ9	VSS	BA9
VSS	P44	VSS	AJ39	VSS	BA19
VSS	T2	VSS	AJ43	VSS	BA23
VSS	T6	VSS	AJ47	VSS	BA27
VSS	T8	VSS	AL3	VSS	BA31
VSS	T40	VSS	AL7	VSS	BA39
VSS	T42	VSS	AL41	VSS	BA43
VSS	T46	VSS	AL45	VSS	BA47
VSS	X2	VSS	AN1	VSS	BC1
VSS	X4	VSS	AN5	VSS	BC3
VSS	X8	VSS	AN9	VSS	BC5
VSS	X40	VSS	AN39	VSS	BC7
VSS	X44	VSS	AN43	VSS	BC9
VSS	X46	VSS	AN47	VSS	BC17
VSS	AB2	VSS	AQ3	VSS	BC21
VSS	AB6	VSS	AQ7	VSS	BC25
VSS	AB8	VSS	AQ41	VSS	BC29
VSS	AB40	VSS	AQ45	VSS	BC39
VSS	AB42	VSS	AU3	VSS	BC41
VSS	AB46	VSS	AU7	VSS	BC43
VSS	AF2	VSS	AU41	VSS	BC45
VSS	AF4	VSS	AU45	VSS	BC47

intel®

16

Tools

Included here is a discussion on the *Pentium Pro processor I/O buffer models* and a description of the Intel recommended debug port implementation. A debug port is used to connect a debug tool to a target system in order to provide run-time control over program execution, register/memory/IO access and breakpoints. A variety of debug tools exist which provide run-time control for the Pentium Pro processor; contact your local Intel sales representative for a list of tools vendors who support the Pentium Pro processor. For the discussion that follows, run-time control tools will be referred to as In-Target Probes, or ITPs.

An ITP uses on-chip debug features of the Pentium Pro processor to provide program execution control. Use of an ITP will not affect the high speed operations of the CPU signals. This ensures that the system can operate at full speed with an ITP attached.

This section describes the debug port as well as raising a number of technical issues that must be taken into account when considering including an ITP in your Pentium Pro processor debug strategy.

16.1. ANALOG MODELING

The Pentium Pro processor I/O buffer models are provided to allow simulation of the system layout. Package and socket parasitics for *each* pin are provided along with the I/O buffer models.

A slow and a fast corner model are provided for both the GTL+ buffer and the CMOS buffer. The fast model is useful for signal integrity analysis, while the slow model is useful for maximum flight time calculations. These models are available in IBIS (I/O Buffer Information Specification) format from World Wide Web site www.intel.com.

16.2. IN-TARGET PROBE FOR THE PENTIUM® PRO PROCESSOR (ITP)

An In-Target Probe (ITP) for the Pentium Pro processor is a debug tool which allows access to on-chip debug features via a small port on the system board called the debug port. An ITP communicates to the Pentium Pro processor through the debug port using a combination of hardware and software. The software is typically an application running on a host PC. The hardware consists of a board in the host PC connected to the signals which make up the Pentium Pro processor's debug interface. Due to the nature of an ITP, the Pentium Pro processor may be controlled without affecting any high speed signals. This ensures that the system can operate at full speed with an ITP attached. Intel uses an ITP for internal debug and system validation and recommends that all Pentium Pro processor-based system designs include a debug port.

16.2.1. Primary Function

The primary function of an ITP is to provide a control and query interface for up to four Pentium Pro processors in one cluster. With an ITP you can control program execution and have the ability to access processor registers, system memory and I/O. Thus, you can start and stop program execution using a variety of breakpoints, single-step your program at the assembly code level, as well as read and write registers, memory and I/O.

16.2.2. Debug Port Connector Description

An ITP will connect to the Pentium Pro processor system through the debug port. Intel recommended connectors, to mate an ITP cable with the debug port on your board, are available in either a vertical or right-angle configuration. Both configurations fit into the same board footprint. The connectors are manufactured by AMP Incorporated and are in their AMPMODU System 50 line. Following are the AMP part numbers for the two connectors:

- Amp 30-pin shrouded vertical header: 104068-3

- Amp 30-pin shrouded right-angle header: 104069-5

NOTE

These are high density through hole connectors with pins on 0.050" by 0.100" centers. Do not confuse these with the more common 0.100" by 0.100" center headers.

16.2.3. Debug Port Signal Descriptions

Table 16-1 describes the debug port signals and provides the pin assignment. The mechanical pinout is shown in Section 16.2.5.2., "Debug Port Connector".

Table 16-1. Debug Port Pinout

Name	Pin	Description
RESET#	1	Reset signal from MP cluster to ITP. See signal note 1
DBRESET#	3	Open drain output from ITP to the system; should be tied into system reset circuitry. This allows the ITP to reset the entire target system. See signal note 2
TCK	5	Boundary scan signal from ITP to MP cluster
TMS	7	Boundary scan signal from ITP to MP cluster
TDI	8	Signal from ITP to first component in boundary scan chain of MP cluster
POWERON	9	From target Vtt to ITP (through a resistor). See signal note 3
TDO	10	Signal from last component in boundary scan chain of MP cluster to ITP

TOOLS

Table 16-1. Debug Port Pinout (Contd.)

Name	Pin	Description
DBINST#	11	Indicates to user system that the ITP is installed (from ITP GND). See signal note 4
TRST#	12	Boundary scan signal from ITP to MP cluster
BSEN#	14	ITP asserts BSEN# while using Boundary Scan
PREQ0#	16	PREQ# signal from ITP to CPU 0 \n\n NOTE: PREQ0# and PRDY0# should be connected to the Pentium® Pro processor which is first (of up to 4) to receive the TDI signal from the debug port; the others should follow in the order of their receipt of TDI
PRDY0#	18	PRDY# signal from CPU 0 to ITP
PREQ1#	20	PREQ# signal from ITP to CPU 1
PRDY1#	22	PRDY# signal from CPU 1 to ITP
PREQ2#	24	PREQ# signal from ITP to CPU 2
PRDY2#	26	PRDY# signal from CPU 2 to ITP
PREQ3#	28	PREQ# signal from ITP to CPU 3
PRDY3#	30	PRDY# signal from CPU 3 to ITP
GND	2, 4, 6, 13, 15, 17, 19, 21, 23, 25, 27, 29	Signal ground

16.2.4. Signal Notes

In general, all open drain GTL+ outputs from the system to the debug port must be placed at a proper logic level, whether or not the debug port is installed. GTL+ signals from the Pentium Pro processor system (RESET#, PRDY#) should be terminated at the debug port, as shown in Figure 16-1.

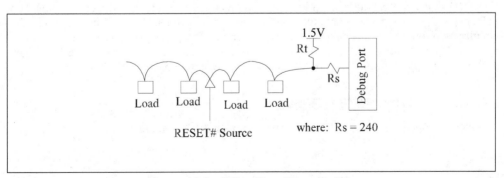

Figure 16-1. GTL+ Signal Termination

16.2.4.1.   SIGNAL NOTE 1: RESET#, PRDYX#

RESET# and PRDY# are GTL+ signals that come from the Pentium Pro processor system to the debug port; they are not driven by an ITP from the debug port. Adding inches of transmission line on to the RESET# or PRDY# signals after they are past the final Pentium Pro processor bus load does not change the timing calculations for the Pentium Pro processor bus agents.

16.2.4.2.   SIGNAL NOTE 2: DBRESET#

The usual implementation for DBRESET# is to connect it to the PWR_GD open drain signal on the 82450GX PCIset as an OR input to initiate a system reset. In order for the DBRESET# signal to work properly, it must actually reset the entire target system. The signal should be pulled up with a resistor that will meet two considerations: (1) the signal must be able to meet V_{ol} of the system and (2) it must allow the signal to meet the specified rise time (suggestion: 240 ohms). When asserted by an ITP, the DBRESET# signal will remain asserted long enough for the system to recognize it and generate a reset. A large capacitance should not be present on this signal as it may not be charged up within the allotted time.

16.2.4.3.   SIGNAL NOTE 3: POWERON

The POWERON input to the debug port has two functions. (1) It is used by an ITP to determine when the system is powered up. (2) The voltage applied to POWERON is internally used to set the GTL+ threshold (or reference) at 2/3 V_{TT} in order to determine the GTL+ logic level.

16.2.4.4.   SIGNAL NOTE 4: DBINST#

Certain target systems use the boundary scan chain for their own purposes, such as manufacturing test of connectivity. DBINST# is used to alert target systems that an ITP has been installed and may need to be active on the boundary scan chain. It should be provided with a weak pull up resistor.

16.2.4.5.   SIGNAL NOTE 5: TDO AND TDI

The TDO signal coming out of each Pentium Pro processor has a 25 ohm driver and should be pulled up to 3.3V using a resistor value of approximately 240 ohms. NOTE: When designing the circuitry to reroute the scan chain around empty Pentium Pro processor sockets, care should be taken so that the multiple TDO pull-up resistors do not end up in parallel (see Figure 16-4). The TDI line coming out of the debug port should be pulled up to 3.3V to 10K ohms.

16.2.4.6.   SIGNAL NOTE 6: PREQ#

The PREQ# signal should be pulled up to 3.3V through a 10K ohm resistor.

16.2.4.7.   SIGNAL NOTE 7: TRST#

If the TRST# signal is connected to the 82454GX, it should be pulled down through a 470 ohm resistor.

16.2.4.8.   SIGNAL NOTE 8: TCK

WARNING: A significant number of target systems have signal integrity issues with the TCK signal. TCK is a high speed signal and must be routed accordingly; make sure to observe power and ground plane integrity for this signal. Follow the guidelines below and assure the quality of the signal when beginning use of an ITP to debug your target.

Due to the number of loads on the TCK signal, special care should be taken when routing it. Poor routing can lead to multiple clocking of some agents on the debug chain, usually on the falling edge of TCK. This causes information to be lost through the chain and can result in bad commands being issued to some agents on the bus. There are two known good routing schemes for the TCK signal: daisy chain and star. Systems using other TCK routing schemes, particularly those with "T" or "Y" configurations where the trace from the source to the "T" is long, invite signal integrity problems.

If the signal is more easily routed as a daisy chain then it is recommended that a pull-up resistor from TCK to 3.3V be placed at the physically most distant node of the TCK route (see Figure 16-2). This resistor should be between 62 and 150 Ohms, depending on the run length of the TCK trace. Use Table 16-2 to select a value:

Table 16-2. TCK Pull-Up Value

Run Length	Resistor
0 - 12"	150 ohms
12 - 15"	120 ohms
15 - 18"	100 ohms
18 - 21"	82 ohms
> 21"	62 ohms

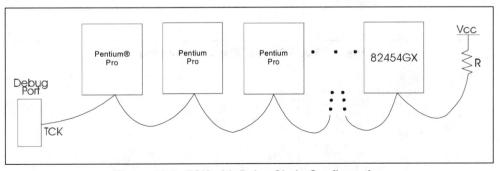

Figure 16-2. TCK with Daisy Chain Configuration

If the signal is more easily routed in a star configuration, each leg that is greater than 8" in length should be terminated with a resistor value R, where: R = (62 ohms) x (the number of legs greater than 8 inches). If all legs are less than 8", terminate only the longest leg with a 62 ohm resistor. If some legs are shorter than 8" and some are longer than 8", terminate the legs longer than 8" using the formula described above and ignore the legs shorter than 8". There should be no more than 4 legs to the star. For example, in Figure 16-3, the star has three legs, where the resistor R value is the same for each leg of the star: 3 x 62 = 186 ohms.

16.2.4.9.   SIGNAL NOTE 9: TMS

TMS should be routed to all components in the boundary scan chain in a daisy chain configuration. Follow the daisy chain guidelines specified for TCK in Section 16.2.4.8., "Signal Note 8: TCK".

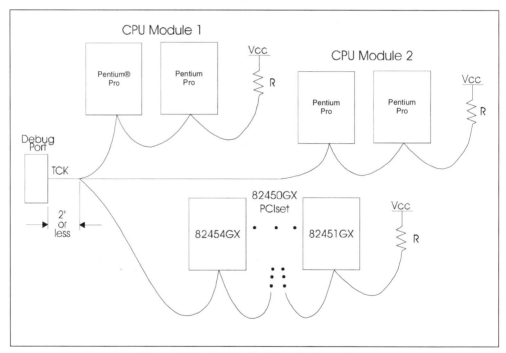

Figure 16-3. TCK with Star Configuration

16.2.5.   Debug Port Layout

Figure 16-4 shows the simplest way to layout the debug port in a multiprocessor system. In this example, the four processors are the only components in the system boundary scan chain. Systems incorporating boundary scan for use other than for an ITP should consider providing a method to partition the boundary scan chain in two distinct sections; one for system debug using the ITP and the other for manufacturing or system test.

System debug using an ITP requires only that the Pentium Pro processors be in the boundary scan chain. During system debug, routing boundary scan signals (particularly TCK and TMS) solely to the Pentium Pro processors enhances the likelihood that the boundary scan signals can be clocked at high speed. This will improve the performance of debug tools that must access large amounts of data via boundary scan. (For example, MP systems that have up to four processor in the chain will require four times as much boundary scan traffic.) Additionally, removing all but the Pentium Pro processors from the boundary scan chain reduces the possibility for errors in the chain when using an ITP for system debug.

If your system includes the use of boundary scan for test during normal system operation, then you should consider including the QST3383 in your layout. This component is used to multiplex the boundary scan lines in order to avoid contention between the system and an ITP. Using the QST3383, the system boundary scan lines are routed directly to the system when an ITP is not installed.

However, if the ITP is installed and is communicating with the Pentium Pro processors, the BS-EN# signal will enable the multiplexer to pass the boundary scan lines from the debug port to the system. Note: When an ITP is installed and communicating with the processors, the TDI line from the system boundary scan control logic does not pass through to the system, but is instead tied back into the TDO line. Thus, while the ITP is communicating with the processors, it is not possible for the system boundary scan control logic to access a processor via the boundary scan chain.

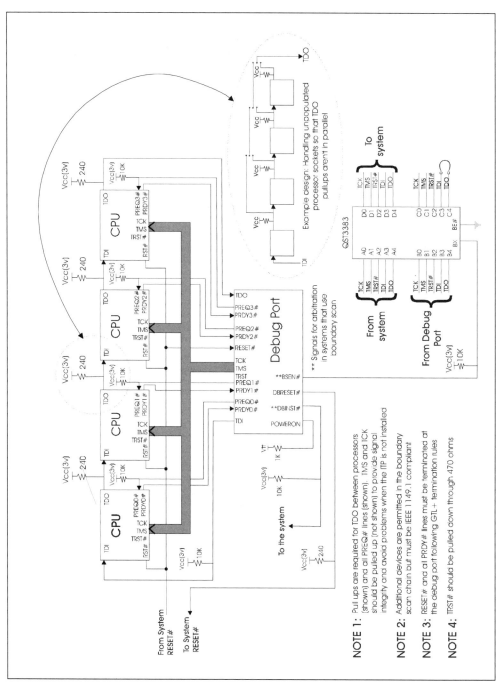

Figure 16-4. Generic MP System Layout for Debug Port Connection

16.2.5.1.   SIGNAL QUALITY NOTES

If system signals to the debug port (i.e. TDO, PRDY[0-3]# and RESET#) are used elsewhere in the system, then dedicated drivers should be used to isolate the signals from reflections coming from the end of the debug port cable. If the Pentium Pro processor boundary scan signals are used elsewhere in the system, then the TDI, TMS, TCK, and TRST# signals from the debug port should be isolated from the system signals with multiplexers as discussed in Section 16.2.5., "Debug Port Layout".

Additionally, it is a general rule that no signals should be left floating. Thus, signals going from the debug port to the Pentium Pro processor-based system should not be left floating. If they are left floating there may be problems when an ITP is not plugged in.

16.2.5.2.   DEBUG PORT CONNECTOR

Figure 16-5 and Figure 16-6 show how the debug port connector should be installed on a circuit board. Note the way the pins are numbered on the connector and how the through holes are laid out on the board. Figure 16-6 shows a dotted line representation of the connector and behind it the through holes as seen from the top side of the circuit board (the side on which the connector will be placed). The through holes are shown so that you can match the pin numbers of the connector to where the connector leads will fall on the circuit board. Although this may appear very simple, it is surprising how often mistakes are made in this aspect of the debug port layout.

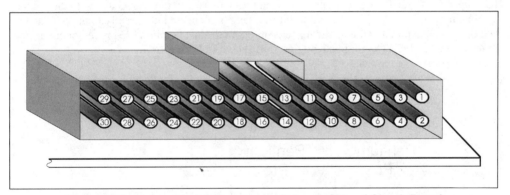

Figure 16-5. Debug Port Connector on Primary Side of Circuit Board

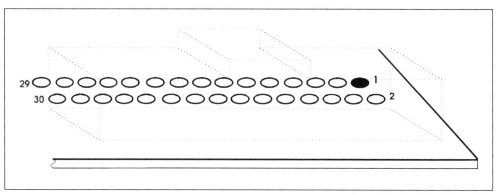

Figure 16-6. Hole Layout for Connector on Primary Side of Circuit Board

16.2.6. Using Boundary Scan to Communicate to the Pentium® Pro Processor

An ITP communicates to the processors in a Pentium Pro processor system by stopping their execution and sending/receiving messages over their boundary scan pins. As long as each Pentium Pro processor is tied into the system boundary scan chain, an ITP can communicate with it. In the simplest case, the Pentium Pro processors are back to back in the scan chain, with the boundary scan input (TDI) of the first Pentium Pro processor connected up directly to the pin labeled TDI on the debug port and the boundary scan output of the last Pentium Pro processor connected up to the pin labeled TDO on the debug port, as shown in Figure 16-7.

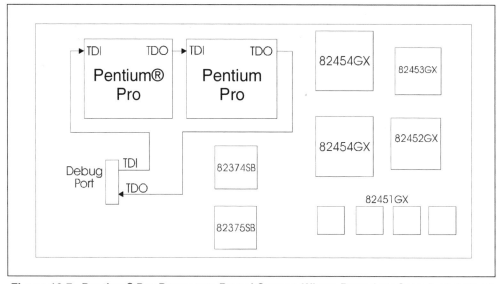

Figure 16-7. Pentium® Pro Processor-Based System Where Boundary Scan is Not Used

While an ITP requires only that the Pentium Pro processors be in the scan chain, Figure 16-8 shows a more complex case. The order in which you place the components in your scan chain is up to you. However, you may need to provide scan chain layout information to the ITP so it knows where the CPUs are in the chain. Note that additional components should not be included in the boundary scan chain unless absolutely necessary. Additional components increase both the complexity of the circuit and the possibility for problems when using the ITP. If possible, lay out the board such that the additional components can be removed from the scan chain for debug.

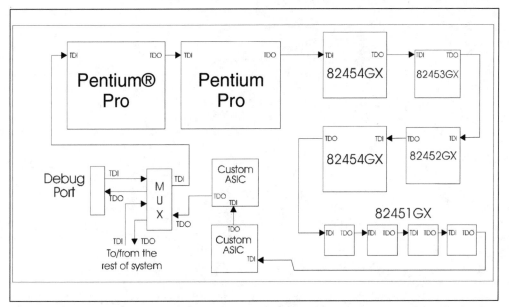

Figure 16-8. Pentium® Pro Processor-Based System Where Boundary Scan is Used

intel

17

OverDrive®
Processor Socket
Specification

CHAPTER 17
OVERDRIVE® PROCESSOR SOCKET
SPECIFICATION

17.1. INTRODUCTION

Intel will offer future OverDrive processors for the Pentium Pro processor. This OverDrive processor will be based on a faster, future Intel processor core.

The future OverDrive processor for Pentium Pro processor-based systems is a processor upgrade that will make all software run faster on an existing Pentium Pro processor system. The OverDrive processor is binary compatible with the Pentium Pro processor. The OverDrive processor is intended for use as a replacement upgrade for single and dual processor Pentium Pro processor designs. The OverDrive processor will be equipped with an integral fan/heatsink and retention clips. Intel plans to ship OverDrive processors with a matched Voltage Regulator Module (OverDrive VRM).

To support processor upgrades, a Zero Insertion Force (ZIF) socket (Socket 8) and a Voltage Regulator Module connector (Header 8) have been defined along with the Pentium Pro processor. Header 8 can be populated with an OEM Pentium Pro processor VRM or with the OverDrive VRM which Intel plans to ship with the OverDrive processor as part of the retail package.

The OverDrive processor will also support Voltage Identification as described in Section 11.6., "Voltage Identification". The four Voltage ID outputs (VID0-VID3) can be used to design a programmable power supply that will meet the power requirements of both the Pentium Pro and OverDrive processors via the Header 8 described in this chapter, or on the motherboard. If you plan to use VID to design a programmable supply for the OverDrive processor, please contact Intel for additional information.

A single socket system should include Socket 8 and Header 8. When this system configuration is upgraded, the Pentium Pro processor and its VRM are replaced with a future OverDrive processor for Pentium Pro processor-based systems and its matching OverDrive VRM. The OverDrive VRM is capable of delivering the lower voltage and higher current required by the upgrade. Other voltage regulation configurations are described in Section 17.3.2., "Upgrade Present Signal (UP#)".

17.1.1. Terminology

Header 8: 40-pin Voltage Regulator Module (VRM) connector defined to contain the OEM VRM and OverDrive VRM.

OverDrive processor: A future OverDrive processor for Pentium Pro processor-based systems.

OverDrive VRM: A VRM designed to provide the specific voltage required by the future OverDrive processor for Pentium Pro processor-based systems.

Socket 8: 387-pin SPGA Zero Insertion Force (ZIF) socket defined to contain either a Pentium Pro or OverDrive processor.

17.2. MECHANICAL SPECIFICATIONS

This section specifies the mechanical features of Socket 8 and Header 8. This section includes the pinout, surrounding space requirements, and standardized clip attachment features.

Figure 17-1 below shows a mechanical representation of the OverDrive processor in Socket 8 and the OverDrive VRM in Header 8.

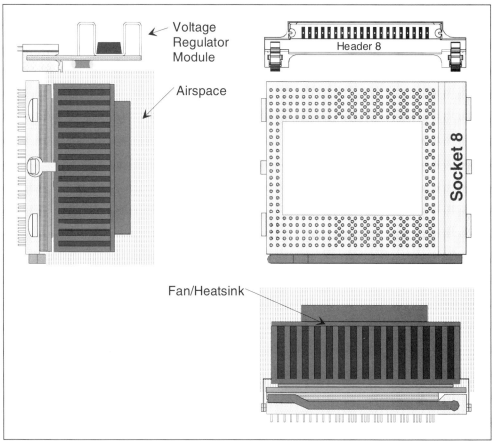

Figure 17-1. Socket 8 Shown with the Fan/heatsink Cooling Solution, Clip Attachment Features and Adjacent Voltage Regulator Module

17.2.1. Vendor Contacts for Socket 8 and Header 8

Contact your local Intel representative for a list of participating Socket 8 and Header 8 suppliers.

17.2.2. Socket 8 Definition

Socket 8 is a 387-pin, modified staggered pin grid array (SPGA), Zero Insertion Force (ZIF) socket. The pinout is identical to the Pentium Pro processor. Two pins are used to support the on-package fan/heatsink included on the OverDrive processor and indicate the presence of the OverDrive processor. The OverDrive processor package is oriented in Socket 8 by the asymmetric use of interstitial pins. Standardized heat sink clip attachment tabs are also defined as part of Socket 8 (Section 17.2.2.3., "Socket 8 Clip Attachment Tabs").

17.2.2.1. SOCKET 8 PINOUT

Socket 8 is shown in Figure 17-2 along with the VRM connector (Header 8). Refer to Chapter 15, *Mechanical Specifications*, for pin listings of the Pentium Pro processor. The OverDrive processor pinout is identical to the Pentium Pro processor. Descriptions of the upgrade specific pins are presented in Table 17-1. Note the location of pin A1 in relation to the cam shelf position. If the socket has the cam shelf located in a different position, then correct insertion of the OverDrive processor may not be possible. See Section 17.2.2.2., "Socket 8 Space Requirements".

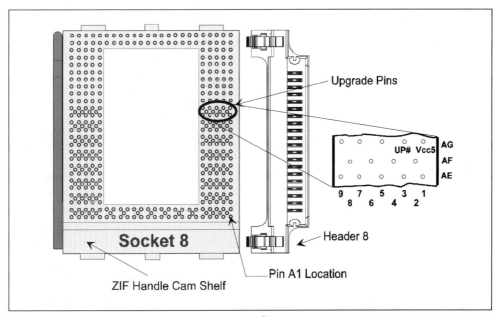

Figure 17-2. OverDrive® Processor Pinout

Table 17-1. OverDrive® Processor Signal Descriptions

Pin Name[1]	Pin #	I/O	Function
$V_{CC}5$	AG1	Input	+5V Supply required for OverDrive® processor fan/heatsink.
UP#	AG3	Output	This output is tied to V_{SS} in the OverDrive processor to indicate the presence of an upgrade processor. This output is an open in the Pentium® Pro processor.

NOTE:

1. Refer to Section 17.3., "Functional Operation of OverDrive® Processor Signals" for a description of the above signals.

17.2.2.2. SOCKET 8 SPACE REQUIREMENTS

The OverDrive processor will be equipped with a fan/heatsink thermal management device. The package envelope dimensions for the OverDrive processor with attached fan/heatsink are shown in Figure 17-3. Clearance is required around the fan/heatsink to ensure unimpeded air flow for proper cooling (refer to Section 17.5.1.1., "Fan/heatsink Cooling Solution" for details). Figure 17-4 shows the Socket 8 space requirements for the OverDrive processor. All dimensions are in inches.

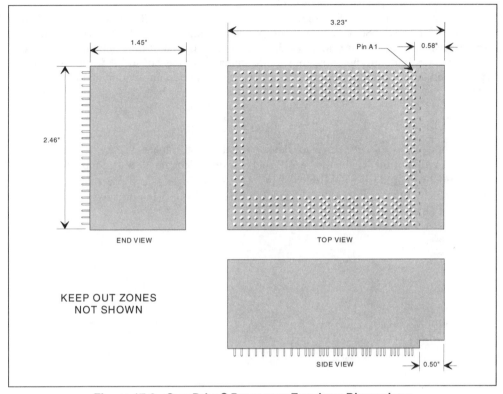

Figure 17-3. OverDrive® Processor Envelope Dimensions

"Keep out zones," also shown in Figure 17-4, have been established around the heat sink clip attachment tabs to prevent damage to surface mounted components during clip installation and removal. The keep out zones extend upwards from the surface of the motherboard to the top of the heat sink. The lateral limits of the keep out zones extend 0.1 inch from the perimeter of each tab.

Immovable objects must not be located less than 1.85 inches above the seating plane of the ZIF socket. Removable objects must also not be located less than the 1.85 inches above the seating plane of the ZIF socket required for the processor and fan/heatsink. These requirements also apply to the area above the cam shelf.

As shown in Figure 17-4 it is acceptable to allow any device (i.e. add-in cards, surface mount device, chassis etc.) to enter within the free space distance of 0.2" from the chip package if it is not taller than the level of the heat sink base. In other words, if a component is taller than height 'B', it cannot be closer to the chip package than distance 'A'. This applies to all four sides of the chip package (the handle side of the ZIF socket will generally meet this specification since its width is typically larger than distance 'A' (0.2")).

For designs which use Header 8, the header itself can violate the 0.2" airspace around the Over-Drive processor package. A VRM (either Pentium Pro processor VRM or OverDrive VRM), once installed in Header 8, and any components on the module, MUST NOT violate the 0.2" airspace. Also, the header must not interfere with the installation of the Pentium Pro or Over-Drive processors, and must not interfere with the operation of the ZIF socket lever. Alternately, Socket 8, and the installed processor must not interfere with the installation and removal of a VRM in Header 8.

NOTE

Components placed close to Socket 8 must not impede access to and operation of the handle of the ZIF socket lever. Adequate clearance must be provided within the proximity of the ZIF socket lever to provide fingertip access to the lever for normal operation, and to allow raising the lever to the full open position.

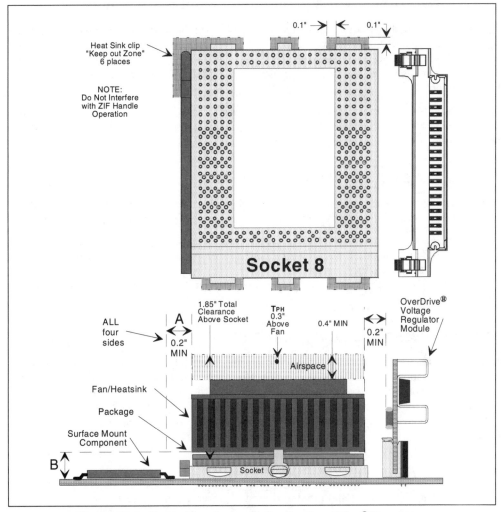

Figure 17-4. Space Requirements for the OverDrive® Processor

17.2.2.3.   SOCKET 8 CLIP ATTACHMENT TABS

Standardized clip attachment tabs will be provided on Socket 8. These will allow clips to secure the OverDrive processor to the socket to enhance shock and vibration protection. OEMs may utilize the attachment tabs for their own thermal solutions. As an option, OEMs may use customized attachment features providing that the additional features do not interfere with the standard tabs used by the upgrade.

Details of the clip attachment tabs and overall dimensions of Intel qualified sockets may be obtained from participating socket suppliers.

17.2.3.   OverDrive® Voltage Regulator Module Definition

Header 8 is a 2-row, 40-pin shrouded header designed to accommodate a Pentium Pro processor VRM, OverDrive VRM, or a programmable VRM. The OverDrive VRM is used to convert the standard 5.0V supply to the OverDrive processor core operating voltage. Integral OverDrive VRM hold down tabs are included as part of the header definition for enhanced shock and vibration protection.

OEMs who plan to design a custom VRM PC Board to fit into Header 8 should refer to the *AP-523 Pentium® Pro Processor Power Distribution Guidelines* Application Note (Order Number 242764).

17.2.3.1.   OVERDRIVE® VRM REQUIREMENT

When upgrading with an OverDrive processor, Intel suggests the use of its matched Voltage Regulator Module, which Intel plans to ship with the OverDrive processor retail package.

If the OEM includes on-board voltage regulation and the Header 8 for the OverDrive VRM, the on-board voltage regulator must be shut off via the UP# output of the CPU. When the OverDrive processor is installed, and the UP# signal is driven LOW, the on-board VR must never power on. This will ensure that there is no contention between the OverDrive VRM and the on-board regulator.

17.2.3.2.   OVERDRIVE® VRM LOCATION

It is recommended that Header 8 be located within approximately 1 inch of Socket 8 to facilitate end user installation. For optimum electrical performance, the Header 8 should be as close as possible to Socket 8. The location must not interfere with the operation of the ZIF socket handle or heatsink attachment clips. To allow system design flexibility, Header 8 placement is optional, but it is recommended that Header 8 NOT be placed on the same side of the ZIF socket as the handle.

17.2.3.3.   OVERDRIVE® VRM PINOUT

The OverDrive VRM pinout and pin description is presented in Figure 17-5 and Table 17-2, respectively.

Pin #	Signal Name	Pin #	Signal Name
A1	5Vin	B1	5Vin
A2	5Vin	B2	5Vin
A3	5Vin	B3	5Vin
A4	12Vin	B4	12Vin
A5	Reserved	B5	Reserved
A6	Reserved	B6	OUTEN
A7	VID0	B7	VID1
A8	VID2	B8	VID3
A9	UP#	B9	PwrGood
A10	Vccp	B10	Vss
A11	Vss	B11	Vccp
A12	Vccp	B12	Vss
A13	Vss	B13	Vccp
A14	Vccp	B14	Vss
A15	Vss	B15	Vccp
A16	Vccp	B16	Vss
A17	Vss	B17	Vccp
A18	Vccp	B18	Vss
A19	Vss	B19	Vccp
A20	Vccp	B20	Vss

Figure 17-5. Header 8 Pinout

Table 17-2. Header 8 Pin Reference

Pin Name	I/O	Usage	Function
12Vin	Input	Required	+12V±5% Supply
5Vin	Input	Required	+5V±5% Supply[1]
V_{SS}	Input	Required	Ground Reference
OUTEN	Input	Optional	When driven high this input will enable the OEM VRM output and float the OverDrive® VRM output. When this input is driven low, the output of the OEM module will float and the OverDrive VRM output will be enabled.
PwrGood	Output	Optional	Power Good is driven high upon the VRM output reaching valid levels. This output requires an external pull-up resistor (~10KΩ).
RES		No connect	Reserved for future use.
UP#	Input	Required	This signal is held high via an external pull-up resistor on the open collector output of the Pentium® Pro processor, and is driven low by the grounded output of the OverDrive processor.
$V_{CC}P$	Output	Required	Voltage Regulator Module core voltage output. Voltage level for the OverDrive processor will be lower than for the Pentium Pro processor.
VID3-VID0	Inputs	Optional	Used by the Pentium Pro processor VRM to determine what output voltage to provide to the CPU. The OverDrive VRM does not require these pins to be connected as it will be voltage matched in advance to the OverDrive processor. Refer to Table 11-1 for Voltage ID pin decoding.

NOTE:

1. The OverDrive® Voltage Regulator Module requires both 5V and 12V. Routing for the 5V VRM supply must support the full requirements of the OverDrive VRM given in Table 17-5 even if the 12V supply is utilized for the OEM VRM.

17.2.3.4. OVERDRIVE® VRM SPACE REQUIREMENTS

Figure 17-6 describes the maximum OverDrive VRM envelope. No part of the OverDrive VRM will extend beyond the defined space.

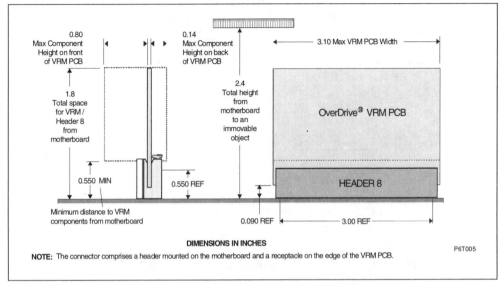

DIMENSIONS IN INCHES

P6T005

NOTE: The connector comprises a header mounted on the motherboard and a receptacle on the edge of the VRM PCB.

Figure 17-6. OverDrive® Voltage Regulator Module Envelope

17.3. FUNCTIONAL OPERATION OF OVERDRIVE® PROCESSOR SIGNALS

17.3.1. Fan/Heatsink Power (V_{CC5})

This 5V supply provides power to the fan of the fan/heatsink assembly. See Table 17-4 for $V_{cc}5$ specifications.

17.3.2. Upgrade Present Signal (UP#)

The Upgrade Present signal is used to prevent operation of voltage regulators providing a potentially harmful voltage to the OverDrive processor, and to prevent contention between on-board regulation and the OverDrive VRM. UP# is an open collector output, held high using a pull-up resistor on the motherboard tied to +5 Volts.

There are several system voltage regulation design options to support both the Pentium Pro processor and its OverDrive processor. The use of the UP# signal for each case is described below:

— Case 1: *Header 8 only*
If the system is designed with voltage regulation from the Header 8 only, then the UP# signal must be connected between the CPU socket (Socket 8) and the VRM connector (Header 8). The Pentium Pro processor VRM should internally connect the UP# input directly to the VRM OUTEN input. If the Pentium Pro processor is replaced with an

OverDrive processor and the OEM VRM is NOT replaced with the OverDrive VRM, the original voltage regulator will never enable its outputs because the lower voltage OverDrive processor could be damaged. Refer to Figure 17-7.

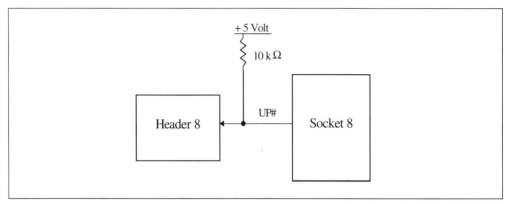

Figure 17-7. Upgrade Presence Detect Schematic - Case 1

— Case 2: *Header 8 AND alternate voltage source*
If the system is designed with alternate voltage source and a Header 8 for future upgrade support, then the UP# signal must be connected between Socket 8, Header 8, and the alternate voltage source. The Pentium Pro processor voltage regulator should use the UP# signal to disable the voltage output when detected low (indicating that an OverDrive processor has been installed). The OverDrive VRM, when installed into the Header 8 will use the UP# signal to enable its outputs (when detected low). When the Pentium Pro processor is replaced with an OverDrive processor and the OverDrive VRM is installed, the original voltage regulator must never enable its outputs because the lower voltage OverDrive processor could be damaged. Refer to Figure 17-8.

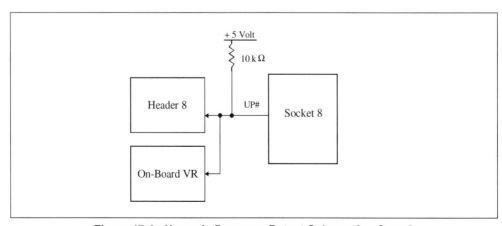

Figure 17-8. Upgrade Presence Detect Schematic - Case 2

— Case 3: *Alternate voltage source only*
If the system is designed with only a programmable voltage source using the VID3-VID0 pins, then the UP# signal need not be used.

NOTE

The programmable voltage source needs to be able to provide the OverDrive processor with it's required power. Refer to Figure 17-9.

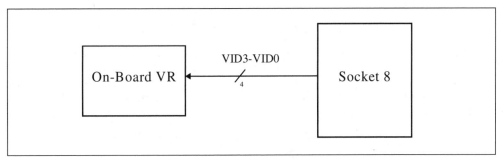

Figure 17-9. Upgrade Presence Detect Schematic - Case 3

17.3.3.   BIOS Considerations

Please refer to the *Pentium® Pro Processor Developer's Manual, Volume 2: Programmer's Reference Manual* (Order Number 242691) for BIOS requirements.

It is the responsibility of the BIOS to detect the type of CPU in the system and program the support hardware accordingly. In most cases, the BIOS does this by reading the CPU signature, comparing it to known signatures, and, upon finding a match, executing the corresponding hardware initialization code.

The CPUID instruction is used to determine several processor parameters. Following execution of the CPUID instruction, bits 12 and 13 of the EAX register can be used to determine if the processor is an OEM or an OverDrive processor. An OverDrive processor is present if bit 13=0 and bit 12=1.

NOTE

Contact your BIOS vendor to ensure that the OverDrive processor BIOS requirements have been included.

17.3.3.1. OVERDRIVE® PROCESSOR CPUID

Following power-on RESET or the CPUID instruction, the EAX register contains the values shown in Table 17-3.

Table 17-3. OverDrive® Processor CPUID

Type [13:12]	Family [11:8]	Model [7:4]	Stepping [3:0]
1	6	3	X

17.3.3.2. COMMON CAUSES OF UPGRADABILITY PROBLEMS DUE TO BIOS

CPU signature detection has been a common cause of current upgradability problems due to BIOS. A few precautions within the BIOS can help to eliminate future upgradability problems with Pentium Pro processor-based systems. When programming or modifying a BIOS, be aware of the impact of future OverDrive processors. The following recommendations should prevent problems in the future:

- Always use the CPU signature and feature flags to identify the processor, including future processors.

- Never use timing loops for delays.

- If an OverDrive processor is detected, report the presence of an "OverDrive processor" to the end-user.

- If an OverDrive processor is detected, don't test on-chip cache sizes or organization. The OverDrive processor cache parameters differ from those of the Pentium Pro processor.

- If an OverDrive processor is detected, don't use the Pentium Pro processor model specific registers and test registers. OverDrive processor MSRs differ from those of the Pentium Pro processor.

- Memory Type Range Registers must be programmed as for a Pentium Pro processor.

17.4. OVERDRIVE® PROCESSOR ELECTRICAL SPECIFICATIONS

This section describes the electrical requirements for the OverDrive processor.

NOTE

ZIF socket electrical parameters may differ from LIF socket parameters; therefore, be sure to use the appropriate ZIF socket parameters for electrical design simulations.

17.4.1. D.C. Specifications

17.4.1.1. OVERDRIVE® PROCESSOR D.C. SPECIFICATIONS

Table 17-4 lists the D.C. specifications for the OverDrive processor that are either different from or in addition to the Pentium Pro processor specifications.

Table 17-4. OverDrive® Processor D.C. Specifications

Symbol	Parameter	Min	Typ	Max	Unit	Notes
IccP	Primary I_{CC} Current	0.100		11.2 12.5 13.9	A	1 2 3
VccP	Primary V_{CC} Voltage	2.375	2.5	2.625		$V_{CCP} = 2.5V \pm 5\%$ 4
IccS	Secondary I_{CC} Current			0	A	
VccS	Secondary V_{CC} Voltage	3.145	3.3	3.465		$V_{CCS} = 3.3V \pm 5\%$
Icc_5FAN	fan/heatsink Current			340	mA	
Vcc_5	fan/heatsink Voltage	4.75	5	5.25		$Vcc5 = 5V \pm 5\%$
P_{Max}	Maximum Thermal Design Power		21.4 23.8 26.3	26.7 29.7 32.9	W	1 2 3

NOTES:

1. This specification applies to the future OverDrive® processor for *150 MHz* Pentium® Pro processor-based systems.

2. This specification applies to the future OverDrive processor for *166 & 180 MHz* Pentium Pro processor-based systems.

3. This specification applies to the future OverDrive processor for *200 MHz* Pentium Pro processor-based systems.

4. This is the *TARGET* OverDrive processor Voltage. It is recommended that the Voltage Identification be used to determine processor voltage for programmable voltage sources and implement a voltage range which adequately covers the OverDrive processor Target Voltage (~2.4-2.7V).

17.4.1.2.   OVERDRIVE® VRM D.C. SPECIFICATIONS

The D.C. specifications for the OverDrive VRM are presented in Table 17-5.

Table 17-5. OverDrive® VRM Specifications

5Vin = 5V ± 5%, T_{CASE} = 0 to 105º C				
Symbol	Parameter	Min	Max	Unit	Notes
V_{IL}	Control Signal Input Low Voltage	-0.3	0.8	V	
V_{IH}	Control Signal Input High Voltage	2.0	Vcc5+0.3	V	
V_{OL}	Control Signal Output Low Voltage		0.4V	V	
V_{OH5}	Control Signal Output High Voltage	2.4	Vcc5+0.3	V	PwrGood
I_{CC5}	5.0V Power Supply Current	0.100	7.0 7.8 8.7	A	1 VRM 2 input 3 current
I_{CC12}	12.0V Power Supply Current		150	mA	VRM input current
I_{OUT}	VRM Output Current		11.2 12.5 13.9	A	1 2 3
L_{MB}	Total inductance between VRM output and processor pins		2.5	nH	
R_{MB}	Total resistance between VRM output and processor pins		2.1	mΩ	4
dicc/dt	Worst Case Input (Icc5) Load Change		100	mA/µS	
T_{Vout}	Valid Input Supply to Output Delay		10	ms	

NOTES:

1. This spec applies to the OverDrive® VRM for *150 MHz* Pentium® Pro processor-based systems.
2. This spec applies to the OverDrive VRM for *166 & 180 MHz* Pentium Pro processor-based systems.
3. This spec applies to the OverDrive VRM for *200 MHz* Pentium Pro processor-based systems.
4. Maximum total resistance from VRM output to CPU pins cannot exceed 2.1 mΩ. For example, a breakdown of the resistive path might be 0.45 mΩ for VRM header, 1.0 mΩ for motherboard power plane resistance, and 0.65 mΩ for ZIF socket.

17.4.2.   OverDrive® Processor Decoupling Requirements

No additional decoupling capacitance is required to support the OverDrive processor beyond what is necessary for the Pentium Pro processor. Any incremental decoupling, both bulk and high speed, required by the OverDrive processor will be provided on the processor package. It is strongly recommended that liberal, low inductance decoupling capacitance be placed near Socket 8 following the guidelines in note [1] of Table 11-4 and the *AP-523 Pentium® Pro Processor Power Distribution Guidelines* Application Note (Order Number 242764). Capacitor values should be chosen to ensure they eliminate both low and high frequency noise components.

17.4.3. A.C. Specifications

Except for internal CPU core Clock frequency, the OverDrive processor will operate within the same A.C. specifications as the Pentium Pro processor.

17.5. THERMAL SPECIFICATIONS

This section describes the cooling solution utilized by the OverDrive processor and the cooling requirements for both the processor and VRM. Heat dissipation by the OverDrive processor will be no greater than the Pentium Pro processor, as described in Chapter 14, *Thermal Specifications*.

17.5.1. OverDrive® Processor Cooling Requirements

The OverDrive processor will be cooled with a fan/heatsink cooling solution. The OverDrive processor will operate properly when the preheat temperature, T_{PH}, is a maximum of 50°C (T_{PH} is the temperature of the air entering the fan/heatsink, measured 0.3" above the center of the fan — See Figure 17-4). When the preheat temperature requirement is met, the fan/heatsink will keep the case temperature, T_C, within the specified range, provided airflow through the fan/heatsink is unimpeded (see Section 17.2.2.2., "Socket 8 Space Requirements").

It is strongly recommended that testing be conducted to determine if the fan inlet temperature requirement is met at the system maximum ambient operating temperature.

NOTE

The OverDrive processor will operate properly when the preheat temperature, T_{PH}, is a maximum of 50°C (T_{PH} is the temperature of the air entering the fan/heatsink, measured 0.3" above the center of the fan — See Figure 17-4).

17.5.1.1. FAN/HEATSINK COOLING SOLUTION

A height of 0.4" airspace above the fan/heatsink unit and a distance of 0.2" around all four sides of the OverDrive processor is REQUIRED to ensure that the airflow through the fan/heatsink is not blocked. The fan/heatsink will reside within the boundaries of the surface of the chip. Blocking the airflow to the fan/heatsink reduces the cooling efficiency and decreases fan life. Figure 17-4 illustrates an acceptable airspace clearance above the fan/heatsink and around the OverDrive processor package.

17.5.2. OEM Processor Cooling Requirements

The OEM processor cooling solution must not impede the upgradability of the system. For example:

- If an OEM fan/heatsink is used, then electrical connections between the OEM fan/heatsink and system must be through an end user separable connector.

- If an OEM fan/heatsink is used, removal of the assembly must not interfere with the operation of the OverDrive processor, for example, by activating cooling failure protection mechanisms employed by the OEM.

- Custom attachment features in addition to the features covered in Section 17.2.2.3., "Socket 8 Clip Attachment Tabs" must not interfere with attachment of the upgrade retention clips.

17.5.3. OverDrive® VRM Cooling Requirements

The OverDrive Voltage Regulator Module will be shipped with a passive heat sink. Voltage regulator case temperature must not exceed 105°C. The ambient temperature, T_A, required to properly cool the VRM can be estimated from the following section.

Table 17-6. OverDrive® VRM Power Dissipation for Thermal Design

Parameter	Typ [1]	Max [1]	Unit	Notes
VRM Power Dissipation	6 6.7 7.5	7 6.5 7.0	Watts	[2] OverDrive® VRM [3] [4]
T_C, Max		105	°C	Voltage Regulator Maximum Case Temperature

NOTES:

1. Specification for the OverDrive® Voltage Regulator Module. A Pentium® Pro processor OEM Module is specific to the design and may differ.
2. This spec applies to the OverDrive VRM for *150 MHz* Pentium Pro processor-based systems.
3. This spec applies to the OverDrive VRM for *166 & 180 MHz* Pentium Pro processor-based systems.
4. This spec applies to the OverDrive VRM for *200 MHz* Pentium Pro processor-based systems.

17.5.4. Thermal Equations and Data

The OverDrive Voltage Regulator Module requires that T_C does not exceed 105°C. T_C is measured on the surface of the hottest component of the VRM. To calculate T_A values for the VRMs at different flow rates, the following equations and data may be used:

$$T_A = T_C - (P \times \Theta_{CA})$$

Where, T_A and T_C = Ambient and Case temperature, respectively. (°C)

Q_{CA} = Case-to-Ambient Thermal Resistance (°C/Watt)

P = Maximum Power Consumption (Watt)

Table 17-7. OverDrive® Processor Thermal Resistance and Maximum Ambient Temperature

Airflow - Ft./Min (M/Sec) [1]					
	100 (0.50)	150 (0.75)	200 (1.01)	250 (1.26)	300 (1.52)
OverDrive® Processor T_A, Max (°C)	Fan/Heatsink requires Ambient of 50°C or less regardless of external airflow.				
OverDrive VRM Θ_{CA} (°C/W)	9.8	8.3	6.8	6.4	6.0
The following specifications apply to the future OverDrive processor for *150 MHz* Pentium® Pro processor-based systems:					
OverDrive VRM T_A, Max (°C)[2]	46	55	64	67	69
The following specifications apply to the future OverDrive processor for *166 & 180 MHz* Pentium Pro processor-based systems:					
OverDrive VRM T_A, Max (°C)	41	51	61	63	66
The following specifications apply to the future OverDrive processor for *200 MHz* Pentium Pro processor-based systems:					
OverDrive VRM T_A, Max (°C)	36	47	57	60	63

NOTES:

1. Airflow direction parallel to long axis of VRM PCB.

2. T_{CASE} = 105°C, Power as per Table 17-6.

17.6. CRITERIA FOR OVERDRIVE® PROCESSOR

This section provides PC system designers with information on the engineering criteria required to ensure that a system is upgradable. The diagrams and checklists will aid the OEM to check specific criteria. Several design tools are available through Intel field representatives which will help the OEM meet the criteria. Refer to Section 17.6.1., "Related Documents".

The criteria are divided into 5 different categories:

- Electrical Criteria

- Thermal Criteria

- Mechanical Criteria

- Functional Criteria

- End User Criteria

17.6.1. Related Documents

All references to related documents within this section imply the latest published revision of the related document, unless specifically stated otherwise. Contact your local Intel Sales representative for latest revisions of the related documents.

Processor and Motherboard Documentation:

● *Pentium® Pro Processor Developer's Manual, Volume 3: Programmer's Reference Manual* (Order Number 242691)

● *AP-523 Pentium® Pro Processor Power Distribution Guidelines* Application Note (Order Number 242764)

17.6.2. Electrical Criteria

The criteria in this section concentrates on the CPU and VRM, and covers pin to plane continuity, signal connections, signal timing and quality, and voltage transients.

17.6.2.1. OVERDRIVE® PROCESSOR ELECTRICAL CRITERIA

The electrical criteria for the OverDrive processor is split into three tables. Most of the criteria refer directly to previous sections of this document.

The criteria for the OverDrive processor that **only** apply to motherboards and systems which employ a Header 8 are presented in Table 17-8. See Table 17-10 for criteria that apply regardless of a Header 8.

Table 17-8. Electrical Test Criteria for Systems Employing Header 8

Criteria	Refer To:	Comment
5Vin Tolerance Header 8 Input	Table 17-2	Measured Under the following Loading Conditions: • Max Icc_5 at Steady-State • Min Icc_5 at Steady-State • Fast Switch between Max and Min Icc_5 Refer to Table 17-5 for OverDrive® VRM Icc_5 specification.
Pentium® Pro processor Vccp Specification	Table 11-4	Measured Under the following Loading Conditions: • Max Iccp at Steady-State • Min Iccp at Steady-State • Fast Switch between Max and Min Iccp Refer to Table 11-5 for Pentium Pro processor Iccp specification.
VRM RES pins	Table 17-2	Must not be connected.
VRM control signals (5Vin, Vss, PwrGood, UP#, Vccp, and VID3-VID0)	Table 17-2	Must be connected as specified. OUTEN is optional.
VRM control input signal quality	Table 17-5	VRM control input signals must meet the D.C. specifications of the VRM.
Maximum Total L_{MB}	Table 17-5	Inductance between VRM output and CPU socket pins.
Maximum Total R_{MB}	Table 17-5	Resistance between VRM output and CPU socket pins.

The criteria for the OverDrive processor that **only** apply to motherboards and systems which **do not** employ a Header 8 are presented in Table 17-9. See Table 17-10 for criteria that apply regardless of a Header 8.

Table 17-9. Electrical Test Criteria for Systems Not Employing Header 8

Criteria	Refer To:	Comment
Vccp Primary CPU Vcc Voltage	Table 17-4 including note 4	Measured Under the following Loading Conditions: • Max Iccp at Steady-State • Min Iccp at Steady-State • Fast Switch between Max and Min Iccp Refer to Table 17-5 for OverDrive® processor Iccp specification.

The criteria for the OverDrive processor that apply to **all** motherboards and systems are presented in Table 17-10.

Table 17-10. Electrical Test Criteria for all Systems

Criteria	Refer To:	Comment
Vcc$_S$ Secondary CPU Vcc Voltage	Table 17-4	Loading Conditions: • Max Icc$_S$ at Steady-State • Min Icc$_S$ at Steady-State • Fast Switch between Max and Min Icc$_S$ Refer to Table 17-4 for OverDrive® processor Icc$_S$ specification.
Vcc$_5$	Table 17-4	Fan/Heatsink Voltage
Vcc continuity to Socket 8	Table 15-3	0.5Ω or less for any single pin from Socket 8 Vcc pins to Vcc supply. Applies to both primary and secondary pins and their respective supplies.
Vss continuity to Socket 8	Table 15-3	0.5Ω or less for any single pin From Socket 8 Vss pins to Vss supply.
RESERVED Pins	Table 15-3	Must not be connected.
Input signal quality	Chapter 13 & Table 11-12	Must meet specification of the Pentium® Pro processor.
AC timing specifications	Section 11.15.	Must meet all A.C. specifications of the Pentium Pro Processor.

17.6.2.2. PENTIUM® PRO PROCESSOR ELECTRICAL CRITERIA

Motherboards and systems will be tested to the specifications of the Pentium Pro processor in Chapter 11, *Electrical Specifications*.

17.6.3. Thermal Criteria

17.6.3.1. OVERDRIVE® PROCESSOR COOLING REQUIREMENTS (SYSTEMS TESTING ONLY)

The maximum preheat temperature, T$_{PH}$, for the OverDrive processor must not be greater than specified in Section 17.5.1., "OverDrive® Processor Cooling Requirements". T$_{PH}$ is the temperature of the air entering the fan heatsink and is measured 0.3 inches (0.76 cm) above the center of the fan. Thermal testing should be performed at the OEM specified maximum system operating temperature (not less than 32°C), and under worst case thermal loading. Worst case thermal loading requires every I/O bus expansion slot to be filled with the longest typical add-in card that will not violate the required clearance for airflow around the OverDrive processor (refer to Section 17.2.2.2., "Socket 8 Space Requirements"). These add-in cards represent typical power dissipation per type and form factor (Full length PCI, VL, ISA, and 1/2 length PCI dissipate 10W; 3/4 length ISA dissipates 7.5W, 1/2 length ISA dissipates 5W, and 1/4 length ISA dissipates 3.3W).

17.6.3.2. PENTIUM® PRO PROCESSOR COOLING REQUIREMENTS (SYSTEMS TESTING ONLY)

The Pentium Pro processor case temperature must meet the specifications of the Pentium Pro processor. Thermal testing should be performed under worst case thermal loading (Refer to Section 17.6.3.1., "OverDrive® Processor Cooling Requirements (Systems Testing Only)" for loading description), and with a cooling solution representative of the OEM's cooling solution. Refer to Table 11-5 for the Pentium Pro processor case temperature specification.

17.6.3.3. VOLTAGE REGULATOR MODULES (SYSTEMS EMPLOYING A HEADER 8 ONLY)

The case temperature of the voltage regulator on the OverDrive VRM must not exceed the specification of Table 17-7.

Table 17-11. Thermal Test Criteria

Criteria	Refer To:	Comment
T_{PH}	Section 17.5.1.	Air temperature entering the fan/heatsink of the OverDrive® processor. Measured 0.3 inches (0.76 cm) above the center of the fan/heatsink.
Pentium® Pro processor Case Temperature	Table 11-5	T_C must meet the specifications of the Pentium Pro Processor. Measured with a cooling solution representative of the OEM's.
Voltage Regulator Case Temperature	Table 17-7	

17.6.4. Mechanical Criteria

17.6.4.1. OVERDRIVE® PROCESSOR CLEARANCE AND AIRSPACE REQUIREMENTS

Refer to Figure 17-4 for a drawing of the various clearance and airspace requirements.

Table 17-12. Mechanical Test Criteria for the OverDrive® Processor

Criteria	Refer To:	Comment
Minimum airspace from top surface of socket to any object.	Figure 17-4	See "Total Clearance Above Socket" in Figure 17-4.
Minimum airspace around all 4 sides of the OverDrive® processor fan/heatsink.	Figure 17-4	Required from the CPU package side to the top of the vertical clearance area. See "A" in Figure 17-4.
Minimum airspace around heatsink clip tabs.	Figure 17-4	Extend from the motherboard surface to the top of the fan/heatsink. See "Keep Out Zones" in Figure 17-4.

Table 17-12. Mechanical Test Criteria for the OverDrive® Processor (Contd.)

Criteria	Refer To:	Comment
ZIF socket lever operation.	Figure 17-4	Must operate from fully closed to fully open position with no interference.

17.6.4.2. OVERDRIVE® VRM CLEARANCE AND AIRSPACE REQUIREMENTS

Refer to Figure 17-6 for a drawing of the various clearance and airspace requirements of the OverDrive VRM. Nothing must intrude into the space envelope, including airspace region, defined in Figure 17-6 with the exception of Header 8 itself.

17.6.5. Functional Criteria

The OverDrive processor is intended to replace the original Pentium Pro processor. The system must boot properly without error messages when the OverDrive processor is installed.

17.6.5.1. SOFTWARE COMPATIBILITY

System hardware and software that operates properly with the original Pentium Pro processor must operate properly with the OverDrive processor.

17.6.5.2. BIOS FUNCTIONALITY

The BIOS must continue to operate correctly with the OverDrive processor installed in the system. Always use the CPU Signature and Feature flags to identify if an OverDrive processor is installed. Please refer to the *Pentium® Pro Processor Developer's Manual: Volume 3, Programmer's Reference Manual* (Order Number 242691) for the BIOS recommendations.

Table 17-13. Functional Test Criteria

Criteria	Refer To:	Comment
Software Compatibility		No incompatibilities resulting from upgrade installation.
BIOS Functionality	Section 17.3.3.	• CPU Type Reported on Screen must be reported correctly or not at all. Intel recommends reporting "OverDrive® Processor". • Never Use Timing Loops. • Do not test the cache, or use model specific registers when the upgrade is detected. • Program MTRRs as for a Pentium® Pro processor.

17.6.6. End User Criteria

17.6.6.1. QUALIFIED OVERDRIVE® PROCESSOR COMPONENTS

To ensure processor upgradability, a system should employ the following Intel-qualified Over-Drive processor components. For a list of qualified components contact your Intel sales representative, or if in the US, contact Intel FaxBACK Information Service at (800) 525-3019.

- Genuine Intel OEM CPU

- Socket 8, 387-hole ZIF

- Header 8, 40-pin shrouded (Systems and Motherboards employing Header 8 solution only.) OR programmable voltage regulator capable of providing the voltage and current required by the OverDrive processor.

17.6.6.2. VISIBILITY AND INSTALLATION

Socket 8 and Header 8 must be visible upon removal of the system cover. Otherwise, the OEM must include diagrams or other indicators visible upon removal of the system cover or clear instructions in the user's manual to guide the end user to the CPU socket and the VRM header. Special tools, other than a screw driver, must not be required for an upgrade installation.

17.6.6.3. JUMPER CONFIGURATION

End user configured jumpers are not recommended. If design requires jumpers or switches to upgrade the system, a detailed jumper description in the manual is required. The jumpers must be easy to locate and set. Jumper identification should be silk-screened on the motherboard if possible. Jumper tables on the inside of the system case are recommended.

17.6.6.4. BIOS CHANGES

BIOS changes or additional software must not be required to upgrade the system with the OverDrive processor.

17.6.6.5. DOCUMENTATION

The system documentation must include installation instructions, with illustrations of the system, Socket 8 and Header 8 location, and any heatsink clip's operation and orientation instructions. Furthermore, there must be no documentation anywhere stating that the warranty is void if the OEM processor is removed.

17.6.6.6. UPGRADE REMOVAL

The upgrade process must be reversible such that upon re-installation of the original CPU, the system must retain original functionality and the cooling solution must return to its original effectiveness.

intel®

A

Signals Reference

This appendix provides an alphabetical listing of all Pentium Pro processor signals. The tables at the end of this appendix summarize the signals by direction: output, input, and I/O.

A.1. ALPHABETICAL SIGNALS REFERENCE

A.1.1. A[35:3]# (I/O)

The A[35:3]# signals are the address signals. They are driven during the two-clock Request Phase by the request initiator. The signals in the two clocks are referenced Aa[35:3]# and Ab[35:3]#. During both clocks, A[35:24]# signals are protected with the AP1# parity signal, and A[23:3]# signals are protected with the AP0# parity signal.

The Aa[35:3]# signals are interpreted based on information carried during the first Request Phase clock on the REQa[4:0]# signals.

For memory transactions as defined by REQa[4:0]# = {XX01X,XX10X,XX11X}, the Aa[35:3]# signals define a 2^{36}-byte physical memory address space. The cacheable agents in the system observe the Aa[35:3]# signals and begin an internal snoop. The memory agents in the system observe the Aa[35:3]# signals and begin address decode to determine if they are responsible for the transaction completion. Aa[4:3]# signals define the critical word, the first data chunk to be transferred on the data bus. Cache line transactions use the burst order described in Section 3.3.4.1., 'Line Transfers" to transfer the remaining three data chunks.

For Pentium Pro processor IO transactions as defined by REQa[4:0]# = 1000X, the signals Aa[16:3]# define a 64K+3 byte physical IO space. The IO agents in the system observe the signals and begin address decode to determine if they are responsible for the transaction completion. Aa[35:17]# are always zero. Aa16# is zero unless the IO space being accessed is the first three bytes of a 64KByte address range.

For deferred reply transactions as defined by REQa[4:0]# = 00000, Aa[23:16]# carry the deferred ID. This signal is the same deferred ID supplied by the request initiator of the original transaction on Ab[23:16]#/DID[7:0]# signals. Pentium Pro processor bus agents that support deferred replies sample the deferred ID and perform an internal match against any outstanding transactions waiting for deferred replies. During a deferred reply, Aa[35:24]# and Aa[15:3]# are reserved.

For the branch-trace message transaction as defined by REQa[4:0]# = 01001 and for special and interrupt acknowledge transactions, as defined by REQa[4:0]# = 01000, the Aa[35:3]# signals are reserved and undefined.

During the second clock of the Request Phase, Ab[35:3]# signals perform identical signal functions for all transactions. For ease of description, these functions are described using new signal names. Ab[31:24]# are renamed the attribute signals ATTR[7:0]#. Ab[23:16]# are renamed the Deferred ID signals DID[7:0]#. Ab[15:8]# are renamed the eight-byte enable signals BE[7:0]#. Ab[7:3]# are renamed the extended function signals EXF[4:0]#.

Ab[31:24]#	Ab[23:16]#	Ab[15:8]#	Ab[7:3]#
ATTR[7:0]#	DID[7:0]#	BE[7:0]#	EXF[4:0]#

On the active-to-inactive transition of RESET#, each Pentium Pro processor bus agent samples A[35:3]# signals to determine its power-on configuration.

A.1.2.   A20M# (I)

The A20M# signal is the address-20 mask signal in the PC Compatibility group. If the A20M# input signal is asserted, the Pentium Pro processor masks physical address bit 20 (A20#) before looking up a line in any internal cache and before driving a read/write transaction on the bus. Asserting A20M# emulates the 8086 processor's address wrap-around at the one Mbyte boundary. Only assert A20M# when the processor is in real mode. The effect of asserting A20M# in protected mode is undefined and may be implemented differently in future processors.

Snoop requests and cache-line writeback transactions are unaffected by A20M# input. Address 20 is not masked when the processor samples external addresses to perform internal snooping.

A20M# is an asynchronous input. However, to guarantee recognition of this signal following an I/O write instruction, A20M# must be valid with active RS[2:0]# signals of the corresponding I/O Write bus transaction. In FRC mode, A20M# must be synchronous to BCLK.

During active RESET#, the Pentium Pro processor begins sampling the A20M#, IGNNE# , and LINT[1:0] values to determine the ratio of core-clock frequency to bus-clock frequency. See Table 9-4. After the PLL-lock time, the core clock becomes stable and is locked to the external bus clock. On the active-to-inactive transition of RESET#, the Pentium Pro processor latches A20M#, IGNNE#, and LINT[1:0] and freezes the frequency ratio internally.

A.1.3.   ADS# (I/O)

The ADS# signal is the address Strobe signal. It is asserted by the current bus owner for one clock to indicate a new Request Phase. A new Request Phase can only begin if the In-order Queue has less than the maximum number of entries defined by the power-on configuration (1 or 8), the Request Phase is not being stalled by an active BNR# sequence and the ADS# associated with the previous Request Phase is sampled inactive. Along with the ADS#, the request initiator drives A[35:3]#, REQ[4:0]#, AP[1:0]#, and RP# signals for two clocks. During the second Request Phase clock, ADS# must be inactive. RP# provides parity protection for REQ[4:0]# and ADS# signals during both clocks. If the transaction is part of a bus locked operation, LOCK# must be active with ADS#.

If the request initiator continues to own the bus after the first Request Phase, it can issue a new request every three clocks. If the request initiator needs to release the bus ownership after the Request Phase, it can deactivate its BREQn#/ BPRI# arbitration signal as early as with the activation of ADS#.

All bus agents observe the ADS# activation to begin parity checking, protocol checking, address decode, internal snoop, or deferred reply ID match operations associated with the new transaction. On sampling the asserted ADS#, all agents load the new transaction in the In-order Queue and update internal counters. The Error, Snoop, Response, and Data Phase of the transaction are defined with respect to ADS# assertion.

A.1.4. AERR# (I/O)

The AERR# signal is the address parity error signal. Assuming the AERR# driver is enabled during the power-on configuration, a bus agent can drive AERR# active for exactly one clock during the Error Phase of a transaction. AERR# must be inactive for a minimum of two clocks. The Error Phase is always three clocks from the beginning of the Request Phase.

On observing active ADS#, all agents begin parity and protocol checks for the signals valid in the two Request Phase clocks. Parity is checked on AP[1:0]# and RP# signals. AP1# protects A[35:24]#, AP0# protects A[23:3]# and RP# protects REQ[4:0]#. A parity error without a protocol violation is signalled by AERR# assertion.

If AERR# observation is enabled during power-on configuration, AERR# assertion in a valid Error Phase aborts the transaction. All bus agents remove the transaction from the In-order Queue and update internal counters. The Snoop Phase, Response Phase, and Data Phase of the transaction are aborted. All signals in these phases must be deasserted two clocks after AERR# is asserted, even if the signals have been asserted before AERR# has been observed. Specifically if the Snoop Phase associated with the aborted transaction is driven in the next clock, the snoop results, including a STALL condition (HIT# and HITM# asserted for one clock), are ignored. All bus agents must also begin an arbitration reset sequence and deassert BREQn#/BPRI# arbitration signals on sampling AERR# active. A current bus owner in the middle of a bus lock operation must keep LOCK# asserted and assert its arbitration request BPRI#/BREQn# after keeping it inactive for two clocks to retain its bus ownership and guarantee lock atomicity. All other agents, including the current bus owner not in the middle of a bus lock operation, must wait at least 4 clocks before asserting BPRI#/BREQn# and beginning a new arbitration.

If AERR# observation is enabled, the Pentium Pro processor retries the transaction once. After a single retry, the request initiator treats the error as a hard error and asserts BERR# or enters the Machine Check Exception handler, as defined by the system configuration.

If AERR# observation is disabled during power-on configuration, AERR# assertion is ignored by all bus agents except a central agent. Based on the Machine Check Architecture of the system, the central agent can ignore AERR#, assert NMI to execute NMI handler, or assert BINIT# to reset the bus units of all agents and execute an MCE handler.

A.1.5. AP[1:0]# (I/O)

The AP[1:0]# signals are the address parity signals. They are driven by the request initiator during the two Request Phase clocks along with ADS#, A[35:3]#, REQ[4:0]#, and RP#. AP1# covers A[35:24]#. AP0# covers A[23:3]#. A correct parity signal is high if an even number of covered signals are low and low if an odd number of covered signals are low. This rule allows parity to be high when all the covered signals are high.

Provided "AERR# drive" is enabled during the power-on configuration, all bus agents begin parity checking on observing active ADS# and determine if there is a parity error. On observing a parity error on any one of the two Request Phase clocks, the bus agent asserts AERR# during the Error Phase of the transaction.

A.1.6. ASZ[1:0]# (I/O)

The ASZ[1:0]# signals are the memory address-space size signals. They are driven by the request initiator during the first Request Phase clock on the REQa[4:3]# pins. The ASZ[1:0]# signals are valid only when REQa[1:0]# signals equal 01B, 10B, or 11B, indicating a memory access transaction. The ASZ[1:0]# decode is defined in Table A-1.

Table A-1. ASZ[1:0]# Signal Decode

ASZ[1:0]#		Description
0	0	0 <= A[35:3]# < 4 GB
0	1	4 GB <= A[35:3]# < 64 GB
1	x	Reserved

If the memory access is within the 0-to-(4GByte -1) address space, ASZ[1:0]# must be 00B. If the memory access is within the 4Gbyte-to-(64GByte -1) address space, ASZ[1:0]# must be 01B. All observing bus agents that support the 4Gbyte (32 bit) address space must respond to the transaction only when ASZ[1:0]# equals 00. All observing bus agents that support the 64GByte (36- bit) address space must respond to the transaction when ASZ[1:0]# equals 00B or 01B.

A.1.7. ATTR[7:0]# (I/O)

The ATTR[7:0]# signals are the attribute signals. They are driven by the request initiator during the second Request Phase clock on the Ab[31:24]# pins. The ATTR[7:0]# signals are valid for all transactions. The ATTR[7:3]# are reserved and undefined. The ATTR[2:0]# are driven based on the Memory Range Register attributes and the Page Table attributes. Table A-2 defines ATTR[3:0]# signals.

Table A-2. ATTR[7:0]# Field Descriptions

ATTR[7:3]#	ATTR[2]#	ATTR[1:0]#			
		11	**10**	**01**	**00**
Reserved (0)	Potentially Speculatable	WriteBack	WriteProtect	WriteThrough	UnCacheable

A.1.8. BCLK (I)

The BCLK (clock) signal is the Execution Control group input signal. It determines the bus frequency. All agents drive their outputs and latch their inputs on the BCLK rising edge.

The BCLK signal indirectly determines the Pentium Pro processor's internal clock frequency. Each Pentium Pro processor derives its internal clock from BCLK by multiplying the BCLK frequency by 2, 3, or 4 as defined and allowed by the power-on configuration.

All external timing parameters are specified with respect to the BCLK signal.

A.1.9. BE[7:0]# (I/O)

The BE[7:0]# signals are the byte-enable signals. They are driven by the request initiator during the second Request Phase clock on the Ab[15:8]# pins. These signals carry various information depending on the REQ[4:0]# value.

For memory or I/O transactions (REQa[4:0]# = {10000B, 10001B, XX01XB, XX10XB, XX11XB}) the byte-enable signals indicate that valid data is requested or being transferred on the corresponding byte on the 64 bit data bus. BE0# indicates D[7:0]# is valid, BE1# indicates D[15:8]# is valid, ..., BE7# indicates D[63:56]# is valid.

For Special transactions ((REQa[4:0]# = 01000B) and (REQb[1:0]# = 01B)), the BE[7:0]# signals carry special cycle encodings as defined in Table A-3. All other encodings are reserved.

Table A-3. Special Transaction Encoding on BE[7:0]#

BE[7:0]#	Special Cycle
0000 0000	Reserved
0000 0001	Shutdown
0000 0010	Flush
0000 0011	Halt
0000 0100	Sync
0000 0101	Flush Acknowledge
0000 0110	Stop Clock Acknowledge
0000 0111	SMI Acknowledge
0000 1000 through 1111 1111	Reserved

For Deferred Reply, Interrupt Acknowledge, and Branch Trace Message transactions, the BE[7:0]# signals are undefined.

A.1.10. BERR# (I/O)

The BERR# signal is the Error group Bus Error signal. It is asserted to indicate an unrecoverable error without a bus protocol violation.

The BERR# protocol is as follows: If an agent detects an unrecoverable error for which BERR# is a valid error response and BERR# is sampled inactive, it asserts BERR# for three clocks. An agent can assert BERR# only after observing that the signal is inactive. An agent asserting BERR# must deassert the signal in two clocks if it observes that another agent began asserting BERR# in the previous clock.

BERR# assertion conditions are defined by the system configuration. Configuration options enable the BERR# driver as follows:

- enabled or disabled

- asserted optionally for internal errors along with IERR#

- optionally asserted by the request initiator of a bus transaction after it observes an error

- asserted by any bus agent when it observes an error in a bus transaction

BERR# *sampling* conditions are also defined by the system configuration. Configuration options enable the BERR# receiver to be enabled or disabled. When the bus agent samples an active BERR# signal and if MCE is enabled, the Pentium Pro processor enters the Machine Check Handler. If MCE is disabled, typically the central agent forwards BERR# as an NMI to one of the processors. The Pentium Pro processor does not support BERR# sampling (always disabled).

A.1.11. BINIT# (I/O)

The BINIT# signal is the bus initialization signal. If the BINIT# driver is enabled during the power on configuration, BINIT# is asserted to signal any bus condition that prevents reliable future information.

The BINIT# protocol is as follows: If an agent detects an error for which BINIT# is a valid error response, and BINIT# is sampled inactive, it asserts BINIT# for three clocks. An agent can assert BINIT# only after observing that the signal is inactive. An agent asserting BINIT# must deassert the signal in two clocks if it observes that another agent began asserting BINIT# in the previous clock.

If BINIT# observation is enabled during power-on configuration, and BINIT# is sampled asserted, all bus state machines are reset. All agents reset their rotating ID for bus arbitration to the state after reset, and internal count information is lost. The L1 and L2 caches are not affected.

If BINIT# observation is disabled during power-on configuration, BINIT# is ignored by all bus agents except a central agent that must handle the error in a manner appropriate to the system architecture.

A.1.12. BNR# (I/O)

The BNR# signal is the Block Next Request signal in the Arbitration group. The BNR# signal is used to assert a bus stall by any bus agent who is unable to accept new bus transactions to avoid an internal transaction queue overflow. During a bus stall, the current bus owner cannot issue any new transactions.

Since multiple agents might need to request a bus stall at the same time, BNR# is a wire-OR signal. In order to avoid wire-OR glitches associated with simultaneous edge transitions driven by multiple drivers, BNR# is activated on specific clock edges and sampled on specific clock edges. A valid bus stall involves assertion of BNR# for one clock on a well-defined clock edge (T1), followed by de-assertion of BNR# for one clock on the next clock edge (T1+1). BNR# can first be sampled on the second clock edge (T1+1) and must always be ignored on the third clock edge (T1+2). An extension of a bus stall requires one clock active (T1+2), one clock inactive (T1+3) BNR# sequence with BNR# sampling points every two clocks (T1+1, T1+3,...).

After the RESET# active-to-inactive transition, bus agents might need to perform hardware initialization of their bus unit logic. Bus agents intending to create a request stall must assert BNR# in the clock after RESET# is sampled inactive.

After BINIT# assertion, all bus agents go through a similar hardware initialization and can create a request stall by asserting BNR# four clocks after BINIT# assertion is sampled.

On the first BNR# sampling clock that BNR# is sampled inactive, the current bus owner is allowed to issue one new request. Any bus agent can immediately reassert BNR# (four clocks from the previous assertion or two clocks from the previous de-assertion) to create a new bus stall. This throttling mechanism enables independent control on every new request generation.

If BNR# is deasserted on two consecutive sampling points, new requests can be freely generated on the bus. After receiving a new transaction, a bus agent can require an address stall due to an anticipated transaction-queue overflow condition. In response, the bus agent can assert BNR#, three clocks from active ADS# assertion and create a bus stall. Once a bus stall is created, the bus remains stalled until BNR# is sampled asserted on subsequent sampling points.

A.1.13. BP[3:2]# (I/O)

The BP[3:2]# signals are the System Support group Breakpoint signals. They are outputs from the Pentium Pro processor that indicate the status of breakpoints.

A.1.14. BPM[1:0]# (I/O)

The BPM[1:0]# signals are more System Support group breakpoint and performance monitor signals. They are outputs from the Pentium Pro processor that indicate the status of breakpoints and programmable counters used for monitoring Pentium Pro processor performance.

A.1.15. BPRI# (I)

The BPRI# signal is the Priority-agent Bus Request signal. The priority agent arbitrates for the bus by asserting BPRI#. The priority agent is always be the next bus owner. Observing BPRI# active causes the current symmetric owner to stop issuing new requests, unless such requests are part of an ongoing locked operation.

If LOCK# is sampled inactive two clocks from BPRI# driven asserted, the priority agent can issue a new request within four clocks of asserting BPRI#. The priority agent can further reduce its arbitration latency to two clocks if it samples active ADS# and inactive LOCK# on the clock in which BPRI# was driven active and to three clocks if it samples active ADS# and inactive LOCK# on the clock in which BPRI# was sampled active. If LOCK# is sampled active, the priority agent must wait for LOCK# deasserted and gains bus ownership in two clocks after LOCK# is sampled deasserted. The priority agent can keep BPRI# asserted until all of its requests are completed and can release the bus by de-asserting BPRI# as early as the same clock edge on which it issues the last request.

On observation of active AERR#, RESET#, or BINIT#, BPRI# must be deasserted in the next clock. BPRI# can be reasserted in the clock after sampling the RESET# active-to-inactive transition or three clocks after sampling BINIT# active and RESET# inactive. On AERR# assertion, if the priority agent is in the middle of a bus-locked operation, BPRI# must be re-asserted after two clocks, otherwise BPRI# must stay inactive for at least 4 clocks.

After the RESET# inactive transition, Pentium Pro processor bus agents begin BPRI# and BNR# sampling on BNR# sample points. When both BNR# and BPRI# are observed inactive on a BNR# sampling point, the APIC units in Pentium Pro processors on a common APIC bus are synchronized. In a system with multiple Pentium Pro processor bus clusters sharing a common APIC bus, BPRI# signals of all clusters must be asserted after RESET# until BNR# is observed inactive on a BNR# sampling point. The BPRI# signal on all Pentium Pro processor buses must then be deasserted within 100ns of each other to accomplish APIC bus synchronization across all processors.

A.1.16. BR0#(I/O), BR[3:1]# (I)

The BR[3:0]# pins are the physical bus request pins that drive the BREQ[3:0]# signals in the system. The BREQ[3:0]# signals are interconnected in a rotating manner to individual processor pins. #. Table A-4 gives the rotating interconnect between the processor and bus signals.

Table A-4. BR0#(I/O), BR1#, BR2#, BR3# Signals Rotating Interconnect

Bus Signal	Agent 0 Pins	Agent 1 Pins	Agent 2 Pins	Agent 3 Pins
BREQ0#	BR0#	BR3#	BR2#	BR1#
BREQ1#	BR1#	BR0#	BR3#	BR2#
BREQ2#	BR2#	BR1#	BR0#	BR3#
BREQ3#	BR3#	BR2#	BR1#	BR0#

During power-up configuration, the central agent must assert the BR0# bus signal. All symmetric agents sample their BR[3:0]# pins on active-to-inactive transition of RESET#. The pin on which the agent samples an active level determines its agent ID. All agents then configure their pins to match the appropriate bus signal protocol, as shown in Table A-5.

Table A-5. BR[3:0]# Signal Agent IDs

Pin Sampled Active on RESET#	Agent ID
BR0#	0
BR3#	1
BR2#	2
BR1#	3

A.1.17. BREQ[3:0]# (I/O)

The BREQ[3:0]# signals are the Symmetric-agent Arbitration Bus signals (called bus request). A symmetric agent n arbitrates for the bus by asserting its BREQn# signal. Agent n drives BREQn# as an output and receives the remaining BREQ[3:0]# signals as inputs.

The symmetric agents support distributed arbitration based on a round-robin mechanism. The rotating ID is an internal state used by all symmetric agents to track the agent with the lowest priority at the next arbitration event. At power-on, the rotating ID is initialized to three, allowing agent 0 to be the highest priority symmetric agent. After a new arbitration event, the rotating ID of all symmetric agents is updated to the agent ID of the symmetric owner. This update gives the new symmetric owner lowest priority in the next arbitration event.

A new arbitration event occurs either when a symmetric agent asserts its BREQn# on an Idle bus (all BREQ[3:0]# previously inactive), or the current symmetric owner de-asserts BREQm# to release the bus ownership to a new bus owner n. On a new arbitration event, based on BREQ[3:0]#, and the rotating ID, all symmetric agents simultaneously determine the new symmetric owner. The symmetric owner can park on the bus (hold the bus) provided that no other symmetric agent is requesting its use. The symmetric owner parks by keeping its BREQn# signal active. On sampling active BREQm# asserted by another symmetric agent, the symmetric owner de-asserts BREQn# as soon as possible to release the bus. A symmetric owner stops issuing new requests that are not part of an existing locked operation upon observing BPRI# active.

A symmetric agent can not deassert BREQn# until it becomes a symmetric owner. A symmetric agent can reassert BREQn# after keeping it inactive for one clock.

On observation of active AERR#, RESET#, or BINIT#, the BREQ[3:0]# signals must be deasserted in the next clock. BREQ[3:0]# can be reasserted in the clock after sampling the RESET# active-to-inactive transition or three clocks after sampling BINIT# active and RESET# inactive. On AERR# assertion, if bus agent n is in the middle of a bus-locked operation, BREQn# must be re-asserted after two clocks, otherwise BREQ[3:0]# must stay inactive for at least 4 clocks.

A.1.18. D[63:0]# (I/O)

The D[63:0]# signals are the data signals. They are driven during the Data Phase by the agent responsible for driving the data. These signals provide a 64-bit data path between various Pentium Pro processor bus agents. 32-byte line transfers require four data transfer clocks with valid data on all eight bytes. Partial transfers require one data transfer clock with valid data on the byte(s) indicated by active byte enables BE[7:0]#. Data signals not valid for a particular transfer must still have correct ECC (if data bus ECC is selected). If BE0# is asserted, D[7:0]# transfers the least significant byte. If BE7# is asserted, D[63:56]# transfers the most significant byte.

The data driver asserts DRDY# to indicate a valid data transfer. If the Data Phase involves more than one clock the data driver also asserts DBSY# at the beginning of the Data Phase and de-asserts DBSY# no earlier than on the same clock that it performs the last data transfer.

A.1.19. DBSY# (I/O)

The DBSY# signal is the Data-bus Busy signal. It indicates that the data bus is busy. It is asserted by the agent responsible for driving the data during the Data Phase, provided the Data Phase involves more than one clock. DBSY# is asserted at the beginning of the Data Phase and may be deasserted on or after the clock on which the last data is driven. The data bus is released one clock after DBSY# is deasserted.

When normal read data is being returned, the Data Phase begins with the Response Phase. Thus the agent returning read data can assert DBSY# when the transaction reaches the top of the In-order Queue and it is ready to return response on RS[2:0]# signals. In response to a write request, the agent driving the write data must drive DBSY# active after the write transaction reaches the top of the In-order Queue and it sees active TRDY# with inactive DBSY# indicating that the target is ready to receive data. For an implicit writeback response, the snoop agent must assert DBSY# active after the target memory agent of the implicit writeback asserts TRDY#. Implicit writeback TRDY# assertion begins after the transaction reaches the top of the In-order Queue, and TRDY# de-assertion associated with the write portion of the transaction, if any is completed. In this case, the memory agent guarantees assertion of implicit writeback response in the same clock in which the snooping agent asserts DBSY#.

A.1.20. DEFER# (I)

The DEFER# signal is the defer signal. It is asserted by an agent during the Snoop Phase to indicate that the transaction cannot be guaranteed in-order completion. Assertion of DEFER# is normally the responsibility of the addressed memory agent or I/O agent. For systems that involve resources on a system bus other than the Pentium Pro processor bus, a bridge agent can accept the DEFER# assertion responsibility on behalf of the addressed agent.

When HITM# and DEFER# are both active during the Snoop Phase, HITM# is given priority and the transaction must be completed with implicit writeback response. If HITM# is inactive, and DEFER# active, the agent asserting DEFER# must complete the transaction with a Deferred or Retry response.

If DEFER# is inactive, or HITM# is active, then the transaction is committed for in-order completion and snoop ownership is transferred normally between the requesting agent, the snooping agents, and the response agent.

If DEFER# is active with HITM# inactive, the transaction commitment is deferred. If the defer agent completes the transaction with a retry response, the requesting agent must retry the transaction. If the defer agent returns a deferred response, the requesting agent must freeze snoop state transitions associated with the deferred transaction and issues of new order-dependent transactions until the corresponding deferred reply transaction. In the meantime, the ownership of the deferred address is transferred to the defer agent and it must guarantee management of conflicting transactions issued to the same address.

If DEFER# is active in response to a newly issued bus-lock transaction, the entire bus-locked operation is re-initiated regardless of HITM#. This feature is useful for a bridge agent in response to a split bus-locked operation. It is recommended that the bridge agent extend the Snoop Phase of the first transaction in a split locked operation until it can either guarantee ownership of all system resources to enable successful completion of the split sequence or assert DEFER# followed by a Retry Response to abort the split sequence.

A.1.21. DEN# (I/0)

The DEN# signal is the defer-enable signal. It is driven to the bus on the second clock of the Request Phase on the EXF1#/Ab4# pin. DEN# is asserted to indicate that the transaction can be deferred by the responding agent.

A.1.22. DEP[7:0]# (I/O)

The DEP[7:0]# signals are the data bus ECC protection signals. They are driven during the Data Phase by the agent responsible for driving D[63:0]#. The DEP[7:0]# signals provide optional ECC protection for the data bus. During power-on configuration, DEP[7:0]# signals can be enabled for either ECC checking or no checking.

The ECC error correcting code can detect and correct single-bit errors and detect double-bit or nibble errors. Chapter 8, *Data Integrity* provides more information about ECC.

DEP[7:0]# provide valid ECC for the entire data bus on each data clock, regardless of which bytes are valid. If checking is enabled, receiving agents check the ECC signals for all 64 data signals.

A.1.23. DID[7:0]# (I/O)

The DID[7:0]# signals are Deferred Identifier signals. They are transferred using A[23:16]# signals by the request initiator. They are transferred on Ab[23:16]# during the second clock of the Request Phase on all transactions, but only defined for deferrable transactions (DEN# asserted). DID[7:0]# is also transferred on Aa[23:16]# during the first clock of the Request Phase for Deferred Reply tranactions.

The deferred identifier defines the token supplied by the request initiator. DID[7:4]# carry the request initiators' agent identifier and DID[3:0]# carry a transaction identifier associated with the request. This configuration limits the bus specification to 16 bus masters with each one of the bus masters capable of making up to sixteen requests.

Every deferrable transaction issued on the Pentium Pro processor bus which has not been guaranteed completion (has not successfully passed its Snoop Result Phase) will have a unique Deferred ID. This includes all outstanding transactions which have not had their snoop result reported, or have had their snoop results deferred. After a deferrable transaction passes its Snoop Result Phase without DEFER# asserted, its Deferred ID may be reused. Similarly, the deferred ID of a transaction which was deferred may be reused after the completion of the snoop window of the deferred reply.

DID[7]# indicates the agent type. Symmetric agents use 0. Priority agents use 1. DID[6:4]# indicates the agent ID. Symmetric agents use their arbitration ID. The Pentium Pro processor has four symmetric agents, so does not assert DID[6]#. DID[3:0]# indicates the transaction ID for an agent. The transaction ID must be unique for all transactions issued by an agent which have not reported their snoop results.

Table A-6. DID[7:0]# Encoding

DID[7]#	DID[6:4]#	DID[3:0]#
Agent Type	Agent ID	Transaction ID

The Deferred Reply agent transmits the DID[7:0]# (Ab[23:16]#) signals received during the original transaction on the Aa[23:16]# signals during the Deferred Reply transaction. This process enables the original request initiator to make an identifier match and wake up the original request waiting for completion.

A.1.24. DRDY# (I/O)

The DRDY# signal is the Data Phase data-ready signal. The data driver asserts DRDY# on each data transfer, indicating valid data on the data bus. In a multi-cycle data transfer, DRDY# can be deasserted to insert idle clocks in the Data Phase. During a line transfer, DRDY# is active for four clocks. During a partial 1-to-8 byte transfer, DRDY# is active for one clock. If a data transfer is exactly one clock, then the entire Data Phase may consist of only one clock active DRDY# and inactive DBSY#. If DBSY# is asserted for a 1-to-8 byte transfer, then the data bus is not released until one clock after DBSY# is deasserted.

A.1.25. DSZ[1:0]# (I/O)

The DSZ[1:0]# signals are the data-size signals. They are transferred on REQb[4:3]# signals in the second clock of Request Phase by the requesting agent. The DSZ[1:0]# signals define the data transfer capability of the requesting agent. For the Pentium Pro processor, DSZ#= 00, always.

A.1.26. EXF[4:0]# (I/O)

The EXF[4:0]# signals are the Extended Function signals. They are transferred on the Ab[7:3]# signals by the request initiator during the second clock of the Request Phase. The signals specify any special functional requirement associated with the transaction based on the requestor mode or capability. The signals are defined in Table A-7.

Table A-7. EFX[4:0]# Signal Definitions

EXF	Name	Extended Functionality	When Activated
EXF4#	SMMEM#	SMM Mode	After entering SMM mode
EXF3#	SPLCK#	Split Lock	The first transaction of a split bus lock operation
EXF2#	Reserved	Reserved	
EXF1#	DEN#	Defer Enable	The transactions for which Defer or Retry Response is acceptable.
EXF0#	Reserved	Reserved	

A.1.27. FERR# (O)

The FERR# signal is the PC Compatibility group Floating-point Error signal. The Pentium Pro processor asserts FERR# when it detects an unmasked floating-point error. FERR# is similar to the ERROR# signal on the Intel387™ coprocessor. FERR# is included for compatibility with systems using DOS-type floating-point error reporting.

A.1.28. FLUSH# (I)

When the FLUSH# input signal is asserted, the Pentium Pro processor bus agent writes back all internal cache lines in the Modified state and invalidates all internal cache lines. At the completion of a flush operation, the Pentium Pro processor issues a Flush Acknowledge transaction to indicate that the cache flush operation is complete. The Pentium Pro processor stops caching any new data while the FLUSH# signal remains asserted.

FLUSH# is an asynchronous input. However, to guarantee recognition of this signal following an I/O write instruction, FLUSH# must be valid along with RS[2:0]# in the Response Phase of the corresponding I/O Write bus transaction. In FRC mode, FLUSH# must be synchronous to BCLK.

On the active-to-inactive transition of RESET#, each Pentium Pro processor bus agent samples FLUSH# to determine its power-on configuration. See Table 9-4.

A.1.29. FRCERR(I/O)

The FRCERR signal is the Error group Functional-redundancy-check Error signal. If two Pentium Pro processors are configured in an FRC pair, as a single "logical" processor, then the checker processor asserts FRCERR if it detects a mismatch between its internally sampled outputs and the master processor's outputs. The checker's FRCERR output pin is connected to the master's FRCERR input pin.

For point-to-point connections, the checker always compares against the master's outputs. For bussed single-driver signals, the checker compares against the signal when the master is the only allowed driver. For bussed multiple-driver Wire-OR signals, the checker compares against the signal only if the master is expected to drive the signal low.

FRCERR is also toggled during the Pentium Pro processor's reset action. A Pentium Pro processor asserts FRCERR for approximately 1 second after RESET's active-to-inactive transition if it executes its built-in self-test (BIST). When BIST execution completes, the Pentium Pro processor de-asserts FRCERR if BIST completed successfully and continues to assert FRCERR if BIST fails. If the Pentium Pro processor does not execute the BIST action, then it keeps FRCERR asserted for approximately 20 clocks and then de-asserts it.

Chapter 9, *Configuration* describes how a Pentium Pro processor can be configured as a master or a checker.

A.1.30. HIT# (I/O), HITM#(I/O)

The HIT# and HITM# signals are Snoop-hit and Hit-modified signals. They are snoop results asserted by any Pentium Pro processor bus agent in the Snoop Phase.

Any bus agent can assert both HIT# and HITM# together for one clock in the Snoop Phase to indicate that it requires a snoop stall. When a stall condition is sampled, all bus agents extend the Snoop Phase by two clocks. The stall can be continued by reasserting HIT# and HITM# together every other clock for one clock.

A caching agent must assert HITM# for one clock in the Snoop Phase if the transaction hits a Modified line, and the snooping agent must perform an implicit writeback to update main memory. The snooping agent with the Modified line makes a transition to Shared state if the original transaction is Read Line or Read Partial, otherwise it transitions to Invalid state. A Deferred Reply transaction may have HITM# asserted to indicate the return of unexpected data.

A snooping agent must assert HIT# for one clock during the Snoop Phase if the line does not hit a Modified line in its writeback cache and if at the end of the transaction it plans to keep the line in Shared state. Multiple caching agents can assert HIT# in the same Snoop Phase. If the requesting agent observes HIT# active during the Snoop Phase it can not cache the line in Exclusive or Modified state.

On observing a snoop stall, the agents asserting HIT# and HITM# independently reassert the signal after one inactive clock so that the correct snoop result is available, in case the Snoop Phase terminates after the two clock extension.

A.1.31. IERR# (O)

The IERR# signal is the Error group Internal Error signal. A Pentium Pro processor asserts IERR# when it observes an internal error. It keeps IERR# asserted until it is turned off as part of the Machine Check Error or the NMI handler in software, or with RESET#, BINIT#, and INIT# assertion.

An internal error can be handled in several ways inside the processor based on its power-on configuration. If Machine Check Exception (MCE) is enabled, IERR# causes an MCE entry. IERR# can also be directed on the BERR# pin to indicate an error. Usually BERR# is sampled back by all processors to enter MCE or it can be redirected as an NMI by the central agent.

A.1.32. IGNNE# (I)

The IGNNE# signal is the PC Compatibility group Ignore Numeric Error signal. If IGNNE# is asserted, the Pentium Pro processor ignores a numeric error and continues to execute non-control floating-point instructions. If IGNNE# is deasserted, the Pentium Pro processor freezes on a non-control floating-point instruction if a previous instruction caused an error.

IGNNE# has no effect when the NE bit in control register 0 is set.

IGNNE# is an asynchronous input. However, to guarantee recognition of this signal following an I/O write instruction, IGNNE# must be valid along with RS[2:0]# in the Response Phase of the corresponding I/O Write bus transaction. In FRC mode, IGNNE# must be synchronous to BCLK.

During active RESET#, the Pentium Pro processor begins sampling the A20M# , IGNNE# and LINT[1:0] values to determine the ratio of core-clock frequency to bus-clock frequency. See Table 9-4. After the PLL-lock time, the core clock becomes stable and is locked to the external bus clock. On the active-to-inactive transition of RESET#, the Pentium Pro processor latches the ratio and freezes the frequency ratio internally.

A.1.33. INIT# (I)

The INIT# signal is the Execution Control group initialization signal. Active INIT# input resets integer registers inside all Pentium Pro processors without affecting their internal (L1 or L2) caches or their floating-point registers. Each Pentium Pro processor begins execution at the power-on reset vector configured during power-on configuration regardless of whether INIT# has gone inactive. The processor continues to handle snoop requests during INIT# assertion.

INIT# can be used to help performance of DOS extenders written for the Intel 80286 processor. INIT# provides a method to switch from protected mode to real mode while maintaining the contents of the internal caches and floating-point state. INIT# can not be used in lieu of RESET# after power-up.

On active-to-inactive transition of RESET#, each Pentium Pro processor bus agent samples INIT# signals to determine its power-on configuration.

INIT# is an asynchronous input. In FRC mode, INIT# must be synchronous to BCLK.

A.1.34. INTR (I)

The INTR signal is the Interrupt Request signal. The INTR input indicates that an external interrupt has been generated. The interrupt is maskable using the IF bit in the EFLAGS register. If the IF bit is set, the Pentium Pro processor vectors to the interrupt handler after the current instruction execution is completed. Upon recognizing the interrupt request, the Pentium Pro processor issues a single Interrupt Acknowledge (INTA) bus transaction. INTR must remain active until the INTA bus transaction to guarantee its recognition.

INTR is sampled on every rising BCLK edge. INTR is an asynchronous input but recognition of INTR is guaranteed in a specific clock if it is asserted synchronously and meets the setup and hold times. INTR must also be deasserted for a minimum of two clocks to guarantee its inactive recognition. In FRC mode, INTR must be synchronous to BCLK. On power-up the LINT[1:0] signals are used for power-on-configuration of clock ratios. Both these signals must be software configured by programming the APIC register space to be used either as NMI/INTR or LINT[1:0] in the BIOS. Because APIC is enabled after reset, LINT[1:0] is the default configuration.

A.1.35. LEN[1:0]# (I/O)

The LEN[1:0]# signals are data-length signals. They are transmitted using REQb[1:0]# signals by the request initiator in the second clock of Request Phase. LEN[1:0]# define the length of the data transfer requested by the request initiator as defined in Table A-8. The LEN[1:0]#, HITM#, and RS[2:0]# signals together define the length of the actual data transfer.

Table A-8. LEN[1:0]# Signals Data Transfer Lengths

LEN[1:0]#	Request Initiator's Data Transfer Length
00	0-8 Bytes
01	16 Bytes
10	32 Bytes
11	Reserved

A.1.36. LINT[1:0] (I)

The LINT[1:0] signals are the Execution Control group Local Interrupt signals. When APIC is disabled, the LINT0 signal becomes INTR, a maskable interrupt request signal, and LINT1 becomes NMI, a non-maskable interrupt. INTR and NMI are backward compatible with the same signals for the Pentium processor. Both signals are asynchronous inputs. In FRC mode, LINT[1:0] must be synchronous to BCLK.

During active RESET#, the Pentium Pro processor continuously samples the A20M#, IGNNE#, and LINT[1:0] values to determine the ratio of core-clock frequency to bus-clock frequency. After the PLL-lock time, the core clock becomes stable and is locked to the external bus clock. On the active-to-inactive transition of RESET#, the Pentium Pro processor freezes the frequency ratio internally.

Both of these signals must be software configured by programming the APIC register space to be used either as NMI/INTR or LINT[1:0] in the BIOS. Because APIC is enabled after reset, LINT[1:0] is the default configuration.

A.1.37. LOCK# (I/O)

The LOCK# signal is the Arbitration group bus lock signal. For a locked sequence of transactions, LOCK# is asserted from the first transaction's Request Phase through the last transaction's Response Phase. A locked operation can be prematurely aborted (and LOCK# deasserted) if AERR# or DEFER# is asserted during the first bus transaction of the sequence. The sequence can also be prematurely aborted if a hard error (such as a hard failure response or AERR# assertion beyond the retry limit) occurs on any one of the transactions during the locked operation.

When the priority agent asserts BPRI# to arbitrate for bus ownership, it waits until it observes LOCK# deasserted. This enables symmetric agents to retain bus ownership throughout the bus locked operation and guarantee the atomicity of lock. If AERR# is asserted up to the retry limit during an ongoing locked operation, the arbitration protocol ensures that the lock owner receives the bus ownership after arbitration logic is reset. This result is accomplished by requiring the lock owner to reactivate its arbitration request one clock ahead of other agents' arbitration request. LOCK# is kept asserted throughout the arbitration reset sequence.

A.1.38. NMI (I)

The NMI signal is the Non-maskable Interrupt signal. It is the state of the LINT1 signal when APIC is disabled. Asserting NMI causes an interrupt with an internally supplied vector value of 2. An external interrupt-acknowledge transaction is not generated. If NMI is asserted during the execution of an NMI service routine, it remains pending and is recognized after the IRET is executed by the NMI service routine. At most, one assertion of NMI is held pending.

NMI is rising-edge sensitive. Recognition of NMI is guaranteed in a specific clock if it is asserted synchronously and meets the setup and hold times. If asserted asynchronously, active and inactive pulse widths must be a minimum of two clocks. In FRC mode, NMI must be synchronous to BCLK.

A.1.39. PICCLK (I)

The PICCLK signal is the Execution Control group APIC Clock signal. It is an input clock to the Pentium Pro processor for synchronous operation of the APIC bus. PICCLK must be synchronous to BCLK in FRC mode.

A.1.40. PICD[1:0] (I/O)

The PICD[1:0] signals are the Execution Control group APIC Data signals. They are used for bidirectional serial message passing on the APIC bus.

A.1.41. PWR_GD (I)

PWR_GD is driven to the Pentium Pro processor by the system to indicate that the clocks and power supplies are within their specification.

This signal is used within the Pentium Pro processor to protect circuits against voltage sequencing issues. While the MTBF of a Pentium Pro processor is on the same order as previous processors without the use of the PWR_GD pin, the use of this signal further increases the Mean Time Between Failures (MTBF) of the Pentium Pro processor component.

This signal will not affect FRC operation.

A.1.42. REQ[4:0]# (I/O)

The REQ[4:0]# signals are the Request Command signals. They are asserted by the current bus owner in both clocks of the Request Phase. In the first clock, the REQa[4:0]# signals define the transaction type to a level of detail that is sufficient to begin a snoop request. In the second clock, REQb[4:0]# signals carry additional information to define the complete transaction type. REQb[4:2]# is reserved. REQb[1:0]# signals transmit LEN[1:0]# (the data transfer length information). In both clocks, REQ[4:0]# and ADS# are protected by parity RP#.

All receiving agents observe the REQ[4:0]# signals to determine the transaction type and participate in the transaction as necessary, as shown in Table A-9.

Table A-9. Transaction Types Defined by REQa#/REQb# Signals

Transaction	REQa[4:0]#					REQb[4:0]#				
	4	3	2	1	0	4	3	2	1	0
Deferred Reply	0	0	0	0	0	x	x	x	x	x
Rsvd (Ignore)	0	0	0	0	1	x	x	x	x	x
Interrupt Acknowledge	0	1	0	0	0	DSZ#		x	0	0
Special Transactions	0	1	0	0	0	DSZ#		x	0	1
Rsvd (Central agent response)	0	1	0	0	0	DSZ#		x	1	x
Branch Trace Message	0	1	0	0	1	DSZ#		x	0	0
Rsvd (Central agent response)	0	1	0	0	1	DSZ#		x	0	1
Rsvd (Central agent response)	0	1	0	0	1	DSZ#		x	1	x
I/O Read	1	0	0	0	0	DSZ#		x	LEN#	

Table A-9. Transaction Types Defined by REQa#/REQb# Signals

Transaction	REQa[4:0]#					REQb[4:0]#				
	4	3	2	1	0	4	3	2	1	0
I/O Write	1	0	0	0	1	DSZ#		x	LEN#	
Rsvd *(Ignore)*	1	1	0	0	x	DSZ#		x	x	x
Memory Read & Invalidate	ASZ#		0	1	0	DSZ#		x	LEN#	
Rsvd *(Memory Write)*	ASZ#		0	1	1	DSZ#		x	LEN#	
Memory Code Read	ASZ#		1	D/C#= 0	0	DSZ#		x	LEN#	
Memory Data Read	ASZ#		1	D/C#= 1	0	DSZ#		x	LEN#	
Memory Write (may not be retried)	ASZ#		1	W/WB #=0	1	DSZ#		x	LEN#	
Memory Write (may be retried)	ASZ#		1	W/WB #=1	1	DSZ#		x	LEN#	

A.1.43. RESET# (I)

The RESET# signal is the Execution Control group reset signal. Asserting RESET# resets all Pentium Pro processors to known states and invalidates their L1 and L2 caches without writing back Modified (M state) lines. RESET# must remain active for one microsecond for a "warm" reset. For a power-on type reset, RESET# must stay active for at least one millisecond after V_{cc} and CLK have reached their proper DC and AC specifications. On observing active RESET#, all bus agents must deassert their outputs within two clocks.

A number of bus signals are sampled at the active-to-inactive transition of RESET# for the power-on configuration. The configuration options are described in Chapter 9, *Configuration* and in every signal description in this chapter.

Unless its outputs are tristated during power-on configuration, after active-to-inactive transition of RESET#, the Pentium Pro processor optionally executes its built-in self-test (BIST) and begins program execution at reset-vector 0_000F_FFF0H or 0_FFFF_FFF0H.

A.1.44. RP# (I/O)

The RP# signal is the Request Parity signal. It is driven by the request initiator in both clocks of the Request Phase. RP# provides parity protection on ADS# and REQ[4:0]#. When a Pentium Pro processor bus agent observes an RP# parity error on any one of the two Request Phase clocks, it must assert AERR# in the Error Phase, provided "AERR# drive" is enabled during the power-on configuration.

A correct parity signal is high if an even number of covered signals are low and low if an odd number of covered signals are low. This definition allows parity to be high when all covered signals are high.

A.1.45. RS[2:0]#(I)

The RS[2:0]# signals are the Response Status signals. They are driven by the response agent (the agent responsible for completion of the transaction at the top of the In-order Queue). Assertion of RS[2:0]# to a non-zero value for one clock completes the Response Phase for a transaction. The response encodings are shown in Table A-10. Only certain response combinations are valid, based on the snoop result signaled during the transaction's Snoop Phase.

Table A-10. Transaction Response Encodings

RS[2:0]#	Description	HITM#	DEFER#
000	Idle State.	NA	NA
001	Retry Response. The transaction is cancelled and must be retried by the initiator.	0	1
010	Defer Response. The transaction is suspended. The defer agent will complete it with a defer reply	0	1
011	Reserved.	0	1
100	Hard Failure. The transaction received a hard error. Exception handling is required.	X	X
101	Normal without data	0	0
110	Implicit Writeback Response. Snooping agent will transfer the modified cache line on the data bus.	1	X
111	Normal with data.	0	0

The RS[2:0]# assertion for a transaction is initiated when all of the following conditions are met:

* All bus agents have observed the Snoop Phase completion of the transaction.

* The transaction is at the top of the In-order Queue.

* RS[2:0]# are sampled in the Idle state

The response driven depends on the transaction as described below:

* The response agent returns a hard-failure response for any transaction in which the response agent observes a hard error.

* The response agent returns a Normal with data response for a read transaction with HITM# and DEFER# deasserted in the Snoop Phase, when the addressed agent is ready to return data and samples inactive DBSY#.

- The response agent returns a Normal without data response for a write transaction with HITM# and DEFER# deasserted in the Snoop Phase, when the addressed agent samples TRDY# active and DBSY# inactive, and it is ready to complete the transaction.

- The response agent must return an Implicit writeback response in the next clock for a read transaction with HITM# asserted in the Snoop Phase, when the addressed agent samples TRDY# active and DBSY# inactive.

- The addressed agent must return an Implicit writeback response in the clock after the following sequence is sampled for a write transaction with HITM# asserted:

  — TRDY# active and DBSY# inactive

  — followed by TRDY# inactive

  — followed by TRDY# active and DBSY# inactive

- The defer agent can return a Deferred, Retry, or Split response anytime for a read transaction with HITM# deasserted and DEFER# asserted.

- The defer agent can return a Deferred or Retry response when it samples TRDY# active and DBSY# inactive for a write transaction with HITM# deasserted and DEFER# asserted.

A.1.46. RSP# (I)

The RSP# signal is the Response Parity signal. It is driven by the response agent during assertion of RS[2:0]#. RSP# provides parity protection for RS[2:0]#.

A correct parity signal is high if an even number of covered signals are low and low if an odd number of covered signals are low. During Idle state of RS[2:0]# (RS[2:0]#=000), RSP# is also high since it is not driven by any agent guaranteeing correct parity.

Pentium Pro processor bus agents can check RSP# at all times and if a parity error is observed, treat it as a protocol violation error. If the BINIT# driver is enabled during configuration, the agent observing RSP# parity error can assert BINIT#.

A.1.47. SMI# (I)

System Management Interrupt is asserted asynchronously by system logic. On accepting a System Management Interrupt, the Pentium Pro processor saves the current state and enters SMM mode. It issues an SMI Acknowledge Bus transaction and then begins program execution from the SMM handler.

A.1.48. SMMEM# (I/O)

The SMMEM# signal is the System Management Mode Memory signal. It is driven on the second clock of the Request Phase on the EXF4#/Ab7# signal. It is asserted by the Pentium Pro processor to indicate that the processor is in System Management Mode and is executing out of SMRAM space.

A.1.49. SPLCK# (I/O)

The SPLCK# signal is the Split Lock signal. It is driven in the second clock of the Request Phase on the EXF3#/Ab6# signal of the first transaction of a locked operation. It is driven to indicate that the locked operation will consist of four locked transactions. Note that SPLCK# is asserted only for locked operations and only in the first transaction of the locked operation.

A.1.50. STPCLK# (I)

The STPCLK# signal is the Stop Clock signal. When asserted, the Pentium Pro processor enters a low power state, the Stop Grant state. The processor issues a Stop Grant Acknowledge special transaction, and stops providing internal clock signals to all units except the bus unit and the APIC unit. The processor continues to snoop bus transactions and service interrupts while in Stop Grant state. When STPCLK# is deasserted, the processor restarts its internal clock to all units and resumes execution. The assertion of STPCLK# has no effect on the bus clock.

STPCLK# is an asynchronous input. In FRC mode, STPCLK# must be synchronous to BCLK.

A.1.51. TCK (I)

The TCK signal is the System Support group Test Clock signal. TCK provides the clock input for the test bus (also known as the test access port). Make certain that TCK is active before initializing the TAP.

A.1.52. TDI(I)

The TDI signal is the System Support group test-data-in signal. TDI transfers serial test data into the Pentium Pro processor. TDI provides the serial input needed for JTAG support.

A.1.53. TDO (O)

The TDO signal is the System Support group test-data-out signal. TDO transfers serial test data out from the Pentium Pro processor. TDO provides the serial output needed for JTAG support.

A.1.54. TMS (I)

The TMS signal is an additional System Support group JTAG-support signal.

A.1.55. TRDY# (I)

The TRDY# signal is the target Ready signal. It is asserted by the target in the Response Phase to indicate that the target is ready to receive write or implicit writeback data transfer. This enables the request initiator or the snooping agent to begin the appropriate data transfer. There will be no data transfer after a TRDY# assertion if a write has zero length indicated in the Request Phase. The data transfer is optional if an implicit writeback occurs for a transaction which writes a full cache line (the Pentium Pro processor will perform the implicit writeback).

TRDY# for a write transaction is driven by the addressed agent when:

- when the transaction has a write or writeback data transfer

- it has a free buffer available to receive the write data

- a minimum of 3 clocks after ADS# for the transaction

- the transaction reaches the top-of-the-In-order Queue

- a minimum of 1 clock after RS[2:0]# active assertion for transaction "n-1".
  (After the transaction reaches the top of the In-order Queue).

TRDY# for an implicit writeback is driven by the addressed agent when:

- transaction has an implicit writeback data transfer indicated in the Snoop Result Phase.

- it has a free cache line buffer to receive the cache line writeback

- if the transaction also has a request initiated transfer, that the request initiated TRDY# was asserted and then deasserted (TRDY# must be deasserted for at least one clock between the TRDY# for the write and the TRDY# for the implicit writeback),

- a minimum of 1 clock after RS[2:0]# active assertion for transaction "n-1".
  (After the transaction reaches the top of the In-order Queue).

TRDY# for a write or an implicit writeback may be deasserted when:

- inactive DBSY# and active TRDY# are observed.

- DBSY# is observed inactive on the clock TRDY# is asserted.

- a minimum of three clocks can be guaranteed between two active-to-inactive transitions of TRDY#

- the response is driven on RS[2:0]#.

- inactive DBSY# and active TRDY# are observed for a write, and TRDY# is required for an implicit writeback.

A.1.56. TRST# (I)

The TRST# signal is an additional System Support group JTAG-support signal.

A.2.   SIGNAL SUMMARIES

The following tables list attributes of the Pentium Pro processor output, input, and I/O signals.

Table A-11. Output Signals[1]

Name	Active Level	Clock	Signal Group
FERR#	Low	Asynch	PC compatibility
IERR#	Low	Asynch	Implementation
PRDY#	Low	BCLK	Implementation
TDO	High	TCK	JTAG
THERMTRIP#	Low	Asynch	Implementation

NOTE:

1. Outputs are not checked in FRC mode.

Table A-12. Input Signals[1]

Name	Active Level	Clock	Signal Group	Qualified
A20M#	Low	Asynch	PC compatibility	Always[2]
BPRI#	Low	BLCK	Pentium® Pro processor bus	Always
BR1#	Low	BLCK	Pentium Pro processor bus	Always
BR2#	Low	BLCK	Pentium Pro processor bus	Always
BR3#	Low	BLCK	Pentium Pro processor bus	Always
BCLK	High	-	Pentium Pro processor bus	Always
DEFER#	Low	BLCK	Pentium Pro processor bus	Snoop Phase
FLUSH#	Low	Asynch	PC compatibility	Always[2]
IGNNE#	Low	Asynch	PC compatibility	Always[2]
INIT#	Low	Asynch	Pentium Pro processor bus	Always[2]
INTR	High	Asynch	PC compatibility	APIC disabled mode
LINT[1:0]	High	Asynch	APIC	APIC enabled mode
NMI	High	Asynch	PC compatibility	APIC disabled mode
PICCLK	High	-	APIC	Always
PWR_GD	High	Asynch	Implementation	
PREQ#	Low	Asynch	Implementation	

Table A-12. Input Signals[1] (Contd.)

Name	Active Level	Clock	Signal Group	Qualified
RESET#	High	BCLK	Pentium Pro processor bus	Always
RS[2:0]#	Low	BCLK	Pentium Pro processor bus	Always
RSP#	Low	BCLK	Pentium Pro processor bus	Always
SMI#	Low	Asynch	PC compatibility	
STPCLK#	Low	Asynch	Implementation	
TCK	High	-	JTAG	
TDI		TCK	JTAG	
TMS		TCK	JTAG	
TRST#	Low	Asynch	JTAG	
TRDY#	Low	TCK	Pentium Pro processor bus	Response Phase

NOTES:

1. All asyncronous input signals must be synchronous in FRC
2. Synchronous assertion with active RS[2:0]# guarantees synchronization.

Table A-13. Input/Output Signals (Single Driver)

Name	Active Level	Clock	Signal Group	Qualified
A[35:3]#	Low	BCLK	Pentium® Pro processor bus	ADS#, ADS#+1
ADS#	Low	BCLK	Pentium Pro processor bus	Always
AP[1:0]#	Low	BCLK	Pentium Pro processor bus	ADS#, ADS#+1
ASZ[1:0]#	Low	BCLK	Pentium Pro processor bus	ADS#
ATTR[7:0]#	Low	BCLK	Pentium Pro processor bus	ADS#+1
BE[7:0]#	Low	BCLK	Pentium Pro processor bus	ADS#+1
BR0#	Low	BCLK	Pentium Pro processor bus	Always
BP[3:2]#	Low	BCLK	Pentium Pro processor bus	Always
BPM[1:0]#	Low	BCLK	Pentium Pro processor bus	Always

Table A-13. Input/Output Signals (Single Driver)(Contd.)

Name	Active Level	Clock	Signal Group	Qualified '
D[63:0]#	Low	BCLK	Pentium Pro processor bus	DRDY#
DBSY#	Low	BCLK	Pentium Pro processor bus	Always
DEN#	Low	BCLK	Pentium Pro processor bus	ADS# + 1
DEP[7:0]#	Low	BCLK	Pentium Pro processor bus	DRDY#
DID[7:0]#	Low	BCLK	Pentium Pro processor bus	ADS#+1
DSZ[1:0]#	Low	BCLK	Pentium Pro processor bus	ADS#+1
DRDY#	Low	BCLK	Pentium Pro processor bus	Always
EXF[4:0]#	Low	BCLK	Pentium Pro processor bus	ADS#+1
FRCERR	High	BCLK	Implementation	Always
LEN[1:0]#	Low	BCLK	Pentium Pro processor bus	ADS#+1
LOCK#	Low	BCLK	Pentium Pro processor bus	Always
REQ[4:0]#	Low	BCLK	Pentium Pro processor bus	ADS#, ADS#+1
RP#	Low	BCLK	Pentium Pro processor bus	Always
SMMEM#	Low	BCLK	Pentium Pro processor bus	ADS# + 1
SPLCK#	Low	BCLK	Pentium Pro processor bus	ADS# + 1

Table A-14. Input/Output Signals (Multiple Driver)

Name	Active Level	Clock	Signal Group	Qualified
AERR#	Low	BCLK	Pentium® Pro processor bus	ADS# + 3
BNR#	Low	BCLK	Pentium Pro processor bus	Always
BERR#	Low	BCLK	Pentium Pro processor bus	Always
BINIT#	Low	BCLK	Pentium Pro processor bus	Always
HIT#	Low	BCLK	Pentium Pro processor bus	Always
HITM#	Low	BCLK	Pentium Pro processor bus	Always
PICD[1:0]	High	PICCLK	APIC	Always

intel ®

Index

intel.

INDEX

W

Z

intel®

NORTH AMERICAN SALES OFFICES

ARIZONA

Intel Corp.
410 North 44th Street
Suite 470
Phoenix 85008
Tel: (800) 628-8686
FAX: (602) 244-0446

CALIFORNIA

Intel Corp.
26707 W. Agoura Road
Suite 203
Calabasas, CA 91302
Tel: (800) 628-8686
FAX: (818)-880-1820

Intel Corp.
3550 Watt Avenue
Suite 140
Sacramento 95821
Tel: (800) 628-8686
FAX: (916) 979-7011

Intel Corp.
9655 Granite Ridge Drive
3rd Floor
Suite 4A
San Diego 92123
Tel: (800) 628-8686
FAX: (619) 467-2460

Intel Corp.
1781 Fox Drive
San Jose 95131
Tel: (800) 628-8686
FAX: (408) 441-9540

Intel Corp.
1551 North Tustin Avenue
Suite 800
Santa Ana 92701
Tel: (800) 628-8686
TWX: (910) 595-1114
FAX: (714) 541-9157

Intel Corp.
514 Via de la Valle
Suite 208-RCO
Solana Beach 92075

Intel Corp.
1960 E. Grand Avenue
Suite 150
El Segundo, CA 90245
Tel: (800) 628-8686
FAX: (310) 640-7133

COLORADO

Intel Corp.
600 South Cherry Street
Suite 700
Denver 80222
Tel: (800) 628-8686
TWX: 910-931-2289
FAX: (303) 322-8670

CONNECTICUT

Intel Corp.
40 Old Ridgebury Road
Suite 311
Danbury 06811
Tel: (800) 628-8686
FAX: (203) 778-2168

FLORIDA

Intel Corp.
600 West Hillsboro Blvd.
Suite 348
Deerfield Beach 33441
Tel: (800) 628-8686
FAX: (305) 421-2444

Intel Corp.
2250 Lucien Way
Suite 100
Suite 8
Maitland 32751
Tel: (800) 628-8686
FAX: (407) 660-1283

GEORGIA

Intel Corp.
20 Technology Park
Suite 150
Norcross 30092
Tel: (800) 628-8686
FAX: (404) 448-0875

IDAHO

Intel Corp.
910 W. Main Street
Suite 236
Boise 83702
Tel: (800) 628-8686
FAX: (208) 331-2295

ILLINOIS

Intel Corp.
300 North Martingale Road
Suite 400
Schaumburg 60173
Tell: (800) 628-8686
FAX: (708) 605-9762

INDIANA

Intel Corp.
8041 Knue Road
Indianapolis 46250
Tel: (800) 628-8686
FAX: (317) 577-4939

MARYLAND

Intel Corp.
131 National Bus. Pkwy
Suite 200
Annapolis Junction 20701
Tel: (800) 628-8686
FAX: (301) 206-3678

MASSACHUSETTS

Intel Corp.
Nagog Park
125 Nagog Park
Acton 01720
Tel: (800) 628-8686
FAX: (508) 266-3867

MICHIGAN

Intel Corp.
32255 North Western Hwy.
Suite 212, Tri Atria
Farmington Hills 48334
Tel: (800) 628-8686
FAX: (313) 851-8770

MINNESOTA

Intel Corp.
3500 West 80th Street
Suite 360
Bloomington 55431
Tel: (800) 628-8686
TWX: 910-576-2867
FAX: (612) 831-6497

NEW JERSEY

Intel Corp.
2001 Route 46
Suite 310
Parsippany 07054
Tel: (800) 628-8686
FAX: (201) 402-4893

Intel Corp.
Lincroft Center
125 Half Mile Road
Red Bank 07701
Tel: (800) 628-8686
FAX: (908) 747-0983

NEW YORK

Intel Corp.
850 Cross Keys Office Pk
Fairport 14450
Tel: (800) 628-8686
TWX: 510-253-7391
FAX: (716) 223-2561

Intel Corp.
2950 Expressway Drive
Islandia 11722
Tel: (800) 628-8686
TWX: 510-227-6236
FAX: (516) 348-7939

OHIO

Intel Corp.
56 Milford Drive
Suite 205
Hudson 44236
Tel: (800) 628-8686
FAX: (216) 528-1026

*†Intel Corp.
3401 Park Center Drive
Suite 220
Dayton 45414
Tel: (800) 628-8686
TWX: 810-450-2528
FAX: (513) 890-8658

OKLAHOMA

Intel Corp.
6801 North Broadway
Suite 115
Oklahoma City 73162
Tel: (800) 628-8686
FAX: (405) 840-9819

OREGON

Intel Corp.
15254 NW Greenbrier
Pkwy
Building B
Beaverton 97006
Tel: (800) 628-8686
TWX: 910-467-8741
FAX: (503) 645-8181

PENNSYLVANIA

Intel Corp.
925 Harvest Drive
Suite 200
Blue Bell 19422
Tel: (800) 628-8686
FAX: (215) 641-0785

SOUTH CAROLINA

Intel Corp.
7403 Parklane Road
Suite 4
Columbia 29223
Tel: (800) 628-8686
FAX: (803) 788-7999

Intel Corp.
100 Executive Center Dr
Suite 109, B183
Greenville 29615
Tel: (800) 628-8686
FAX: (803) 297-3401

TEXAS

Intel Corp.
8911 Capital of Texas Hwy
Suite 4230
Austin 78759
Tel: (800) 628-8686
FAX: (512) 338-9335

Intel Corp.
5000 Quorum Drive
Suite 750
Dallas 75240
Tel: (800) 628-8686
FAX: (214) 233-1325

Intel Corp.
20405 State Hwy 249
Suite 880
Houston 77070
Tel: (800) 628-8686
TWX: 910-881-2490
FAX: (713) 376-2891

UTAH

Intel Corp.
428 East 6400 South
Suite 135
Murray 84107
Tel: (800) 628-8686
FAX: (801) 268-1457

WASHINGTON

Intel Corp.
2800 156th Avenue SE
Suite 105
Bellevue 98007
Tel: (800) 628-8686
FAX: (206) 746-4495

WISCONSIN

Intel Corp.
400 North Executive Drive
Suite 401
Brookfield 53005
Tel: (800) 628-8686
FAX: (414) 789-2746

CANADA

BRITISH COLUMBIA

Intel of Canada, Ltd.
999 Canada Place
Suite 404
Suite 11
Vancouver V6C 3E2
Tel: (800) 628-8686
FAX: (604) 844-2813

ONTARIO

Intel of Canada, Ltd.
2650 Queensview Drive
Suite 250
Ottawa K2B 8H6
Tel: (800) 628-8686
FAX: (613) 820-5936

Intel of Canada, Ltd.
190 Attwell Drive
Suite 500
Rexdale M9W 6H8
Tel: (800) 628-8686
FAX: (416) 675-2438

QUEBEC

Intel of Canada, Ltd.
1 Rue Holiday, Tour West
Suite 320
Pt. Claire H9R 5N3
Tel: (800) 628-8686
FAX: 514-694-0064

NORTH AMERICAN DISTRIBUTORS

ALABAMA

Anthem Electronics
600 Boulevard South
Suite 104F & H
Huntsville 35802
Tel: (205) 890-0302

Arrow/Schweber Electronics
1015 Henderson Road
Huntsville 35805
Tel: (205) 837-6955
FAX: (205) 721-1581

Hall-Mark Computer
4890 University Square
Huntsville 35816
Tel: (800) 409-1483

Hamilton Hallmark
4890 University Square
Suite 1
Huntsville 35816
Tel: (205) 837-8706
FAX: (205) 830-2565

MTI Systems Sales
4950 Corporate Drive
Suite 120
Huntsville 35805
Tel: (205) 830-9526
FAX: (205) 830-9557

Pioneer Technologies Group
4835 University Square
Suite 5
Huntsville 35805
Tel: (205) 837-9300
FAX: (205) 837-9358

Wyle Electronics
7800 Governers Dr., W.
Tower Building, 2nd Floor
Huntsville 35807
Tel: (205) 830-1119
FAX: (205) 830-1520

ARIZONA

Alliance Electronics
7550 East Redfield Rd
Scottsdale 85260
Tel: (602) 261-7988

Anthem Electronics
1555 West 10th Place
Suite 101
Tempe 85281
Tel: (602) 966-6600
FAX: (602) 966-4826

Arrow/Schweber Electronics
2415 West Erie Drive
Tempe 85282
Tel: (602) 431-0030
FAX: (602) 431-9555

Avnet Computer
1626 South Edwards Dr
Tempe 85281
Tel: (800) 426-7999

Hall-Mark Computer
4637 South 37th Place
Phoenix 85040
Tel: (800) 409-1483

Pioneer Standard
1438 West Broadway
Suite B-140
Tempe 85282
Tel: (602) 350-9335

Hamilton Hallmark
4637 South 36th Place
Phoenix 85040
Tel: (602) 437-1200
FAX: (602) 437-2348

Wyle Electronics
4141 East Raymond
Phoenix 85040
Tel: (602) 437-2088
FAX: (602) 437-2124

CALIFORNIA

Anthem Electronics
9131 Oakdale Avenue
Chatsworth 91311
Tel: (818) 775-1333
FAX: (818) 775-1302

Anthem Electronics
1 Oldfield Drive
Irvine 92718-2809
Tel: (714) 768-4444
FAX: (714) 768-6456

Anthem Electronics
580 Menlo Drive
Suite 8
Rocklin 95677
Tel: (916) 624-9744
FAX: (916) 624-9750

Anthem Electronics
9369 Carroll Park Drive
San Diego 92121
Tel: (619) 453-9005
FAX: (619) 546-7893

Anthem Electronics
1160 Ridder Park Drive
San Jose 95131
Tel: (408) 453-1200
FAX: (408) 441-4504

Arrow/Schweber Electronics
26707 West Agoura Road
Calabasas 91302
Tel: (818) 880-9686
FAX: (818) 772-8930

Arrow/Schweber Electronics
48834 Kato Road
Suite 103
Fremont 94538
Tel: (510) 490-9477
FAX: (510) 490-1084

Arrow/Schweber Electronics
6 Cromwell
Suite 100
Irvine 92718
Tel: (714) 581-4622
FAX: (714) 454-4206

Arrow/Schweber Electronics
9511 Ridgehaven Court
San Diego 92123
Tel: (619) 565-4800
FAX: (619) 279-8062

Arrow/Schweber Electronics
1180 Murphy Avenue
San Jose 95131
Tel: (408) 441-9700
FAX: (408) 453-4810

Avnet Computer
1 Mauchley
Irvine 92718
Tel: (800) 426-7999

Avnet Computer
371 Van Ness Way
Torrance 90501
Tel: (800) 426-7999

Avnet Computer
15950 Bernardo Ctr Dr
Suite 6
San Diego 92127
Tel: (800) 426-7999

Avnet Computer
1175 Bordeaux Drive
Suite A
Sunnyvale 94089
Tel: (800) 426-7999

Hall-Mark Computer
21150 Califa Street
Woodland Hills 91367
Tel: (800) 409-1483

Hall-Mark Computer
15950 Bernardo Ctr Dr
Suite C
San Diego 92127
Tel: (800) 409-1483

Hall-Mark Computer
1175 Bordeaux Drive
Sunnyvale 94089
Tel: (800) 409-1483

Hall-Mark Computer
1 Mauchly
Irvine 92718
Tel: (800) 409-1483

Hall-Mark Computer
580 Menlo Drive
Suite 2
Rocklin 95765
Tel: (800) 409-1483

Hamilton Hallmark
3170 Pullman Street
Costa Mesa 92626
Tel: (714) 641-4100
FAX: (714) 641-4122

Hamilton Hallmark
2105 Lundy Avenue
San Jose 95131
Tel: (408) 435-3500
FAX: (408) 435-3720

Hamilton Hallmark
4545 Viewridge Avenue
San Diego 92123
Tel: (619) 571-7540
FAX: (619) 277-6136

Hamilton Hallmark
21150 Califa Street
Woodland Hills 91367
Tel: (818) 594-0404
FAX: (818) 594-8234

Hamilton Hallmark
580 Menlo Drive
Suite 2
Rocklin 95762
Tel: (916) 624-9781
FAX: (916) 961-0922

Pioneer Standard
5126 Clareton Drive
Suite 106
Agoura Hills 91301
Tel: (818) 865-5800

Pioneer Standard
217 Technology Drive
Suite 110
Irvine 92718
Tel: (714) 753-5090

Pioneer Technologies Group
134 Rio Robles
San Jose 95134
Tel: (408) 954-9100
FAX: (408) 954-9113

Pioneer Standard
4370 La Jolla Village Drive
San Diego 92122
Tel: (619) 546-4906

Wyle Electronics
15370 Barranca Pkwy
Irvine 92713
Tel: (714) 753-9953
FAX: (714) 753-9877

Wyle Electronics
15360 Barranca Pkwy
Suite 200
Irvine 92713
Tel: (714) 753-9953
FAX: (714) 753-9877

Wyle Electronics
2951 Sunrise Blvd.
Suite 175
Rancho Cordova 95742
Tel: (916) 638-5282
FAX: (916) 638-1491

Hall-Mark Computer
15950 Bernardo Ctr Dr
Suite C
San Diego 92127
Tel: (800) 409-1483

Hall-Mark Computer
1175 Bordeaux Drive
Sunnyvale 94089
Tel: (800) 409-1483

Hall-Mark Computer
1 Mauchly
Irvine 92718
Tel: (800) 409-1483

Hall-Mark Computer
580 Menlo Drive
Suite 2
Rocklin 95765
Tel: (800) 409-1483

Hamilton Hallmark
3170 Pullman Street
Costa Mesa 92626
Tel: (714) 641-4100
FAX: (714) 641-4122

Hamilton Hallmark
2105 Lundy Avenue
San Jose 95131
Tel: (408) 435-3500
FAX: (408) 435-3720

Hamilton Hallmark
4545 Viewridge Avenue
San Diego 92123
Tel: (619) 571-7540
FAX: (619) 277-6136

Hamilton Hallmark
21150 Califa Street
Woodland Hills 91367
Tel: (818) 594-0404
FAX: (818) 594-8234

Hamilton Hallmark
580 Menlo Drive
Suite 2
Rocklin 95762
Tel: (916) 624-9781
FAX: (916) 961-0922

Pioneer Standard
5126 Clareton Drive
Suite 106
Agoura Hills 91301
Tel: (818) 865-5800

Pioneer Standard
217 Technology Drive
Suite 110
Irvine 92718
Tel: (714) 753-5090

Pioneer Technologies Group
134 Rio Robles
San Jose 95134
Tel: (408) 954-9100
FAX: (408) 954-9113

Pioneer Standard
4370 La Jolla Village Drive
San Diego 92122
Tel: (619) 546-4906

Wyle Electronics
15370 Barranca Pkwy
Irvine 92713
Tel: (714) 753-9953
FAX: (714) 753-9877

Wyle Electronics
9525 Chesapeake Dr.
San Diego 92123
Tel: (619) 565-9171
FAX: (619) 365-0512

Wyle Electronics
3000 Bowers Avenue
Santa Clara 95051
Tel: (408) 727-2500
FAX: (408) 727-5896

Wyle Electronics
17872 Cowan Avenue
Irvine 92714
Tel: (714) 863-9953
FAX: (714) 263-0473

Wyle Electronics
26010 Mureau Road
Suite 150
Calabasas 91302
Tel: (818) 880-9000
FAX: (818) 880-5510

Zeus Arrow Electronics
6276 San Ignacio Avenue
Suite E
San Jose 95119
Tel: (408) 629-4689
FAX: (408) 629-4792

Zeus Arrow Electronics
6 Cromwell Street
Suite 100
Irvine 92718
Tel: (714) 581-4622
FAX: (714) 454-4355

COLORADO

Anthem Electronics
373 Inverness Dr. S.
Englewood 80112
Tel: (303) 790-4500
FAX: (303) 790-4532

Arrow/Schweber Electronics
61 Inverness Dr East
Suite 105
Englewood 80112
Tel: (303) 799-0258
FAX: (303) 799-0730

Avnet Computer
9605 Maroon Circle
Englewood 80111
Tel: (800) 426-7999

Hall-Mark Computer
9605 Maroon Circle
Englewood 80111
Tel: (800) 409-1483

Hamilton Hallmark
12503 East Euclid Dr
Suite 20
Englewood 80111
Tel: (303) 790-1662
FAX: (303) 790-4991

Hamilton Hallmark
710 Wooten Road
Suite 28
Colorado Springs 80915
Tel: (719) 637-0055
FAX: (719) 637-0088

Pioneer Technologies
5600 Greenwood Plaza Blvd.
Suite 201
Englewood 80111
Tel: (303) 773-8090

Wyle Electronics
451 East 124th Avenue
Thornton 80241
Tel: (303) 457-9953
FAX: (303) 457-4831

CONNECTICUT

Anthem Electronics
61 Mattatuck Heights Road
Waterburg 06705
Tel: (203) 575-1575
FAX: (203) 596-3232

Arrow/Schweber Electronics
860 N. Main St. Ext.
Wallingford 06492
Tel: (203) 265-7741
FAX: (203) 265-7988

Hall-Mark Computer
Still River Corporate Ctr
55 Federal Road
Danbury 06810
Tel: (800) 409-1483

Hamilton Hallmark
125 Commerce Court, Unit 6
Cheshire 06410
Tel: (203) 271-2844
FAX: (203) 272-1704

Pioneer Standard
2 Trap Falls Road
Shelton 06484
Tel: (203) 929-5600

FLORIDA

Anthem Electronics
5200 NW 3rd Avenue
Suite 206
Ft. Lauderdale 33309
Tel: (305) 484-0990

Anthem Electronics
598 S. Northlake Blvd.
Suite 1024
Altamonte Sprgs 32701
Tel: (813) 797-2900
FAX: (813) 796-4880

Arrow/Schweber Electronics
400 Fairway Drive
Suite 102
Deerfield Beach 33441
Tel: (305) 429-8200
FAX: (305) 428-3991

Arrow/Schweber Electronics
37 Skyline Drive
Suite 3101
Lake Mary 32746
Tel: (407) 333-9300
FAX: (407) 333-9320

Arrow/Schweber Electronics
4010 Boy Scout Dr.
Suite 295
Tampa 33607
Tel: (813) 873-1030
FAX: (813) 873-0077

Avnet Computer
541 S. Orlando Ave.
Suite 203
Maitland 32751
Tel: (800) 426-7999

Hall-Mark Computer
10491 72nd St. North
Largo 34647
Tel: (800) 409-1483

Hall-Mark Computer
13700 58th St. North
Suite 206
Clearwater 34620
Tel: (800) 409-1483

Hamilton Hallmark
3350 N.W. 53rd Street
Suite 105-107
Ft. Lauderdale 33309
Tel: (305) 484-5482
FAX: (305) 484-2995

Hamilton Hallmark
10491 72nd St. North
Largo 34647
Tel: (813) 541-7440
FAX: (813) 544-4394

Hamilton Hallmark
7079 University Blvd.
Winter Park 32792
Tel: (407) 657-3300
FAX: (407) 678-4414

Pioneer Technologies Group
337 Northlake Blvd
Suite 1000
Alta Monte Spgs 32701
Tel: (407) 834-9090
FAX: (407) 834-0865

Pioneer Technologies Group
674 South Military Trail
Deerfield Beach 33442
Tel: (305) 428-8877
FAX: (305) 481-2950

Wyle Electronics
1000 112th Circle North
St. Petersburg 33716
Suite 800
Tel: (813) 579-1518
FAX: (813) 579-1518

Zeus Arrow Electronics
37 Skyline Drive
Bldg D., Suite 3101
Lake Mary 32746
Suite 800
Tel: (407) 333-3055
FAX: (407) 333-9681

GEORGIA

Anthem Electronics
2400 Pleasant Hill Rd
Suites 9 & 10
Duluth 30136
Tel: (404) 931-3900
FAX: (404) 931-3902

Arrow/Schweber Electronics
4250 E Rivergreen Pkwy
Suite E
Duluth 30136
Tel: (404) 497-1300
FAX: (404) 476-1493

Avnet Computer
3425 Corporate Way
Suite G
Duluth 30136
Tel: (800) 426-7999

Hall-Mark Computer
3425 Corporate Way
Suite G
Duluth 30136
Tel: (800) 409-1483

Hamilton Hallmark
3425 Corporate Way
Suite G & A
Duluth 30136
Tel: (404) 623-5475
FAX: (404) 623-5490

Pioneer Technologies Group
4250C Rivergreen Pkwy
Duluth 30136
Tel: (404) 623-1003
FAX: (404) 623-0665

Wyle Electronics
6025 The Corners Pkwy
Suite 111
Norcross 30092
Tel: (404) 441-9045
FAX: (404) 441-9086

ILLINOIS

Anthem Electronics
1300 Remington Road
Suite A
Schaumburg 60173
Tel: (708) 884-0200
FAX: (708) 885-0480

Arrow/Schweber Electronics
1140 W Thorndale Rd
Itasca 60143
Tel: (708) 250-0500

Avnet Computer
1124 Thorndale Ave
Bensenville 60106
Tel: (800) 426-7999

Hall-Mark Computer
1124 Thorndale Ave
Bensenville 60106
Tel: (800) 409-1483

Hamilton Hallmark
1130 Thorndale Ave
Bensenville 60106
Tel: (800) 426-7999

MTI Systems Sales
1140 West Thorndale
Avenue
Itasca 60143
Tel: (708) 250-8222
FAX: (708) 250-8275

Pioneer Standard
2171 Executive Drive
Suite 200
Addison 60101
Tel: (708) 495-9680
FAX: (708) 495-9831

Wyle Electronics
2055 Army Trail Road
Suite 140
Addison 60101
Tel: (800) 853-9953

Zeus Arrow Electronics
1140 W Thorndale Ave
Itasca 60143
Tel: (708) 250-0500

INDIANA

Arrow/Schweber Electronics
7108 Lakeview
Parkway West Drive
Indianapolis 46268
Tel: (317) 299-2071
FAX: (317) 299-2379

Avnet Computer
655 West Carmel Drive
Suite 160
Carmel 46032
Tel: (800) 426-7999

Hall-Mark Computer
655 West Carmel Drive
Carmel 46032
Tel: (800) 409-1483

Hamilton Hallmark
655 West Carmel Drive
Suite 160
Carmel 46032
Tel: (317) 575-3500
FAX: (317) 575-3535

Pioneer Standard
9350 Priority Way W Dr
Indianapolis 46250
Tel: (317) 573-0880
FAX: (317) 573-0979

KANSAS

Arrow/Schweber Electronics
9801 Legler Road
Lenexa 66219
Tel: (913) 541-9542
FAX: (913) 541-0328

Hall-Mark Computer
10809 Lakeview Ave
Lenexa 66219
Tel: (800) 409-1483

Hamilton Hallmark
10809 Lakeview
Avenue
Lenexa 66215
Tel: (913) 888-4747
FAX: (913) 888-0523

MARYLAND

Anthem Electronics
7168A Columbia
Gateway Drive
Columbia 21046
Tel: (800) 239-6039

Arrow/Schweber Electronics
9800J Patuxent Woods
Drive
Columbia 21046
Tel: (301) 596-7800
FAX: (301) 596-7821

Avnet Computer
7172 Columbia
Gateway Drive
Suite G
Columbia 21045
Tel: (800) 426-7999

Hall-Mark Computer
7172 Columbia
Gateway Drive
Suite G
Columbia 21046
Tel: (800) 409-1483

Hamilton Hallmark
10240 Old Columbia
Road
Columbia 21046
Tel: (410) 988-9800
FAX: (410) 381-2036

North Atlantic Industries
Systems Division
7125 River Wood Drive
Columbia 21046
Tel: (301) 312-5800
FAX: (301) 312-5850

Pioneer Technologies Group
15810 Gaither Road
Gaithersburg 20877
Tel: (301) 921-0660
FAX: (301) 670-6746

Wyle Electronics
9101 Guilford Road
Suite 120
Columbia 21046
Tel: (301) 490-2170
FAX: (301) 490-2190

MASSACHUSETTS

Anthem Electronics
200 Research Drive
Wilmington 01887
Tel: (508) 657-5170
FAX: (508) 657-6008

Arrow/Schweber Electronics
25 Upton Drive
Wilmington 01887
Tel: (508) 658-0900
FAX: (508) 694-1754

Avnet Computer
10 D Centennial Drive
Peabody 01960
Tel: (800) 426-7999

Hall-Mark Computer
10 D Centennial Drive
Peabody 01960
Tel: (800) 409-1483

Hamilton Hallmark
10 D Centennial Drive
Peabody 01960
Tel: (508) 531-7430
FAX: (508) 532-9802

Pioneer Standard
44 Hartwell Avenue
Lexington 02173
Tel: (617) 861-9200
FAX: (617) 863-1547

Wyle Electronics
5 Oak Park Drive
Bedford 01803
Tel: (617) 271-9953
FAX: (617) 275-3809

Zeus Arrow Electronics
25 Upton Drive
Wilmington 01887
Tel: (508) 658-4776
FAX: (508) 694-2199

MICHIGAN

Arrow/Schweber Electronics
44720 Helm Street
Plymouth 48170
Tel: (313) 462-2290
FAX: (313) 462-2686

Avnet Computer
41650 Garden Brk Rd
Suite 120
Novi 48375
Tel: (800) 426-7999

Hall-Mark Computer
41650 Garden Brk Rd
Suite 120
Novi 48375
Tel: (800) 409-1483

Hamilton Hallmark
44191 Plymouth Oaks
Blvd.
Suite 1300
Plymouth 48170
Tel: (313) 416-5806
FAX: (313) 416-5811

Hamilton Hallmark
41650 Garden Brk Rd
Suite 100
Novi 49418
Tel: (313) 347-4271
FAX: (313) 347-4021

Pioneer Standard
4505 Broadmoor S.E.
Grand Rapids 49512
Tel: (616) 698-1800
FAX: (616) 698-1831

Pioneer Standard
44190 Plymouth Oaks
Blvd.
Plymouth 48170
Tel: (313) 525-1800
FAX: (313) 427-3720

MINNESOTA

Anthem Electronics
7646 Golden Triangle
Drive
Eden Prairie 55344
Tel: (612) 944-5454
FAX: (612) 944-3045

Arrow/Schweber Electronics
10100 Viking Drive
Suite 100
Eden Prairie 55344
Tel: (612) 941-5280
FAX: (612) 942-7803

Avnet Computer
9800 Bren Roaqd East
Suite 410
Minnetonka 55343
Tel: (800) 426-7999

Hall-Mark Computer
9800 Bren Road East
Suite 410
Minnetonka 55343
Tel: (800) 409-1483

Hamilton Hallmark
9401 James Ave South
Suite 140
Bloomington 55431
Tel: (612) 881-2600
FAX: (612) 881-9461

Pioneer Standard
7625 Golden Triangle
Drive
Suite G
Eden Prairie 55344
Tel: (612) 944-3355
FAX: (612) 944-3794

Zeus Arrow Electronics
25 Upton Drive
Wilmington 01887
Tel: (508) 658-4776
FAX: (508) 694-2199

Wyle Electronics
1325 East 79th Street
Suite 1
Bloomington 55425
Tel: (612) 853-2280
FAX: (612) 853-2298

MISSOURI

Arrow/Schweber Electronics
2380 Schuetz Road
St. Louis 63141
Tel: (314) 567-6888
FAX: (314) 567-1164

Avnet Computer
3783 Rider Train South
Earth City 63045
Tel: (800) 426-7999

Hall-Mark Computer
3783 Rider Trail South
Earth City 63045
Tel: (800) 409-1483

Hamilton Hallmark
3783 Rider Trail South
Earth City 63045
Tel: (314) 291-5350
FAX: (314) 291-0362

NEW HAMPSHIRE

Avnet Computer
2 Executive Park Drive
Bedford 03102
Tel: (800) 426-7999

NEW JERSEY

Anthem Electronics
26 Chapin Road, Unit K
Pine Brook 07058
Tel: (201) 227-7960
FAX: (201) 227-9246

Arrow/Schweber Electronics
4 East Stow Road
Unit 11
Marlton 08053
Tel: (609) 596-8000
FAX: (609) 596-9632

Arrow/Schweber Electronics
43 Route 46 East
Pine Brook 07058
Tel: (201) 227-7880
FAX: (201) 227-2064

Avnet Computer
1-B Keystone Avenue
Building 36
Cherry Hill 08003
Tel: (800) 426-7999

Hall-Mark Computer
1-B Keystone Avenue
Building 36
Cherry Hill 08003
Tel: (800) 409-1483

Hall-Mark Computer
10 Lanidex Plaza West
Parsippany 07054
Tel: (800) 409-1483

Hamilton Hallmark
1 Keystone Avenue
Building 36
Cherry Hill 08003
Tel: (609) 424-0110
FAX: (609) 751-2552

Hamilton Hallmark
10 Lanidex Plaza West
Parsippany 07054
Tel: (201) 515-5300
FAX: (201) 515-1601

MTI Systems Sales
43 Route 46 East
Pinebrook 07058
Tel: (201) 882-8780
FAX: (201) 539-6430

NORTH AMERICAN DISTRIBUTORS (Cont'd)

PioneerStandard
14-A Madison Road
Fairfield 07006
Tel: (201) 575-3510
FAX: (201) 575-3454

Wyle Electronics
115 Route 46, Bldg F
Mountain Lakes 07046
Tel: (201) 402-4970

NEW MEXICO

Alliance Electronics, Inc.
3411 Bryn Mawr N.E.
Albuquerque 87101
Tel: (505) 292-3360
FAX: (505) 275-6392

Avnet Computer
7801 Academy Road
Building 1, Suite 204
Albuquerque 87109
Tel: (800) 426-7999

NEW YORK

Anthem Electronics
47 Mall Drive
Commack 11725
Tel: (516) 864-6600
FAX: (516) 493-2244

Arrow/Schweber Electronics
3375 Brighton Henrietta
Townline Road
Rochester 14623
Tel: (716) 427-0300
FAX: (716) 427-0735

Arrow/Schweber Electronics
20 Oser Avenue
Hauppauge 11788
Tel: (516) 231-1000
FAX: (516) 231-1072

Avnet Computer
2 Penn Plaza
Suite 1245
New York 10121
Tel: (800) 426-7999

Avnet Computer
1057 E. Henrietta Road
Rochester 14623
Tel: (800) 426-7999

Hall-Mark Computer
2 Penn Plaza
New York 10121
Tel: (800) 409-1483

Hall-Mark Computer
1057 E Henrietta Road
Rochester 14623
Tel: (800) 409-1483

Hamilton Hallmark
933 Motor Parkway
Hauppauge 11788
Tel: (516) 434-7470
FAX: (516) 434-7491

Hamilton Hallmark
1057 E Henrietta Road
Rochester 14623
Tel: (716) 475-9130
FAX: (716) 475-9119

Hamilton Hallmark
3075 Veterans
Memorial Hwy.
Ronkonkoma 11779
Tel: (516) 737-0600
FAX: (516) 737-0838

MTI Systems Sales
1 Penn Plaza
250 West 34th Street
New York 10119
Tel: (212) 643-1280
FAX: (212) 643-1288

Pioneer Standard
68 Corporate Drive
Binghamton 13904
Tel: (607) 722-9300
FAX: (607) 722-9562

Pioneer Standard
60 Crossway Pk West
Woodbury, Long Island
11797
Tel: (516) 921-8700
FAX: (516) 921-2143

Pioneer Standard
840 Fairport Park
Fairport 14450
Tel: (716) 381-7070
FAX: (716) 381-5955

Zeus Arrow Electronics
100 Midland Avenue
Port Chester 10573
Tel: (914) 937-7400
FAX: (914) 937-2553

NORTH CAROLINA

Anthem Electronics
4805 Greenwood
Suite 100
Raleigh 27604
Tel: (919) 782-3550

Arrow/Schweber Electronics
5240 Greensdairy
Road
Raleigh 27604
Tel: (919) 876-3132
FAX: (919) 878-9517

Avnet Computer
4421 Stuart Andrew
Boulevard
Suite 600
Charlotte 28217
Tel: (800) 426-7999

Hall-Mark Computer
3510 Spring Forest Rd
Suite B
Raleigh 27604
Tel: (800) 409-1483

Hamilton Hallmark
3510 Spring Forest Rd
Suite B
Raleigh 27604
Tel: (800) 409-1483

Hamilton Hallmark
5234 Greens Dairy Rd
Raleigh 27604
Tel: (919) 878-0819

Pioneer Technologies Group
2200 Gateway Ctr. Blvd
Suite 215
Morrisville 27560
Tel: (919) 460-1530

OHIO

Arrow/Schweber Electronics
6573 Cochran Road
Suite E
Solon 44139
Tel: (216) 248-3990
FAX: (216) 248-1106

Arrow/Schweber Electronics
8200 Washington
Village Drive
Centerville 45458
Tel: (513) 435-5563
FAX: (513) 435-2049

Avnet Computer
7764 Washington
Village Drive
Dayton 45459
Tel: (800) 426-7999

Avnet Computer
2 Summit Park Drive
Suite 520
Independence 44131
Tel: (800) 426-7999

Hall-Mark Computer
5821 Harper Road
Solon 44139
Tel: (800) 409-1483

Hall-Mark Computer
777 Dearborn Pk Lane
Suite L
Worthington 43085
Tel: (800) 409-1483

Hamilton Hallmark
5821 Harper Road
Solon 44139
Tel: (216) 498-1100
FAX: (216) 248-4803

Hamilton Hallmark
777 Dearborn Pk Lane
Suite L
Worthington 43085
Tel: (614) 888-3313
FAX: (614) 888-0767

MTI Systems Sales
23404 Commerce Pk
Road
Beachwood 44122
Tel: (216) 464-6688
FAX: (216) 464-3564

Pioneer Standard
4433 Interpoint Blvd
Dayton 45424
Tel: (513) 236-9900
FAX: (513) 236-8133

Pioneer Standard
4800 East 131st Street
Cleveland 44105
Tel: (216) 587-3600
FAX: (216) 663-1004

Wyle Electronics
6835 Cochran Rd.
Solon 44139
Tel: (216) 248-9996

OKLAHOMA

Arrow/Schweber Electronics
12101 East 51st Street
Suite 106
Tulsa 74146
Tel: (918) 252-7537
FAX: (918) 254-0917

Hamilton Hallmark
5411 S. 125th E. Ave
Suite 305
Tulsa 74146
Tel: (918) 254-6110
FAX: (918) 254-6207

Pioneer Standard
9717 East 42nd Street
Suite 105
Tulsa 74146
Tel: (918) 665-7840
FAX: (918) 665-1891

OREGON

Almac Arrow Electronics
9500 S.W. Nimbus Ave
Suite E
Beaverton 97008
Tel: (503) 629-8090
FAX: (503) 645-0611

Anthem Electronics
9090 SW Gemini Drive
Beaverton 97005
Tel: (503) 643-1114
FAX: (503) 626-7928

Avnet Computer
9750 SW Nimbus Ave.
Beaverton 97005
Tel: (800) 426-7999

Hall-Mark Computer
9750 SW Nimbus Ave.
Beaverton 97005
Tel: (800) 409-1483

Hamilton Hallmark
9750 SW Nimbus Ave.
Beaverton 97005
Tel: (503) 526-6200
FAX: (503) 641-5939

Pioneer Technologies
8905 Southwest
Numbus Ave.
Suite 160
Beaverton 97005
Tel: (503) 626-7300
FAX: (503) 626-5300

Wyle Electronics
9640 Sunshine Court
Building G
Suite 200
Beaverton 97005
Tel: (503) 643-7900
FAX: (503) 646-5466

PENNSYLVANIA

Anthem Electronics
355 Business Ctr Drive
Horsham 19044
Tel: (215) 443-5150
FAX: (215) 675-9875

Avnet Computer
213 Executive Drive
Suite 320
Mars 16046
Tel: (800) 426-7999

Arrow/Schweber Electronics
2681 Mosside Blvd
Suite 204
Monroeville 15146
Tel: (412) 856-9490

Pioneer Technologies Group
259 Kappa Drive
Pittsburgh 15238
Tel: (412) 782-2300
FAX: (412) 963-8255

Pioneer Technologies Group
500 Enterprise Road
Keith Valley Bus.Ctr
Horsham 19044
Tel: (215) 674-4000

Wyle Electronics
1 Eves Drive
Suite 111
Marlton 08053-3185
Tel: (609) 985-7953
FAX: (609) 985-8757

TEXAS

Anthem Electronics
651 N. Plano Road
Suite 401
Richardson 75081
Tel: (214) 238-7100
FAX: (214) 238-0237

Anthem Electronics
14050 Summit Drive
Suite 119
Tel: (512) 388-0049
FAX: (512) 388-0271

Arrow/Schweber Electronics
Brake Ctr III, Bldg M1
11500 Metric Boulevard
Suite 160
Austin 78758
Tel: (512) 835-4180
FAX: (512) 832-5921

Arrow/Schweber Electronics
3220 Commander Drive
Carrollton 75006
Tel: (214) 380-6464
FAX: (214) 248-7208

Arrow/Schweber Electronics
19416 Park Row
Suite 190
Houston 77084
Tel: (713) 647-6868
FAX: (713) 492-8722

Avnet Computer
4004 Beltline
Suite 200
Dallas 75244
Tel: (800) 426-799

Avnet Computer
1235 North Loop West
Suite 525
Houston 77008
Tel: (800) 426-7999

Hall-Mark Computer
12211 Technology Blvd
Austin 78727
Tel: (800) 409-1483

Hall-Mark Computer
4004 Beltline Road
Suite 200
Dallas 75244
Tel: (800) 409-1483

Hall-Mark Computer
1235 North Loop West
Houston 77008
Tel: (800) 409-1483

Hamilton Hallmark
12211 Technology
Boulevard
Austin 78727
Tel: (512) 258-8848
FAX: (512) 258-3777

Hamilton Hallmark
11420 Page Mill Road
Dallas 75243
Tel: (214) 553-4300
FAX: (214) 553-4395

Hamilton Hallmark
8000 Westglen
Houston 77063
Tel: (713) 781-6100
FAX: (713) 953-8420

Pioneer Standard
1826D Kramer Lane
Austin 78758
Tel: (512) 835-4000
FAX: (512) 835-9829

Pioneer Standard
13765 Beta Road
Dallas 75244
Tel: (214) 263-3168
FAX: (214) 490-6419

Pioneer Standard
10530 Rockley Road
Suite 100
Houston 77099
Tel: (713) 495-4700
FAX: (713) 495-5642

Wyle Electronics
1810 Greenville Ave
Richardson 75081
Tel: (214) 235-9953
FAX: (214) 644-5064

Wyle Electronics
9208 Waterford Center
Blvd
Suite 150
Austin 78750
Tel: (512) 345-8853
FAX: (512) 345-9330

Wyle Electronics
2901 Wilcrest
Suite 120
Houston 77099
Tel: (713) 879-9953
FAX: (713) 879-9953

Zeus Arrow Electronics
3220 Commander Dr
Carrollton 75006
Tel: (214) 380-4330
FAX: (214) 447-2222

UTAH

Anthem Electronics
1279 West 2200 South
Salt Lake City 84119
Tel: (801) 973-8555
FAX: (801) 973-8909

Arrow/Schweber Electronics
1946 West Parkway
Boulevard
Salt Lake City 84119
Tel: (801) 973-6913
FAX: (801) 972-0200

NORTH AMERICAN DISTRIBUTORS (Cont'd)

Avnet Computer
1100 East 6600 South
Suite 150
Salt Lake City 84121
Tel: (800) 426-7999

Hall-Mark Computer
1100 East 6600 South
Suite 150
Salt Lake City
Tel: (800) 409-1483

Hamilton Hallmark
1100 East 6600 South
Suite 120
Salt Lake City 84121
Tel: (801) 266-2022
FAX: (801) 263-0104

Wyle Electronics
1325 West 2200 South
Suite E
West Valley 84119
Tel: (801) 974-9953
FAX: (801) 972-2524

WASHINGTON

**Almac Arrow
Electronics**
14360 S.E. Eastgate
Way
Bellevue 98007
Tel: (206) 643-9992
FAX: (206) 643-9709

Anthem Electronics
19017 120th Ave N.E.
Suite 102
Bothell 98011
Tel: (206) 483-1700
FAX: (206) 486-0571

Avnet Computer
8630 154th Ave, NE
Redmond 98052
Tel: (800) 426-7999

Hamilton Hallmark
8630 154th Avenue
Redmond 98052
Tel: (206) 881-6697
FAX: (206) 867-0159

Pioneer Technologies
2800 156th Ave S.E.
Suite 100
Bellevue 98007
Tel: (206) 644-7500

Wyle Electronics
15385 NE 90th St
Redmond 98052
Tel: (206) 881-1150
FAX: (206) 881-1567

WISCONSIN

**Arrow/Schweber
Electronics**
200 N. Patrick
Suite 100
Brookfield 53045
Tel: (414) 792-0150
FAX: (414) 792-0156

Avnet Computer
2440 South 179th St
New Berlin 53416
Tel: (800) 426-7999

Hall-Mark Computer
2440 South 179th St
New Berlin 53146
Tel: (800) 409-1483

Hamilton Hallmark
2440 South 179th St
New Berlin 53146
Tel: (414) 797-7844
FAX: (414) 797-9259

Pioneer Standard
120 Bishops Way
Suite 163
Brookfield 53005
Tel: (414) 780-3600
FAX: (414) 780-3613

Wyle Electronics
150 North Patrick
Building 7, Suite 150
Brookfield 53045
Tel: (414) 879-0434
FAX: (414) 879-0474

ALASKA

Avnet Computer
1400 W Benson Blvd
Suite 400
Anchorage 99503
Tel: (800) 426-7999

CANADA

ALBERTA

Avnet Computer
1144 29th Avenue NE
Suite 108
Calgary T2E 7P1
Tel: (800) 387-3406

Pioneer/Pioneer
560, 1212-31 Ave. NE
Calgary T2E 7S8
Tel: (403) 291-1988
FAX: (403) 295-8714

BRITISH COLUMBIA

**Almac Arrow
Electronics**
8544 Baxter Place
Burnaby V5A 4T8
Tel: (604) 421-2333
FAX: (604) 421-5030

Hamilton Hallmark
8610 Commerce Court
Burnaby V5A 4N6
Tel: (604) 420-4101
FAX: (604) 420-5376

Pioneer/Pioneer
4455 North 6 Road
Rochmond V6V 1P6
Tel: (604) 273-5575
FAX: (604) 273-2413

MANITOBA

Pioneer/Pioneer
540 Marjorie Street
Winnipeg R3H 0S9

ONTARIO

**Arrow/Schweber
Electronics**
36 Antares Drive
Unit 100
Nepean K2E 7W5
Tel: (613) 226-6903
FAX: (613) 723-2018

**Arrow/Schweber
Electronics**
1093 Meyerside, Unit 2
Mississauga L5T 1M4
Tel: (416) 670-2010
FAX: (416) 670-5863

Avnet Computer
Canada System
Engineering Group
151 Superior Blvd.
Mississauga L5T 2L1
Tel: (800) 387-3406

Avnet Computer
190 Colonade Road
Nepean K2E 7J5
Tel: (800) 387-3406

**Canada System
Engineering Group**
151 Superior Boulevard
Mississuaga L5T 2L1
Tel: (800) 387-3406

Hamilton Hallmark
151 Superior Blvd.,
Unit 1-6
Mississauga L5T 2L1
Tel: (416) 564-6060
FAX: (416) 564-6033

Hamilton Hallmark
190 Colonade Road
Nepean K2E 7J5
Tel: (613) 226-1700
FAX: (613) 226-1184

Pioneer/Pioneer
3415 American Drive
Mississauga L4V 1T6
Tel: (416) 507-2600
FAX: (416) 507-2831

Pioneer/Pioneer
155 Colonnade Rd., S.
Suite 17
Nepean K2E 7K3
Tel: (613) 226-8840
FAX: (613) 226-6352

QUEBEC

**Arrow/Schweber
Electronics**
1100 Street Regis Blvd
Dorval H9P 2T5
Tel: (514) 421-7411
FAX: (514) 421-7430

**Gates Arrow
Electronics**
500 Boul.
St-Jean-Baptiste Ave
Quebec H2E 5R9
Tel: (418) 871-7500
FAX: (418) 871-6816

Avnet Computer
7575 Trans Canada
Suite 601
St. Laurent H4T 1V6
Tel: (800) 265-1135

Hamilton Hallmark
7575 Transcanada Hwy
Suite 600
Street Laurent H4T 2V6
Tel: (514) 335-1000
FAX: (514) 335-2481

Pioneer/Pioneer
520 McCaffrey
Street Laurent H4T 1N1
Tel: (514) 737-9700
FAX: (514) 737-5212

NORTH AMERICAN SERVICE OFFICES

Computervision

Intel Corporation's North American Preferred Service Provider

Central Dispatch: 1-800-876-SERV (1-800-876-7378)

ALABAMA
Birmingham
Huntsville

ALASKA
Anchorage

ARIZONA
Phoenix
Tucson

ARKANSAS
North Little Rock

CALIFORNIA
Concord
Los Angeles
Ontario
Orange
Redwood City
Sacramento
San Diego
San Francisco
Van Nuys

COLORADO
Colorado Springs
Denver

CONNECTICUT
E. Windsor
Middlebury

FLORIDA
Ft. Lauderdale
Jacksonville
Miami
Orlando
Pensacola
Tampa

GEORGIA
Atlanta

HAWAII
Honolulu

ILLINOIS
Chicago
Wood Dale

INDIANA
Carmel
Evansville
Ft. Wayne
South Bend

IOWA
Cedar Rapids
Davenport
West Des Moines

KANSAS
Kansas City
Wichita

KENTUCKY
Louisville
Madisonville

LOUISIANA
Baton Rouge
New Orleans

MAINE
Auburn

MARYLAND
Baltimore

MASSACHUSETTS
Bedfoird
S. Easton

MICHIGAN
Detroit
Flint
Grand Rapids
Lansing
Troy

MINNESOTA
Minneapolis

MISSOURI
Springfield
Street Louis

MISSISSIPPI
Jackson

NEW HAMPSHIRE
Manchester*

MONTANA
Butte

NEBRASKA
Omaha

NEW JERSEY
Cherry Hill
Hamilton Township
Westfield

NEW MEXICO
Albuquerque

NEW YORK
Albany
Binghampton
Buffalo
Farmingdale
New York City
Rochester
Dryden

NORTH CAROLINA
Ashville
Charlotte
Greensboro
Raleigh
Wilmington

OHIO
Cincinnati
Cleveland
Columbus
Dayton

OKLAHOMA
Oklahoma City
Tulsa

OREGON
Beaverton

PENNSYLVANIA
Camp Hill
Erie
Pittsburgh
Wayne

SOUTH CAROLINA
Charleston
Columbia
Greenville

TENNESSEE
Chattanooga
Knoxville
Memphis
Nashville

TEXAS
Austin
Houston
Dallas
Tyler

UTAH
Salt Lake City

VERMONT
White River Junction

VIRGINIA
Charlottesville
Richmond
Roanoke
Virginia Beach

WASHINGTON
Renton
Richland

WASHINGTON D.C.*

WEST VIRGINIA
Charleston

WISCONSIN
Milwaukee

CANADA
Calgary
Edmonton
Fredericton
Halifax
Mississauga
Montreal
Ottawa
Toronto
Vancouver, BC*
Winnipeg
Quebec City
Regina
St.John's